Film Noir

Inside Film Series

Forthcoming Titles

Contemporary US Cinema	Dr Michael Allen
Russian Cinema	Dr David Gillespie
The Western	David Lusted
Documentary	Dr Alan Marcus
The Horror Film	Dr Peter Hutchings
Shakespeare on Film	Dr Judith Buchanan
Women and Film	Pamela Church Gibson
French Cinema	Dr Lucy Mazdon
Italian Cinema	Dr Mary Wood

More information can be found at:
www.booksites.net/mclean

FILM NOIR

Andrew Spicer

Longman

An imprint of **Pearson Education**

Harlow, England · London · New York · Reading, Massachusetts · San Francisco
Toronto · Don Mills, Ontario · Sydney · Tokyo · Singapore · Hong Kong · Seoul
Taipei · Cape Town · Madrid · Mexico City · Amsterdam · Munich · Paris · Milan

For Joyce

Pearson Education Limited
Edinburgh Gate
Harlow
Essex CM20 2JE
England

and Associated Companies throughout the world

Visit us on the World Wide Web at:
www.pearsoned.co.uk

First published 2002

© Pearson Education Limited 2002

ISBN 0 582 43712 1

British Library Cataloguing-in-Publication Data
A catalogue record for this book is available from the British Library

10   9   8   7   6   5   4
08   07   06   05   04

Typeset in 10/13pt Giovanni Book by 35
Printed and bound in China
EPC/04

CONTENTS

PREFACE AND ACKNOWLEDGEMENTS

Any study of film noir, however objective, has to engage with what could be called the 'noir myth': that film noir is quintessentially those black and white 1940s films, bathed in deep shadows, which offered a 'dark mirror' to American society and questioned the fundamental optimism of the American dream. There is, as with any myth, a great deal of truth to this image, but film noir needs to be understood as a cultural phenomenon which is much more historically extensive, complex and diverse. Although the present study gives due weight to the range of formal devices that often mark out film noir – its arresting visual and aural style and its complex modes of narration – it argues that film noir cannot be understood simply as a set of textual conventions which reflected a wider social malaise. Rather, it was also the product of a multifaceted interaction between developments within particular genres – the gangster/crime film and the Gothic melodrama – fluctuating conditions of production and reception within the American film industry, and more diffuse cultural movements: modernism and postmodernism. Film noir was also the product of the complex interface between European and American cinema.

This study attempts an introductory overview of film noir conceived as both a dynamic, fluid and evolving cultural phenomenon, and also as a contested discursive construction. Film noir is, famously, a retrospective categorization and therefore not only which films should be included, but also its whole function as a classificatory and evaluative label have been questioned. The present study, following James Naremore (1998), argues that film noir is an imprecise but necessary cultural category which helps to make sense of a complex phenomenon. As my primary purpose is to give a broad overview, *Film Noir* is as inclusive as possible, exploring both the 'classical' period (1940–59) and also neo-noir. A final chapter analyses how film noir developed in Britain. As the book assumes an acquaintanceship with film noir rather than a deep familiarity, it often concentrates on films that have been widely celebrated and discussed, including *Double Indemnity*, *Scarlet Street*, *Kiss Me Deadly*, *Touch of Evil* and *The Third Man*, and neo-noirs such as *Taxi Driver*, *Body Heat* and *Pulp Fiction*. However, it also ranges widely across the (disputed) noir canon, attempting to do justice to the range and variety of noir films and to the complexity of the 'noir phenomenon'.

Although the literature on film noir is extensive as the bibliography (which is selective rather than comprehensive) shows, much work remains to be done: on the marketing and reception of the films, on the development of American noir in the 1950s, on the current evolution of neo-noir, and on noir's presence within European cinemas. However, as these powerful and fascinating films retain their ability to shock and surprise, there is every indication that many further studies will be forthcoming.

The preparation of any book incurs many debts. I am grateful to the Faculty of Art, Media and Design at the University of the West of England for a small research grant, which provided some teaching relief that enabled me to devote more time to writing. I am especially grateful to the staff in the Faculty's library at Bower Ashton for dealing with an avalanche of interlibrary loan requests. The enthusiasm of the university's students for film noir and their readiness to discuss its intricacies, was always encouraging. The British Film Institute Library was an important source of material and its staff helpful as ever. The National Film and Television Archive provided some viewing prints, particularly *Christmas Holiday*, which were essential to aspects of my argument. I am indebted to Ian Conrich for supplying copies of films that I could not otherwise have seen. I am particularly grateful to Robert Murphy and Brian Neve who read through the entire manuscript and offered many helpful observations and suggestions. What faults remain are entirely my own. Alex Ballinger at the McLean Press was an enthusiastic and energetic editor who has encouraged me at every stage in the book's production. My partner Joyce Woolridge read through several drafts of each chapter and made many perceptive comments that made me think again about the films, or prevented the argument from straying. Joyce's help in preparing the final manuscript and in preparing the index was invaluable. This book is dedicated to her.

LIST OF PHOTOGRAPHS

The Background to Film Noir

1. The birth of the modern thriller: Peter Lorre in *M* (Fritz Lang, 1931) **p.13**

Conditions of Production and Reception

2. The clandestine couple: Alan Ladd and Veronica Lake in *The Blue Dahlia* (George Marshall, 1946) **p.39**

Noir Style

3. The vulnerable private eye: Marlowe (Dick Powell) in a vertiginous setting in *Murder, My Sweet* (Edward Dmytryk, 1944) **p.53**
4. Semi-documentary noir: *The Naked City* (Jules Dassin, 1948) **p.58**

Themes and Narrative Strategies

5. The outsider as patriotic hero? Skip McCoy (Richard Widmark) interrogating Candy (Jean Peters) in *Pickup on South Street* (Samuel Fuller, 1953) **p.71**
6. Femme fatale Phyllis Dietrichson (Barbara Stanwyck) provokes Walter Neff (Fred MacMurray) to 'explore the angles' in *Double Indemnity* (Billy Wilder, 1944) **p.77**

Gender in Film Noir

7. The working-class loser meets his fate: John Garfield in *He Ran All the Way* (John Berry, 1951) **p.95**

The Noir Auteur

8. The noir victim: Joe Norson (Farley Granger) at the mercy of gangster Georgie Garsell (James Craig) in *Side Street* (Anthony Mann, 1950) **p.111**
9. The middle-aged victim: Professor Warnley (Edward G. Robinson) in *The Woman in the Window* (Fritz Lang, 1944) **p.122**

Neo-Noir 1: Modernist Film Noir

10. New wave noir: Charles Aznavour in *Tirez sur le pianiste* (François Truffaut, 1960) **p.132**

Neo-Noir 2: Postmodern Film Noir

British Film Noir

CHAPTER ONE

The Background to Film Noir

THE EVOLUTION OF THE TERM 'FILM NOIR'

Of late there has been a trend in Hollywood toward the wholesale production of lusty, gut-and-gore crime stories, all fashioned on a theme with a combination of plausibly motivated murder and studded with high-powered Freudian implication. Of the quantity of such films now in vogue, Double Indemnity, Murder, My Sweet, Conflict *and* Laura *are a quartet of the most popular which quickly come to mind . . . This quartet constitutes a mere vanguard of the cinematic homicide to come. Every studio in town has at least two or three similar blood-freezers before the camera right now, which means that within the next year or so movie murder – particularly with a psychological twist – will become almost as common as the weekly newsreel or musical.*

(Shearer, 1945, in Silver and Ursini, 1999a, p.9)

The reviewer who made these comments in the summer of 1945 was clearly fascinated by what he took to be a new phenomenon in Hollywood film production: 'murder with a psychological twist'. The subject matter, sex and violence, has clear continuities with the tradition of American crime fiction, but the injection of 'high-powered Freudian implication' is new. A few months earlier, another reviewer had labelled these films ' "red meat" stories of illicit romance and crime' (Stanley, 1944, in Biesen, 1998, p.137). A third, writing two years later, used the term 'morbid drama' for this cycle of thrillers whose chief characteristics were 'deep shadows, clutching hands, exploding revolvers, sadistic villains and heroines tormented with deeply rooted diseases of the mind' (D. Marsham, *Life* August 25, 1947, in Schatz, 1981, p.111). Clearly groping for the most appropriate label for these films, American reviewers most frequently called them 'psychological thrillers', a term that the film industry itself employed (Neale, 2000, p.169).

The origins of the label 'film noir' have been traced to the French film critic Nino Frank who used the term in his response to the release of four crime thrillers – *The Maltese Falcon* (1941), *Murder, My Sweet* (UK title: *Farewell My Lovely*, 1944), *Double Indemnity* (1944) and *Laura* (1944) – in Paris in August 1946. Film noir was employed through its analogy with *'série noire'*, the label given to French translations of American 'hard-boiled' fiction from which several of these films had been adapted. After the five-year absence of Hollywood films during the Occupation, Frank, even more than his American counterparts, was stimulated by what he perceived as a new type of crime film that would render obsolete the traditional detective film with its emphasis on plot convolutions and the unmasking of the killer, through a radical visual style, a complex mode of narration, and a pronounced interest in the characters' 'uncertain psychology'. Frank averred: 'The essential quality is no longer "who-done-it?" but how does this protagonist act?' (Frank, 1946, in Silver and Ursini, 1999a, p.16).

In France, especially through the work of left-wing critics writing for the film journal *Positif*, film noir became an important component of a self-questioning intellectual climate dominated by Existentialism. This philosophy emphasizes contingency and chance, a world where there are no values or moral absolutes, and which is devoid of meaning except those that are self-created by the alienated and confused 'non-heroic hero'. French intellectuals saw in film noir a reflection of their own pessimism and angst. As *cinéastes* they were looking for American films that were 'art' rather than merely commercial entertainment, but which were also popular (Naremore, 1995–6, pp.12–28). The nature of American film noir continued to be debated over the next decade, culminating in the first book-length study in 1955, *Panorama du film noir américain*, by Raymonde Borde and Etienne Chaumeton, who characterized film noir as 'nightmarish, weird, erotic, ambivalent, and cruel' (Borde and Chaumeton, 1955, in Silver and Ursini, 1996, p.16). They concluded that 'the moral ambivalence, the criminality, the complex contradictions in motives and events, all conspire to make the viewer co-experience the anguish and insecurity which are the true emotions of contemporary *film noir*', whose aim was 'to create a *specific alienation*' (ibid., p.25, original emphasis). Film noir therefore was deemed to unsettle spectators, forming a disruptive component of an American cinema that had habitually sought to reassure and comfort its audience. With its modernist sensibility, film noir embodied a critical strand in popular cinema. Borde and Chaumeton's high valuation of film noir was supported by the work of a new generation of French critics-turned-directors, Claude Chabrol, Jean-Luc Godard and François Truffaut, whose appropriation of film noir became an important component in their construction of a radical French cinema, the nouvelle vague, as discussed in Chapter 7.

As there was no equivalent intellectual film culture in America at this point, it was not until the late 1960s that the term film noir, and with it the intense interest in this body of films and the positive valuation placed on them that the French commentators had established, became widespread. The opening chapter of Charles Higham and Joel Greenberg's *Hollywood in the Forties* (1968) was entitled 'Black Cinema', but they used the term film noir within the text itself and placed a high value on a body of films seen as cynical, subversive, erotic and visually sophisticated (Higham and Greenberg, 1968, pp.19–50). Raymond Durgnat wrote a typically wide-ranging and provocative essay in 1970, 'Paint It Black: The Family Tree of the Film Noir' which helped to locate film noir within more general cultural formations (Durgnat, 1970, pp.48–56). However, it was Paul Schrader's 1972 essay 'Notes on *Film Noir*', originally issued to accompany a Los Angeles Museum retrospective, that was particularly influential, not only in defining noir 'stylistics', but also in its subdivision of what he regarded as a 'specific period of film history'. Schrader saw film noir as an inevitable development of the gangster film delayed by the war, which divided into three broad and overlapping phases: 1941–6 was the phase of the private eye and the lone wolf; 1945–9 showed a preoccupation with the problems of crime, political corruption and police routine; while 1949–53 was the 'period of psychotic action and suicidal impulse' that he regards as the 'cream'. Like Borde and Chaumeton, Schrader considered film noir's masterpiece to be a 'straggler', Robert Aldrich's *Kiss Me Deadly* (1955), while Orson Welles's *Touch of Evil* (1958) provided its 'epitaph' (Schrader, 1972, pp.8–13).

Schrader's enthusiasm echoed that of the earlier French writers, offering film noir to a rapidly developing American film culture as an exciting and iconoclastic element of Hollywood cinema that was ripe for revaluation and reappropriation following the widespread disillusionment consequent upon the war in Vietnam. Schrader observed, 'as the current political mood hardens, filmgoers and filmmakers will find the *film noir* of the late forties increasingly attractive', and its influence will be felt at a time when 'American movies are again taking a look at the underside of the American character' (ibid., p.8). Schrader himself wrote the screenplay for Martin Scorsese's *Taxi Driver* (1976), which, with its angst-ridden, alienated Vietnam veteran, updated film noir for a new generation and formed part of noir's revival as discussed in Chapter 7.

Since this formative period there has been a steady stream of academic articles, book-length studies and anthologies of essays. Alain Silver and Elizabeth Ward's encyclopedic *Film Noir*, first published in 1980, was highly influential in defining the noir 'canon', providing commentaries on over 250 films and tabulations of creative personnel and studio output (Silver and Ward, 1993). Slightly earlier, in 1978, *Women in Film Noir* edited by E. Ann

Kaplan, part of a wider feminist movement within cultural studies, raised the complex issue of noir's representation of women, the ways in which its female types, centrally the *femme fatale*, were expressive of ideological tensions within patriarchy over female sexuality. The reissue of an extended edition of *Women in Film Noir* twenty years later was testimony to the importance of these essays and to the continued interest in noir's construction of gender. Richard Dyer's essay on *Gilda* observed that 'film noir is characterised by a certain anxiety over the existence and definition of masculinity and normality' (Kaplan, 1998, p.115). Frank Krutnik's *In a Lonely Street*, was the first book-length study to discuss the complexities of masculinity within film noir (Krutnik, 1991). Chapter 5 discusses this issue in detail, and pays attention to the neglected area of actors' performances, which are central to the representation of gender. Of more recent studies of film noir, the outstanding contribution has been James Naremore's *More Than Night*, which attempted to place the 'noir phenomenon' within its various intellectual, cultural and social contexts (Naremore, 1998). However, film noir remains a contested term, a point that will be explored in the concluding section of this chapter.

THE CHARACTERISTICS OF FILM NOIR

The label 'film noir' designates a cycle of films that share a similar iconography, visual style, narrative strategies, subject matter and characterisation. Their iconography (repeated visual patterning) consists of images of the dark, night-time city, its streets damp with rain which reflects the flashing neon signs. Its sleazy milieu of claustrophobic alleyways and deserted docklands alternates with gaudy nightclubs and swank apartments. The visual style habitually employs high contrast (chiaroscuro) lighting, where deep, enveloping shadows are fractured by shafts of light from a single source, and dark, claustrophobic interiors have shadowy shapes on the walls. The decentred, unstable compositions are further distorted by the use of odd angles and wide-angle lenses; fog or mist obscures the action and characters' faces are often lit with strange highlights or partially shadowed to create hidden and threatening spaces. Noir's highly complex narrative patterning is created by the use of first-person voice-overs, multiple narrators, flashbacks and ellipses which often create ambiguous or inconclusive endings. Noir narratives are frequently oneiric (dream-like), where every object and encounter seems unnaturally charged.

Thematically, film noir is dominated by a mixture of existential and Freudian motifs, discussed in a separate section. The noir universe is dark, malign and unstable where individuals are trapped through fear and paranoia, or overwhelmed by the power of sexual desire. Noir's principal protagonists consist of the alienated, often psychologically disturbed, male anti-hero and the hard, deceitful *femme fatale* he encounters. But the range of noir characters is more complex than is usually thought. All these elements of film noir will be discussed in detail in the chapters that follow. The rest of this chapter will examine the cultural influences that gave rise to the noir cycle.

CULTURAL INFLUENCES

James Naremore has identified film noir as the interface between an avant-garde European modernism and an older, more conservative tradition of 'blood melodrama', stories of violence and erotic love that included crime films but also Gothic romance (Naremore, 1998, p.220). In examining the influence of these traditions on film noir it is useful to bear in mind Richard Maltby's observation that: 'Cultural history is too diffuse to allow for clear causal relationships; the most it can attempt is to establish a chain of plausibility' (Maltby, 1998, p.38).

'Hard-Boiled' Crime Fiction

> I first heard Personville called Poisonville by a red-haired mucker named Hickey Dewey in the Big Ship at Butte. He also called a shirt a shoit. I didn't think anything of what he had done to the city's name. Later I heard men who couldn't manage their r's give it the same pronunciation. I still didn't see anything in it but the meaningless sort of humour that used to make richardsnary the thieves' word for dictionary. A few years later I went to Personville and learned better.
>
> *(Dashiell Hammett,* Red Harvest, *1929)*

The work of the American 'hard-boiled' writers, such as Dashiell Hammett, Raymond Chandler and James M. Cain, was frequently used as the basis for films noirs: almost 20 per cent of noir thrillers produced between 1941 and 1948 were direct adaptations of 'hard-boiled' novels and short stories (Krutnik, 1991, pp.33–4, 182–7). In addition, numerous films noirs imitated or reworked hard-boiled sources and many hard-boiled writers, including Raymond Chandler who wrote an original screenplay for *The Blue Dahlia* (1946) and co-adapted Cain's *Double Indemnity*, were hired by Hollywood studios during this period. As Borde and Chaumeton argued, hard-boiled fiction formed the central and 'immediate' influence on film noir's subject matter and characterization.

Hard-boiled writing was a development of the nineteenth-century 'dime novel' where writers developed a vernacular style and promoted working-class attitudes and values that were expressive of American republican democracy (Denning, 1987). Hard-boiled writing formed part of what became known generically as 'pulp fiction', i.e. stories produced on cheap wood-pulp paper. The first cheap magazine devoted to crime fiction was the *Detective Story Magazine* established by 1915, but the most significant of well over twenty such titles was *Black Mask*, which was almost entirely devoted to hard-boiled fiction by the end of the 1920s. Towards the end of the 1930s this fiction began to appear in the new form of the paperback whose lurid covers promised a crime thriller laced with graphic sex and violence (O'Brien, 1997). Pulp fiction's readership was largely the male urban working class who enjoyed the fast-paced violence and eroticism.

Dashiell Hammett is often regarded as the 'father' of this tradition, with *Red Harvest*, quoted from above, a watershed between the older dime novelists and a more modern conception of an American society that is corrupt and alienated. Hammett developed a tough, terse, understated vernacular idiom that kept close to the rhythms of ordinary speech and is often directly narrated by the main male protagonist. In many ways this first-person narration was an 'essentially radio aesthetic' and indeed many of these stories were adapted for that new cultural form (Jameson, 1993, p.36). The short, declarative sentences of hard-boiled writing created a sense of speed and urgency that resembled reportage. Joseph T. Shaw, editor of *Black Mask*, encouraged his other writers to emulate Hammett's style with its 'objectivity, economy and restraint', and it was Shaw who persuaded Hammett himself to move into full-length fiction. Hammett and other exponents of the art were masters of the laconic wisecrack, which combined wit, verbal aggression and a sense of self-esteem. These characteristics made hard-boiled writing the opposite of the more polite, refined and middle-class 'English school' of detective fiction, which included Agatha Christie and Dorothy L. Sayers. In Raymond Chandler's famous description, 'Hammett took murder out of the Venetian vase and dropped it into the alley' (Chandler, 1964, p.194). American writers replaced ratiocination by action, and the drawing rooms of country houses with the 'mean streets' of the fast-growing American city (Porter, 1981).

This concentration on urban life was distinctive and modern, reflecting the major cultural and social transformation that America was undergoing (Marling, 1995). Although Hammett's 'Poisonville' is any modern American town, his disciple Chandler became the great chronicler of Los Angeles, *the* modern metropolis. In hard-boiled writing, the city is corrupt, disorientating and threatening, often depicted as a dark, confusing labyrinth, a nightmare city that is the seamy but enticing underside to respectable American life (Christopher, 1997). This city is an emphatically masculine world, concentrating on male ambitions and lusts; and, it must be emphasized, their fears and paranoias. The male protagonists of hard-boiled fiction are obsessed with women, but only with their looks and bodies, the way they move or wear make-up and clothes. Most frequently, women are characterized as *femmes fatales*, overwhelmingly desirable but duplicitous.

The most famous male protagonist was the private eye. In Hammett's fiction the figure is either the anonymous 'The Continental Op', an employee of a detective agency, or the self-employed gumshoe Sam Spade whose over-riding obsession is never to be a 'sap'. Chandler's serial detective, Philip Marlowe, was a more refined and honourable character. American reviewers thought his name sounded resonantly English, connoting elegance and erudi-tion. Marlowe is independent, incorruptible, intelligent, cultured and sensit-ive, but also tough, hard-drinking and good with his fists. Like Sam Spade, he is a lone outsider, who lives in a cheap, comfortless flat free from family ties. Marlowe's investigations as the modern knight of the city streets do not form part of any wider crusade. Unlike Sherlock Holmes, Marlowe realizes that although he may solve an individual case, it is part of a wider corruption that is too deep to be eradicated. The private eye was the new urban folk hero who mediated between respectable society and the criminal underworld (Donald, 1999, p.70). His real significance lay in his ability to interpret modern urban life, 'to reveal whatever the city conceals: secret passions, liaisons, crimes and corruptions' (Willett, 1996, p.6).

After Hammett and Chandler, James M. Cain was the most influential pulp writer. Edmund Wilson dubbed Cain the leader of the 'poets of tabloid murder', observing that 'Cain himself is particularly ingenious in tracing from their first beginnings the tangles that gradually tighten around the necks of the people involved in those bizarre and brutal crimes that figure in the Amer-ican papers' (Wilson, 1962, p.21). Cain never uses a private eye protagonist, instead his narrators are themselves criminals, therefore his novels took the form of the extended 'confession' so beloved of tabloid readers, though his fiction also had an educated readership. His protagonists are victims of the Depression, ordinary people forced by circumstances into crime, becoming drifters who turn to violence, in a world where individual effort is no longer rewarded with financial security. Cain's fiction focused on the rootless lower class who poured, from the prairies and deserts, into Los Angeles, a city which functions, as in Chandler's novels, as a seductive Eldorado. Cain concen-trates on the alliance between money and sexual desire, particularly male fears of female sexuality: the *femme fatale* with whom the narrators become enmeshed. His narrators have no capacity for self-analysis or reflection and do not develop as characters, but are gripped by the obsessive 'fatal passion' that dominates their lives.

Cornell Woolrich's influence on film noir is not so widely recognized, and yet no less significant: eleven of his stories were adapted in the classic period. Woolrich wrote for a whole range of magazines in the 1930s and 1940s and his output was prodigious (Nevins, 1988). Although his prose has the typically pared-down, urgent idiom of the 'hard-boiled' school, it contains tortuously elaborate passages of masochistic delirium through which his characters, who are almost always victims, acknowledge that 'defeat, dispossession, fear and pursuit [are] the shaping energies of life' (Lee, 1990, p.185). His stories take to new extremes the metaphor of the city as a nightmare labyrinth in which his paranoid protagonists are trapped and from which they try frantically to escape. His fictional world is therefore more overtly expressionist. Any sense of objective reality is engulfed in subjective fantasies, which Woolrich often describes in detail. For instance, the scene in *Phantom Lady* (1942) in which the female protagonist visits a nightclub where black jazz musicians are playing: 'The next two hours were spent in a sort of Dante-esque inferno . . . It wasn't the music, the music was good. It was the phantasmagoria of their shadows, looming black, wavering ceiling-high on the walls. It was the actuality of their faces, possessed, demonic, peering out here and there on sudden notes, then seeming to recede again' (quoted in Tuska, 1984, p.88). Passages like these were readily translatable into noir's visual idiom, and Robert Siodmak's 1944 adaptation is discussed in detail in Chapter 6.

James Naremore argues that the work of these hard-boiled writers developed 'blood melodrama' into a modernist art form, but one that was populist rather than avant-garde (Naremore, 1998, pp.40–95). Their influence on film was delayed until the 1940s because, as will be discussed in the next chapter, Hollywood films were aimed at a 'family audience', and were subject to close censorship, which prose fiction escaped. The major studios, sensing the potential problems in such suggestive subject matter, translated hard-boiled fiction into a more restrained and less combative idiom. Two early adaptations of *The Maltese Falcon* – Roy del Ruth's 1931 version and William Dieterle's *Satan Met a Lady* (1936) – significantly modified Hammett's style, softening the characterization of the detective so that he became the much more respectable figure of the gentleman amateur. Even in 1942, in RKO's *The Falcon Takes Over*, an adaptation of Chandler's *Farewell, My Lovely*, George Sanders plays the detective as the debonair socialite, breezing through a well-lit, upper-crust world in what was then the dominant form of the comedy thriller. It was John Huston's *The Maltese Falcon* (1941) – the first adaptation that was true to the spirit of the original – that began to close the gulf between the hard-boiled tradition and its screen equivalent.

The Gangster Film

Although it was not as central as hard-boiled fiction, the gangster film did exert an important cultural influence on film noir, because it represented another development of 'blood melodrama' that was centrally concerned with crime, violence and the modern American city. The gangster, like the private eye, contributed to the 'cultural mapping of new social territory', the city (Ruth, 1996, p.8). As Robert Warshow memorably articulated: 'The gangster is a man of the city, with the city's language and knowledge, with its queer and dishonest skills and its terrible daring . . . not the real city, but that dangerous and sad city of the imagination' (Warshow, 1962, p.131). The gangster was another authentic American folk hero, 'the archetypal American dreamer' whose actions live out the contradictions of capitalism, the price of being a successful competitive individualist.

Although the gangster was a staple of pulp fiction, the figure was also a screen presence as far back as D.W. Griffith's *The Musketeers of Pig Alley* (1912), or *Alias Jimmy Valentine* (1915) which was remade in 1920 and 1928. Joseph Von Sternberg's *Underworld* (1927) scripted by Ben Hecht, was the story of Bull Weed (George Bancroft), a top Chicago mobster arrested for killing his arch rival. In prison he becomes convinced that he has been betrayed by his moll, Feathers McCoy (Evelyn Brent), in league with an alcoholic intellectual Rolls Royce (Clive Brook), whom Bull befriended when he discovered him begging on a street corner. After breaking out, Bull realizes they are both loyal to him and in love. He lets the pair escape, facing certain death at the hands of the police cordon alone. *Underworld* was the first film to depict a criminal milieu sympathetically and Von Sternberg's shadowy, atmospheric direction lends the cityscape a spectral suggestiveness that complements Hecht's taut, idiomatic script. *Underworld*'s themes of alienation, paranoia, betrayal, revenge and the desire for death, all prefigure film noir.[1]

The major cycle of gangster films occurred shortly after Hollywood's transition to sound enabled it to capture the dramatic sound of machine-gun fire and the fast patter of the gangster's speech. The three seminal films of the early 1930s – Mervyn LeRoy's *Little Caesar* (1930), William Wellman's *The Public Enemy* (UK title: Enemies of the Public, 1931) and Howard Hawks's *Scarface* (1932) – all contributed to the development of a subversive image of the gangster as the modern entrepreneur. Author and screenwriter W.R. Burnett emphasised that *Little Caesar*'s dialogue attempted to treat criminals as human beings, showing the world through their eyes, and also developed 'a style of writing based on the way American people spoke – not literary English. Of course, that the Chicago slang was all around me made it easy to pick up' (McGilligan, 1986, p.58). James Cagney's role as Tom Powers in *The Public Enemy* incarnated the modern 'city boy', the man from a deprived background whose toughness, dynamic energy and quick wits allow him to succeed through his own efforts in a competitive world (Sklar, 1992). As Jonathan Munby has argued, gangster fiction constituted a dissident tradition which represented lower-class and ethnically marginalized American interests in the

1920s and 1930s, their 'frustrated desire for cultural and economic inclusion' in an era of Prohibition and the Depression (Munby, 1999a, p.40).

It is for this reason that Munby argues that film noir is a cycle or particular development within the broad generic history of the crime/gangster film. Munby argues that to place film noir outside that context is to run the risk of 'an ahistorical vision of crime film forms' that negates the strong links and continuities between the 1930s and the 1940s. However, while the influence of 1930s gangster films on film noir is profound, many commentators have pointed out that the heroic self-assertion of the gangster – intensely *public* figures who represent the pleasures of conspicuous consumption and whose story is one of rapid rise and inevitable fall – is very different from the doom-laden withdrawal of the typical small-time, unheroic noir protagonist. Noir's antiheroes do not dominate their environments and often do not deserve what happens to them. The archetypal gangster becomes a marginal presence in film noir. With the exception of *Underworld*, the visual texture of the gangster film is typically flatter and less self-conscious than film noir, a straightforward realism, direct and economical.[2]

The Gothic Romance

Accounts of film noir have over-privileged its debt to the hard-boiled tradition, and therefore its male-centredness, at the expense of the Gothic legacy, the other great tradition of 'blood melodrama'. In his recent authoritative study of 1940s Hollywood, Thomas Schatz rightly argues that the Gothic romance was equally important in generating the noir style and that Gothic noirs such as *Gaslight* (1944) share a close 'family resemblance' to hard-boiled noirs in both style and themes (Schatz, 1997, pp.232–9). As film noir continued into the 1950s, it became dominated by the male-orientated crime thriller, but the importance of the Gothic romance to early film noir is immense.

The Gothic romance was a literary tradition that originated in the late eighteenth century as part of a European revival of Gothicism in the arts, a shift in taste that embraced the wild, the morbid and the supernatural, a new preoccupation with death, solitude and the horrific or terrifying (Punter, 1996). The key Gothic setting is the ruin or the labyrinthine mansion with its secret, shadowy passageways and locked rooms containing dark secrets. The most influential Gothic romance was Anne Radcliffe's *The Mysteries of Udolpho* (1794) with its persecuted heroine imprisoned in the decaying castle of Udolpho by her aunt's sinister husband. The Gothic tradition migrated to America as early as the end of the eighteenth century, in the work of Charles Brockenden Brown, and was developed by Nathaniel Hawthorne and Edgar Allan Poe. Old World Gothic was refracted into a preoccupation with evil Europeans and with the pathology of guilt (ibid., pp.165–85).

The Gothic romance modulated through the nineteenth century 'sensation novel' to become one of the staples of popular fiction targeted at a female audience (Modleski, 1982, pp.59–84). The modern Gothic romance continues to have at its centre the imperilled victim-heroine, often recently married to an enigmatic older man to whom she feels intensely attracted and repelled, and who feels helpless, confused, frightened and despised; her paranoias include the strong sensation that the past is repeating itself. She has a desperate desire to know her husband's secret, but is terrified about what that knowledge may bring. Hollywood drew extensively on this Gothic tradition in the 1940s as a branch of the 'woman's film', aimed at the numerically dominant female audience and displaying an ambivalent attitude towards the Victorian period. The first Gothic noir was Alfred Hitchcock's *Rebecca* (1940) discussed in Chapter 3, adapted from Daphne du Maurier's 1939 novel.[3]

European Influences 1: German Expressionism

German Expressionism is always cited as the major influence on film noir's arresting visual style and also its pessimistic mood. However, it was the influence of Weimar cinema (1919–33) as a whole, rather than just 'Expressionism', that was profound, and also more complex, multifaceted and indirect than is often supposed.

The origins of German Expressionism lay deep in the Gothic-Romantic movement in European culture. Expressionism was a cross-cultural movement encompassing music, dance, painting, sculpture, architecture, design, literature, theatre and film, which lasted roughly between 1906 and 1924. In essence it was a philosophical and artistic critique of bourgeois rationalism; an attempt to express the distortions, alienation, fragmentation and dislocation, the 'irrationality', of modern life. Expressionism was concerned to represent subjective experience: states of mind, feelings, ideas, perceptions, dreams and visions, often paranoid states. The protagonists of many Expressionist films – including the most famous and influential, Robert Wiene's *Das Cabinet des Dr Caligari* (*The Cabinet of Dr Caligari*, 1919) – are frequently tormented or unbalanced. *Der Student von Prag* (*The Student of Prague*), first released in 1913, but remade in Expressionist style in 1926, was the archetypal *Doppelgänger* story in which a student sells his mirror image to a sorcerer who turns that image into the young man's evil, murderous second self. *The Student of Prague* was eloquent testimony to Expressionism's concern with the instability and fluidity of identity, which found resonant echoes in film noir. Expressionism created an embracing *stimmung* (mood) and texture, dependent on a distinct visual style that used high contrast, chiaroscuro lighting where shafts of intense light contrast starkly with deep, black shadows, and where space is fractured into an assortment of unstable lines and surfaces, often fragmented or twisted into odd angles. Overall, Expressionist cinema used a highly designed and carefully composed mise-en-scène that was anti-naturalistic. In a recent study, Thomas Elsaesser emphasizes the complexity of narration as another key characteristic. Expressionist cinema cultivated displaced, decentred narratives, nested in frame tales, split or doubled stories, voice-overs and flashback narration (Elsaesser, 2000). Both Expressionism's style and its narrative patterns influenced film noir.

The Weimar 'Street Film' and the Urban Thriller

Without denying the importance of Expressionism, Janice Morgan has emphasized the significance of the *Strassenfilm*, the 'street film', as an influence on film noir (Morgan, 1996, pp.31–53). The street film was part of what is usually known as *Neue Sachlichkeit* or 'New Objectivity' which departed from the Gothic scenarios of Expressionism to concentrate on the social realities of contemporary German life. The subject matter of this cycle of films, beginning with Karl Grune's *Die Strasse* (*The Street*, 1923), was the descent of a respectable middle-class protagonist into the 'overcharged landscape' – fascinating, thrilling, but dangerous – of city streets at night. In these films one can perceive a proto-noir urban milieu consisting of deep shadows, rushing traffic, flashing lights and cast of underworld characters: black marketeers, gamblers and con men and, above all, the *femme fatale* who embodies the temptation and threat of illicit desire. The cycle was most associated with G.W. Pabst, notably *Die freudlose Gasse* (*The Joyless Street*, 1923) set in Vienna in the period of hyperinflation, but also Joe May's *Asphalt* (1928) where an up and coming policeman from a good family falls in love with a prostitute. The 'street film', and the later development of the *Milieuonfilm* ('milieu talkie'), were realistic and ordinary, delineating the characteristic psychic and social ills of modern day urban life. Von Sternberg's *Der blaue Engel* (*The Blue Angel*, 1930), made simultaneously in German and English, depicted the descent of a school teacher (Emil Jannings) who becomes enthralled by a *femme fatale*, a nightclub singer played by Marlene Dietrich.

Fritz Lang's urban crime thrillers about the master criminal Dr Mabuse – *Dr Mabuse der Spieler* (*Dr Mabuse the Gambler*) parts one and two (1922) and *Das Testament von Dr Mabuse* (*The Last Will of Dr Mabuse*, 1932) – and his study of a paedophile in his best known film, *M* (1931), showed a preoccupation with the fluidity of identity, depicting the city as a dark labyrinth (Kaes, 2000; Gunning, 2000, pp.87–202). In *M*, Franz Becker (Peter Lorre) is a tortured outsider caught between the rival forces of police and organized crime. Becker is painfully aware of his condition, that the desires that dictate his actions are beyond his rational control. Lang combined dispassionate observation with an intense subjectivity in the frequent scenes where the action is shown from

The birth of the modern thriller: Peter Lorre in *M* (Fritz Lang, 1931)

the viewpoint of the protagonist. Lang commented: 'I use my camera in such a way as to show things, wherever possible, from the viewpoint of the protagonist; in that way my audience identifies itself with the character on the screen and thinks with him' (Bogdanovich, 1967, p.85). To 'think with' such characters is deeply disturbing, suggesting as it does that criminality and deviance are not 'out there' safely distanced, but a potential within the modern subject, a possible identity to inhabit.

Émigrés

Lang was one of many German film-makers who pursued a second career in America. The reputation of Weimar cinema and the technical expertise of its creative personnel made them a highly desirable commodity for Hollywood. The rise of Nazism and Hitler's assumption of power in 1933 served to intensify an already established exodus. These émigrés included directors: William Dieterle, Lang, Otto Preminger, Siodmak and the writer-director Billy Wilder; cinematographers: John Alton, Karl Freund and Rudolph Maté; and also actors, set designers, scriptwriters and composers. Their influence was pervasive but by no means simple. Many worked on other types of pictures than film noir and many films noirs bear no trace of Austro-German involvement. As Marc Vernet has pointed out, Expressionist lighting techniques were already part of Hollywood's stylistic repertoire and predated any direct influence (Vernet, 1993, pp.1–32). As this study will show, Hollywood's 'classical narrative' style with its continuity editing was only capable of partial deformation by the more severe expressionist techniques. American films, made within a more nakedly commercial system, did not strive for the 'landscape of delirium' that Expressionism used. The direct influence of Expressionist techniques, as Foster Hirsch has observed, comes out most strongly in nightmare sequences, 'where for a few moments, under the protection of a dream interlude, the film becomes overtly subjective, entering into the hero's consciousness to portray its disordered fragments' (Hirsch, 1983, p.57). However, rather than direct transplantation, one is looking at a process of diffusion and reappropriation where a modified Expressionism could be superimposed over existing generic conventions through a more self-conscious deployment of mise-en-scène, chiaroscuro lighting, minimalist sets, mobile camerawork and the use of fractured narratives.

What the detailed studies of Siodmak and Lang in Chapter 6 seek to demonstrate is that successful émigrés were those who could assimilate to some degree their host culture. Both Wilder – whose *Double Indemnity* (1944) was the single most influential film noir – and Lang were fascinated by, but also critical of, American life; they were what Elsaesser has called 'doubly estranged' from both their homeland and their hosts, producing a schizophrenic artistic vision that was neither wholly European nor fully American (Elsaesser, 2000, p.374). Jonathan Munby has shown how the sensibility of the Austrian-Jewish directors – Wilder, Preminger and Edgar Ulmer – was shaped by their early experience of 'internal exile', as Jews in Catholic Vienna, before they emigrated to America (Munby, 1999b, pp.138–62). Munby also emphasizes their extensive Americanization in the 1930s. Each developed a close and detailed knowledge of their country of adoption, an affection and concern for American democracy and the American way of life, whilst remaining outsiders, a process of partial assimilation and continued critical detachment that was especially wary of any attempt to suppress freedom of thought and expression, notoriously McCarthyism, analysed later. The émigrés were able to mould 'blood melodrama' so that it also bore the trace of European modernism, which was in turn influenced by American Expressionism, discussed below.

European Influences 2: French Poetic Realism

The effect of French Poetic Realism on film noir is less appreciated, but Ginette Vincendeau has provided a cogent and persuasive case for its stylistic and thematic influence, which, she argues, ' "filled the gap" between German Expressionism and classical Hollywood cinema' (Vincendeau, 1992b, p.54). The term Poetic Realism was first used in 1933 to describe 'a genre of urban drama, often set among the Paris proletariat or lower middle classes, with romantic/criminal narratives emphasising doom and despair. In these films, "poetry" and mystery are found in everyday objects and settings – hence the proletarian milieu' (ibid., p.52). The alternative label was *le fantastique social* – one that radiated eeriness in an ordinary, not Gothic milieu. Prewar French critics and reviewers did use the term film noir to describe these films (O'Brien, 1996, pp.7–20). This cycle of films, whose central period was 1936–9, was dominated by the collaboration of scriptwriter Jacques Prévert and director Marcel Carné. The pair made seven films together, including the two that are considered to be definitive: *Quai des brumes* (*Port of Shadows*, 1938) and *Le Jour se lève* (*Daybreak*, 1939).

Poetic Realism drew on an indigenous tradition of crime fiction that concentrated on the everyday, the ordinary and the banal. The chief exponent was Georges Simenon who rose to prominence in the early 1930s and was popular with both the intelligentsia and a broad public. However, Simenon competed with a strong Gallic taste for hard-boiled American crime writers: Carné was enthralled by the hard boiled American *policier*. Revealingly, the first adaptation of Cain's *The Postman Always Rings Twice* was made in France in 1939 as *Le Dernier Tournant* (*The Final Twist*), directed by Pierre Chenal.

Poetic Realism's visual style was indebted to Weimar cinema and German cameramen and set designers were frequently employed. Several German directors, including Lang and Siodmak, worked in French cinema before going to America, and French creative personnel had almost invariably worked in Germany. However, Poetic Realism was a distinctive modification of Expressionism, exhibiting a softer and less extreme use of chiaroscuro. Poetic Realism is concerned to create a distinctive milieu with shiny cobblestones and neon-lit nightclubs that are sites of danger and desire, and much atmospheric use is made of shadow or fog. But the city was rendered less abstractly than in the Weimar 'street film'. The sets were designed to have solidity, and to render a specific milieu, not a generalized one, hence the terms *Films de milieu* or *Films d'atmosphère*. The pace of Poetic Realism is closer to Weimar than to Hollywood, using tightly controlled camera movements and long takes, reframing rather than cutting within their deep focus settings.

As Dudley Andrew observes, the pace and insistent mise-en-scène makes Poetic Realism a cinema of character rather than events, and its typical protagonists anticipate film noir (Andrew, 1995). The dangers of desire, as in the 'street film', were represented by the *femme fatale*, or 'lost girl', in her beret and shiny raincoat that transferred the reflections of the night-time city onto her body as if she were all surface, without substance. The male protagonists tend to be confused, passive, divided and deeply introspective. The dominant actor was Jean Gabin, always marked as an outsider, romantic, but possessed by self-destructive forces. Such was Gabin's stature that he created a new type of male hero, a modern Everyman who is complex and ambivalent, both sexually and socially. His tough masculine power is often outweighed by a 'feminine' sensitivity and vulnerability, a clear difference from his American counterparts, and his social status is ambiguous or confused. He often plays a decent workman or soldier who, through circumstances beyond his control, is criminalized. Like many noir heroes, his past is constantly alluded to, but never fully revealed. Unlike his American successors, Gabin always dies, making these French films, for instance *Pépé le Moko* (1937) where he kills himself, generally bleaker and more heavily fatalistic than film noir. The lighting, milieu, iconography and characterization, especially Gabin's angst-ridden hero, all prefigure noir.

These films were not only popular in France – *Quai des brumes* was the most successful film released in 1938 – but they were also intensely admired within English and American intellectual circles as adult in content and visually sophisticated (ibid., pp.13–14, 89, 255). As Vincendeau points out, there were also direct American remakes. Renoir's *La Chienne* (*The Bitch*, 1931), a dark drama about a respectable clerk's victimization by a prostitute and her pimp, based on a best-selling crime thriller by George de la Fouchardière, was remade by Lang as *Scarlet Street* (1945), its Parisian locale transferred to New York's Greenwich Village. *Le Jour se lève* was remade as *The Long Night* (1947), directed by Anatole Litvak and starring Henry Fonda in the Gabin role.

American Expressionism: Universal Horrors, Val Lewton and Orson Welles

The most direct influence of German Expressionism was felt on a cycle of horror films produced by Universal Studios in the early 1930s. Universal, led by the German-born Carl Laemmle, had a tradition of hiring Weimar talent including Edgar Ulmer who directed the extraordinary *The Black Cat* (UK title: *House of Doom*, 1934). The horror cycle was initiated by the American Tod Browning's *Dracula* and the Englishman James Whale's *Frankenstein*, both released in 1931. Whale, a sophisticated intellectual with a great feeling for Gothic forms, was the key director, also making *The Old Dark House* (1932), and *The Bride of Frankenstein* (1935), the most celebrated of these films. Robert Florey's *Murders in the Rue Morgue* (1932) was the most directly Expressionist, with strong echoes of *Caligari* in the twisted streets, oddly contorted houses that lean over the glistening cobblestones, and gloomy shadows (Dettmann and Bedford, 1976, p.24). The German émigré Karl Freund photographed *Murders* (and *Dracula*) and also directed *The Mummy* (1932). In the opening scene the assistant of the English archaeologist who has been investigating the Pharaoh's tomb opens the sacred chest thereby releasing the protective curse that brings the Mummy (Boris Karloff) gradually to life. The pacing of this silent scene, its acting, and its lighting – the glowing white light and deep, velvety shadows – are all pure Weimar.

The best of the Universal horror films take great care over composition (both design and decor), camera angles and lighting, and their slow pace allows the subtle suggestiveness of the mise-en-scène to create the meaning. Universal's second horror cycle, beginning with *Son of Frankenstein* (1939), was less distinguished, but both cycles were a major influence on the studio's early experimentation with film noir, beginning with Hitchcock's *Shadow of a Doubt* (1943) and Siodmak's *Phantom Lady* (1944) which influenced the development of the whole noir cycle.

As discussed in Chapter 3, the other studio most associated with film noir was RKO, whose evolution of the form was indebted to both Val Lewton and Orson Welles. The Russian-born Lewton started at RKO in 1942, running his own 'B' feature unit to produce horror films that would compete with Universal's (Siegel, 1972). Their frugal budgets and low status meant that Lewton enjoyed almost complete creative control, free of front office inter-ference save for the lurid titles that were established by production chief Charles Koerner through market pre-testing. Despite his budgetary limitations, Lewton's erudition and painstaking meticulousness over every aspect of production created a series of eleven films that were coherent, visually dis-tinctive and of high aesthetic quality. He shaped and encouraged the work of his directors, including Jacques Tourneur who directed the first three features, Robert Wise and Mark Robson, all of whom went on to make distinguished films noirs. Unlike Universal's monsters, Lewton's horrors featured ordinary men and women in what were usually contemporary, often urban, settings. The principal cinematographer was Nicholas Musuraca, already known as a specialist in 'mood lighting', who honed his craft on these films where impoverished sets could be disguised by the use of atmospheric lighting effects. Musuraca became one of the most significant noir cameramen.

Lewton's first film *Cat People* (1942) was a supernatural 'chiller', the third, *The Leopard Man* (1943), was adapted from Woolrich's *Black Alibi* in which a deranged serial killer distracts attention by casting suspicion on the activities of an escaped leopard. Perhaps the most atmospheric, subtly suggestive and chilling film was the fourth, *The Seventh Victim* (1943). Its epigraph is from one of John Donne's Holy Sonnets – 'I run to Death, and Death meets me as fast, and all my Pleasures are like Yesterdays' – which inaugurates a tale of isolation and morbid despair in which a young woman, Jacqueline, takes her own life, seeing death as a release from the intolerable existentialist pressures of living. *The Seventh Victim* is a complex modernist film that can pass as a genre product through its use of a satanic cult – the Palladists – which pursue Jacqueline, and its quest story in which Jacqueline's sister and her lover try to unravel the mystery of her disappearance. It contained a famous visual set-piece where Jacqueline, released by the Palladists to walk the deserted midnight streets, is assailed by the threatening shadows, that alternate with the bright shafts of light from street lamps, and menacing but obscure sounds. At the height of tension a city bus arrives, and the sound of its brakes and the opening of the pneumatic doors are as startling as an appearance of the monster in a conventional horror film. Lewton worked on audiences' imaginations, knowing that given the right suggestions, the viewer 'will populate the darkness with more horrors than all the horror writers in Hollywood could think of' (quoted in ibid., p.32). As J.P. Telotte argues, Lewton's films question the nature of perception and expose the fictiveness of rationality and the processes of reason, emphasizing the dreamlike qualities of experience, the power of myths and psychic fantasies and the constant threat of meaninglessness (Telotte, 1985). In both subject manner and style they helped generate film noir.

Orson Welles's interest in cinematic modernism and avant-garde practice was well known (Arthur, 1996b, pp.367–82). He made several important contributions to film noir, but his astonishingly innovative *Citizen Kane* (1940) has often been identified as *the* key example of 'American Expressionism' and therefore another bridge between European modernism and film noir. *Citizen Kane*'s investigation of its enigmatic subject, Charles Foster Kane the newspaper magnate, uses a number of Expressionist techniques in set design, lighting, the use of mirrors, superimpositions and distorted perspectives as well as a multiple flashback narration. The film's complex design, involving an unprecedented number of separate sets, facilitated the dramatic choreography of Welles's camerawork, which was indebted to the Weimar *Kammerspielfilm* (literally 'chamber film'). The most sophisticated *Kammerspielfilm* was *The Last Laugh* (1924), where director F.W. Murnau and his cinematographer Karl Freund developed the *entfesselte kamera*, the 'unfastened' or 'unchained' camera, using cranes, dollies and holsters strapped to the cameraman to free the camera from its tripod. The camera's mobility was the means through which subjective experience, an intimate individual psychology, could be realized, often through complex point-of-view shots.

Welles's innovations were developed through his intense collaboration with the highly experienced cinematographer Greg Toland (Carringer, 1985, pp.67–86). *Kane* is famous for its use of deep-focus photography, which allows objects in the foreground and background to be seen with equal clarity. Toland had not invented this technique and had used it on several of his earlier films, including Samuel Goldwyn's *Dead End* (1938), that have been identified as forerunners of film noir; but *Kane* was an audaciously bold application of what was, at this point, an unconventional method (Cormack, 1994, pp.123–37). Toland also makes consistent and creative use of wide-angle lenses and low-angle compositions that distort the foreground with figures elongated or slightly ballooned out. Welles's use of sound effects, deriving from his radio work, was also innovative and Bernard Herrmann's unconventional score, which used unorthodox combinations of instruments, was the first of many he would contribute to film noir.

Kane was the product of Welles's exceptional artistic ability and the unheard-of creative freedom he was offered, as the 'boy wonder', by George J. Schaefer, head of production at RKO, in a bid to add more cultured films to the studio's rather 'assembly-line' product (Jewell, 1996, pp.122–31). Although *Kane* was not popular with a broad public, it was a critical success, voted best picture of 1941 by the New York film critics and the National Board of Review, and receiving Academy Nominations in nine categories. The development of deep-focus photography was brought to a halt by the war, but Expressionist lighting came into vogue shortly after *Kane*'s release, in part at least, attributable to the influence of Welles's extraordinary achievement. Elaborate tracking shots, long takes, compositions in depth and set designs reminiscent of *Kane* are all evident in 1940s films noirs. *Kane* was also influential in its use of subjective narration through a complex use of flashbacks, which opened up a whole range of possibilities that Hollywood's conventional omniscient narration foregoes.

The characteristics of film noir that were outlined at the end of the first section can now be understood as the complex synthesis of American and European cultural traditions. But this synthesis occurred at a particular historical moment, which also needs to be analysed in detail.

FILM NOIR AS A 'DARK MIRROR' TO AMERICAN SOCIETY

In attempting to explain the eruption of film noir's dark, cynical and often pessimistic stories into the sunlit pastures of Hollywood's characteristically optimistic and affirmative cinema, film historians have often resorted to the metaphor of the 'dark mirror': 'However briefly, then, *film noir* held up a dark mirror to post-war America and reflected its moral anarchy' (Cook, 1990, p.471). At its broadest this 'moral anarchy' or, as it is often termed, 'social malaise', is related to several overarching factors: America's entry into the Second World War and the end of isolationism; paranoias about the 'red menace' that developed into McCarthyism as the Cold War penetrated deeply into popular consciousness; and the reverberations of dropping the hydrogen bombs on Hiroshima and Nagasaki. Silver and Ward argue that 'McCarthyism and the specter of the Bomb became the unspoken inspirations for a leitmotif of fear or, more specifically, paranoia that resounded through the noir cycle after the war' (Silver and Ward, 1980, p.2). Historians have tended to see the late 1940s in America as a period of uncertainty, an 'age of anxiety', in which there seemed to be a significant tension between an outward stability and prosperity, and strong inner doubts and a sense of alienation.[4] One historian has recently described this condition of fear and paranoia as 'triumphalist despair' (Engelhart, 1995, p.9). Dana Polan argues that film noir was one of the outgrowths of the change from a unified, collective war culture to a much more fragmented postwar society uncertain of its direction (Polan, 1986). It is possible to support these contentions through contemporary views. The reviewer I quoted at the beginning commented, 'psychologists explain that [the moviegoer] likes [this type of film because] it serves as a violent escape in tune with the violence of the times, a cathartic for pent-up emotions . . . the war has made us psychologically and emotionally ripe for pictures of this sort' (Shearer, 1945, in Silver and Ursini, 1999a, p.10).

Postwar Readjustment

Films noirs are littered with maladjusted veterans, the product of the difficult and traumatic readjustment to peace and civilian life after a period of severe disruption and the dangers, and excitements, of active service. Like other extended conflicts, the Second World War had profound psychological effects upon its combatants, often making their reintegration into civilian society difficult or impossible. The problem of the 'psychoneurotic vet' who had been traumatized by his wartime experiences and whose unpredictable violence, instability and aimlessness made him unsuited for civilian life, was well documented. He often became disillusioned by returning to his mundane prewar occupation after becoming used to both action and command. Kaya Silverman, quoting Siegfried Kracauer's observation that the returning veteran was an 'average individual stunned by the shock of readjustment', argues that he became the representative postwar male whose problems indicted the breakdown of established notions of social functioning, inducing an 'historical trauma' where males felt impotent and dysfunctional, compulsive and passive (Silverman, 1992, pp.52–124). The preoccupation with these 'difficult', 'damaged' men – who had disturbing similarities to the 'shell-shocked' victims of the Great War – extended to magazine journalism, lodging the problem in popular consciousness. William Wyler's *The Best Years of Our Lives*, which dramatized these issues, was the most popular film released in 1946. Films noirs' veterans, in such examples as *Cornered* (1945) or *Ride the Pink Horse* (1947), thus formed part of a wider concern, but, as will be argued in Chapters 4 and 5, the narrative patterns and visual style of film noir enabled it to explore this problem most extensively. Maladjustment was an important preoccupation in the immediate aftermath of the war, rarely surfacing after 1950.

Clearly interwoven with this concern for the returning serviceman were the wartime changes in the role of women. The temporary but widespread use of women in the labour force brought with it a new sense of social and economic independence and this fostered fears of male displacement and unease which was condensed in the figure of the *femme fatale* (Harvey, 1998, pp.35–46). But the preponderance of these strong-willed, manipulative and sexually active females in film noir was also a challenge to the dominant Hollywood conventions of representing women. The relations between the sexes are often played out in the nightclub rather than the home, which, like family life, is a notable absence in films noirs (Sobchak, 1998, pp.129–70). These issues of male paranoia and the independent woman will be explored in detail in Chapter 5.

McCarthyism

After the initial upheavals created by the return to peace subsided, the most abiding preoccupation of American society became the Communist 'threat'. The intense anti-Communist campaign that grew up after the war has come to be referred to as 'McCarthyism' after the Republican Senator Joseph McCarthy who tirelessly rooted out the 'enemy within' that was supposedly undermining the fabric of American society and values.[5] The Republican resurgence after the war gave the party the confidence for a renewed assault on what it regarded as subversive elements that included an attack on those who still adhered to the social welfare doctrines of Roosevelt's New Deal, forged in the early 1930s in response to the Depression. McCarthy, constantly trying to grab attention through the media, was the mouthpiece for these ideas. The actual instrument was the House Committee on UnAmerican Activities (HUAC) formed in 1938, but now given a vigorous new lease of life. A sub-committee descended on Hollywood for preliminary hearings into alleged 'communist infiltration of the motion picture industry' in May 1947. In October the Committee conducted public hearings in Washington in which 'friendly' and 'unfriendly' witnesses from the film industry were summoned. The 'friendly' ones dutifully complained of Communist infiltration in the film industry while the eleven 'unfriendly' witnesses refused to co-operate. One, Bertolt Brecht, fled back to Europe, but the remainder, the 'Hollywood Ten', were imprisoned for contempt of Congress. Among the Ten were director Edward Dmytryk, writer-producer Adrian Scott and influential scriptwriters Dalton Trumbo and Albert Matz. A meeting of studio executives and members of the industry's regulating body, the Motion Pictures Producers Association, agreed to suspend the Ten without pay and deny employment to anyone re-fusing to co-operate with HUAC's investigations, thereby effectively institut-ing a blacklist of unemployable artists. After a second more protracted and virulent round of investigations, which happened intermittently during 1951–4, over 200 suspected Communists had been blacklisted. The list went un-challenged until 1960 when Dalton Trumbo was re-employed, but Dmytryk re-appeared before the Committee in 1951 and, because he had named twenty-four former Communists, was reinstated (Belton, 1994, pp.328–44).

The anti-Communist witch hunt helped to create a climate of fear and paranoia in American society and curtailed the efforts of an important group of left-liberal writers and directors that included Dmytryk, Trumbo and also Abraham Polonsky, Robert Rossen, Joseph Losey, and the actor John Garfield whose work is analysed in detail in Chapter 4, and their films noirs make a clear critique of the social and emotional costs of American society's unfettered competitive capitalism. In the longer term McCarthyism and the Cold War against Communism formed part of a pronounced shift to the right in American culture, which is often reflected in films noirs, particularly those in the 1950s. As will be discussed in Chapter 4, many 1950s noirs are preoccupied with the threat of organized crime syndicates or with psycho-pathic criminals who are threats to the suburban home. The threat of nuclear destruction haunts several noirs, notably Robert Aldrich's *Kiss Me Deadly* (1955), analysed in detail.

Existentialism and Freudianism

Although film noir does explore social issues, commentators have linked its dominant concerns with individual paranoia and psychological disturbance to the popularization of Existentialism and Freudianism. Robert Porfirio has argued persuasively for the pervasive presence of 'existential motifs' in film noir, noting that as, a general attitude rather than a specific school of thought that developed in wartime France, Existentialism was a late outgrowth of Romanticism, present in the 'hard-boiled' novel and resurfacing powerfully during and after the war. Noir's non-heroic protagonists are entrapped, often by mischance, in an alienating, lonely world, usually the night-time city, where they face the threat of death. The chaotic, random violence of this world gives rise to feelings of persecution and paranoia; a sense that life is absurd, meaningless, without order or purpose (Porfirio, 1996, pp.77–93). This existentialism was another response by liberal intellectuals disillusioned by the failure of American society to embrace socialism and therefore becom-ing disenchanted with the values and objectives of prewar radicalism (Pell, 1985, pp.41–9, 181). A despondent old intelligentsia was joined by a younger generation which was similarly despairing and pessimistic (Tallack, 1991, p.198). David Riesman's influential *The Lonely Crowd* (1950) argued that the individual was increasingly alienated from the amorphous indeterminacy of modern urban life.

As has been shown, both American and French reviewers were struck by the abundance of Freudian motifs in the crime thrillers that were emerging towards the end of the war. Film noir's depiction of a wide variety of disturbed mental states is one of its most arresting features and linked to the growth of psychoanalysis in America during the interwar period so that its terminology and concepts had penetrated into popular consciousness (Thomas, 1992, pp.71–87). As Frank Krutnik has argued, the importance of psychoanalysis to film noir goes well beyond 'particular references to psychoanalytic concepts or the presence of psychiatrists/analysts as characters', as it provided a way of understanding and dramatizing characters' motivations, sexuality, disturbed states of mind – noir's whole emotional landscape (Krutnik, 1991, p.46). Dana Polan notes that the effect of deploying Freudian psychoanalysis was double-edged. On the one hand it was a rational, positive science that provided the solution, a 'cure', to an array of social and psychic ills. On the other it was a discourse that could be appropriated for the dramatic depiction, often through dreams, of these ills wrenched free from an explanatory or recuperative framework (Polan, 1986, pp.14–15). As will be discussed in later chapters, film noir is extremely adept at suggesting, often through the mise-en-scène, repressed or hidden sexual longings and murderous impulses, where violence and desire are often disturbingly melded. As with its use of existentialism, film noir's use of psychoanalysis does not represent a detached and in-depth understanding of psychoanalysis per se, but rather an acute sense of its potential to add depth to the conventions of 'blood melodrama' (Gabbard and Gabbard, 1987, pp.16–37, 73–4).

However, an important caveat to the theory that film noir reflects the 'postwar mood', is the fact that film noir emerged *during* the war, and the early noirs, including those mentioned at the head of the chapter such as *Double Indemnity*, cannot therefore exemplify postwar angst. As discussed in Chapters 2 and 3, film noir's emergence was partly as a result of wartime conditions: restrictions on costs, technological developments in lighting and photography, less prohibitive censorship practices, and on the film industry's gradually increasing willingness to tackle difficult issues. Robert Sklar identifies a wartime *Zeitgeist* (spirit of the times) in which the early noirs represent a more extreme example of a general mood of 'claustrophobia and entrapment' felt by film-makers and audiences alike, an introversion and gloom very different from the usually 'extrovert' American cinema (Sklar, 1978, pp.252–5). Certainly the protagonists of some early noirs, the wartime spy thrillers made by Hitchcock, Lang and Welles, whose *Journey into Fear* (1943) was the first example, were paranoid men-on-the-run, besieged by Nazi agents or fifth columnists. Although the most prolific period of film noir production was 1946–51, it is very important to understand film noir as a wartime as well as a postwar phenomenon.

However, Richard Maltby has warned against understanding film noir as simply a reflection of the *Zeitgeist*. He argues that the *Zeitgeist* theory of culture is notoriously selective and circular: the angst-ridden narratives of film noir become 'evidence' of social problems which in turn are considered to have generated the films themselves. In the postwar period, those commentators who did see film noir (by whatever label) as symptomatic of a widespread malaise were usually anxious liberal intellectuals, worried about the apparent direction of American society, a group that was by no means fully representative (Maltby, 1992, pp.39–48). What often alarmed critics was that film noir thrillers, unlike their predecessors, foregrounded criminal psychology or that of the victim and seemed to suggest that psychoneuroses were common in American society. One of the most influential was Siegfried Kracauer, another German émigré, who argued that these disturbed crime thrillers reflected a world of irrational confusion and 'ideological fatigue' that used 'psychological motifs in place of social solutions' (quoted in ibid., p.40). At this time Kracauer was in the process of composing his study of German Expressionism, *From Caligari to Hitler* (1947), that tied the darkness of those films to the disillusioned and demoralized state of Germany after the First World War. Kracauer was one of many writers who detected disturbing parallels between the two postwar movements. Intellectual commentators and reviewers adopted a very similar position in Britain, as discussed in Chapter 9. However, there were very many wartime films that had stirring messages of hope, courage and ultimate victory, and the most popular postwar films were often strikingly upbeat, for instance *Blue Skies* (1946), one of a number of buoyant musicals that were perhaps as characteristic of the postwar period as film noir (Ray, 1985, p.165).

PROBLEMS OF DEFINITION: WHAT IS FILM NOIR?

I have already shown how film noir is a discursive critical construction that has evolved over time. What must now be acknowledged is that it is a *contested* construction. Film noir has been defined as a genre, a movement, a visual style, a prevailing mood or tone, a period, or as a transgeneric phenomenon. This uncertainty partly stems from its retrospective status; as Steve Neale has pointed out, film noir cannot be verified by 'reference to contemporary studio documents, discussions or reviews, or to any other contemporary intertextual source' (Neale, 2000, p.153). Neale argues that this is not an insuperable problem, 'provided that the nature and status of the term are acknowledged, and provided that the canon is established by applying a clear and consistent set of criteria to as broad an initial corpus of films as is possible' (ibid.). The fundamental problem, as he suggests, is that this is not the case; there remains, even now, significant disagreement about which films to include and what to exclude. One key issue, raised by Neale and discussed already, is that the habitual concentration on film noir's derivation from hard-boiled crime fiction obscures the importance of noirs derived from Gothic melodrama. I have included discussion of these films and the semi-documentaries and 'police procedurals' such as Jules Dassin's *The Naked City* (1948) which evolved after the war in response to calls for greater 'realism' in American films, again profoundly influenced by European developments, in this instance Italian neo-realism as discussed in detail in Chapter 3. My inclusion of these films is a response to Neale's demand for discussion of film noir to be based on as broad a corpus of films as possible.

As Neale also points out, in addition to problems about which films constitute the noir 'canon', many of the elements that are used to define film noir – its particular treatment of gender and sexuality, its devices of flashback and voice-over narration, its concentration on abnormal psychological states and its visual style – can all be found in contemporaneous films that are not classified as noir (ibid., pp.162–73). Hence the frequent reliance on terms other than genre to define film noir, including R. Barton Palmer's 'transgeneric phenomenon.' However, as James Damico observes, as with other genres, the fact that salient features can be found elsewhere does not invalidate the significance of their *particular combination* within film noir (Damico, 1996, pp.95–105). But, a different problem occurs with Damico's classificatory rigour through a paradigmatic master narrative that involves a triangular relationship between the main male protagonist, the 'not-innocent woman' he encounters and a second man to whom she is unwillingly attached; this relationship becomes a tale of deceit, murder and betrayal. This formulation obscures as much as it clarifies as there are many other, quite dissimilar, noir plots.[6] Any attempt at defining film noir solely through its 'essential' formal components proves to be reductive and unsatisfactory because film noir, as the French critics asserted from the beginning, also involves a sensibility, a particular way of looking at the world.

A fundamental shift has occurred in the understanding of film noir with the widespread use of the term 'neo-noir', used to designate films noirs made after the 'classic' 1940–59 period and which derive their inspiration from those earlier films. Neo-noir, which now forms an important component within postmodern American film culture, as discussed fully in Chapters 7 and 8, indicates a high degree of self-consciousness about film noir amongst current film-makers. The label 'neo-noir' mobilizes the high cultural capital – the connotations of sexy, chic 'artiness', visual sophistication and 'adult' subject matter – that the term film noir has accumulated. Rick Altman observes that 'noir has over the last twenty years become as much a part of film journalism as biopic, sci-fi and docudrama' (Altman, 1999, p.61). As James Naremore argues, film noir has become an imprecise but necessary 'intellectual category', comparable to romantic or classic, whose use helps to make sense of diverse but important phenomena (Naremore, 1998, pp.2–6, 276–7). What the present study hopes to demonstrate is that film noir – in its classical and modern forms – is an evolving cultural phenomenon whose fullest development occurs within American cinema but which has also influenced European cinema, notably French, and also British, the subject of Chapter 9.

NOTES

1. Other Von Sternberg films – *The Docks of New York* (1928), *Thunderbolt* (1929), and especially *The Shanghai Gesture* (1941) – are considered to have influenced the development of film noir, along with the suggestive eroticism of his six films with Marlene Dietrich, especially *The Blue Angel* (1930). Von Sternberg's single noir, *Macao* (1952) has the trademark exoticism, but was a troubled film, largely reshot by Nicholas Ray.
2. Silver and Ward's identify elements of 'existential anguish' and noir visual style in some 1930s gangster films, notably *Beast of the City* (1932), but they insist on keeping the two cycles separate (1993, pp.323–5).
3. For further discussion see Waldman (1983), Walsh (1985), Doane (1987), Basinger (1993). For an informative overview see Barefoot (2001).
4. A highly informative recent study is Henriksen *Dr Strangelove's America* (1997), which includes consideration of film noir. See also Lary May, *The Big Tomorrow* (2000) described in 'Further Reading'.
5. The literature on McCarthyism is extensive. For studies of its impact on Hollywood see Ceplair and Englund (1983), Andersen (1986, pp.141–96) and May (1989, pp.125–53). The most detailed study of the 'Hollywood Ten' is Dick, *Radical Innocence* (1989).
6. Krutnik (1991) has a fairly elaborate taxonomy of 'crime film cycles' (Appendix 2, pp.188–226). These are helpful in grouping films, but not fundamental to a definition of noir.

CHAPTER TWO

Conditions of Production and Reception

The background chapter has established that film noir is an amalgam of varied cultural influences and has a complex relationship to its historical moment. This chapter will demonstrate that film noir also bears the marks of the specific conditions of production and reception that pertained in the 1940–59 period during which the American film industry underwent a gradual but profound transformation.[1]

FILM NOIR AS A PRODUCTION CYCLE

Richard Maltby has argued that Hollywood feature film production is best understood as volatile cycles of films initiated by the success of an originating film or films rather than as a stable arrangement of genres (Maltby, 1995, p.107). Rick Altman argues that such cycles are produced by 'associating a new type of material or approach with already existing genres' that emerge from a narrow base often in one particular studio but which gradually build into industry-wide genres (Altman, 1999, pp.59–62). In the case of film noir, as discussed in the previous chapter, its generic status was only established retrospectively. However, as a production cycle one can discern three phases of film noir's development: uncertain beginnings (1940–3), a major burst of energy (1944–52), and a longer period of fragmentation and decline (1952–9). The 'major phase' was consequent upon the success of *Double Indemnity*, *Laura* and *Murder, My Sweet* all released in 1944, which sparked a host of similar productions.

Table 2.1, drawn from the three principal noir filmographies – Alain Silver and Elizabeth Ward's *Film Noir: An Encyclopedic Reference to the American Style* (1993), Jon Tuska's *Dark Cinema: American 'Film Noir' in a Cultural Perspective* (1984) and Spencer Selby's *Dark City: The Film Noir* (1997) – show this

Table 2.1 Numbers of films noirs released by year

	Silver & Ward	Tuska	Selby
1940	2	1	5
1941	4	8	11
1942	4	5	5
1943	2	3	5
1944	7	14	18
1945	16	19	22
1946	24	31	42
1947	29	35	53
1948	24	32	43
1949	27	33	52
1950	31	36	57
1951	25	29	39
1952	14	15	26
1953	10	10	21
1954	13	13	26
1955	12	13	20
1956	9	11	19
1957	9	8	12
1958	3	3	7
1959	3	3	7
Total	268	322	490

pattern clearly. Both Tuska and Selby include 'period' or Gothic noirs and Selby includes a wider range of crime thrillers, particularly those from the 1950s.

At its height in 1950, film noir represents roughly 8 per cent of American feature films in the lowest estimate (Silver and Ward) or 14.8 per cent in the highest calculation (Selby). These are impressive figures and show the scale of the noir phenomenon, a vigorous cycle that included a substantial number of films from all the main production companies, as Table 2.2 shows.

The relatively high figures for Columbia, Warner Bros., and especially RKO, are an indication that noir was particularly attractive to cost-conscious production companies. The motto of RKO's head of production Charles Koerner was 'Showmanship in Place of Genius' and he favoured the production of inexpensive black and white thrillers (Lasky, 1985, p.176). Columbia, which came late to film noir, saw this style as both attractively cheap, and a way of reinventing itself in the crime fiction market after the hiatus of the war. As J.P. Telotte notes, Columbia's noirs specialized in brooding, interior narratives which 'outnoired' other studios' product (Telotte, 1992, p.109). Noir was not as appealing to studios that had traditionally been more lavish: Paramount, Twentieth Century-Fox and MGM. MGM's production head Louis B. Mayer despised 'fancy photographic effects', expressionist set distortions or excessive

Table 2.2 Numbers of films noirs released by production companies

	Silver & Ward	Tuska	Selby
Allied Artists	6	6	17
Columbia	33	33	55
Eagle-Lion	5	9	15
MGM	24	25	36
Monogram	7	7	9
Paramount	27	31	33
Producers Releasing Corporation (PRC)	3	3	6
RKO	42	49	64
Republic	3	4	17
Twentieth Century-Fox	28	39	46
United Artists	35	46	76
Universal	20	33	48
Warner Bros.	29	33	58

stylization of any kind. He thought cinemagoers went to see films for the actors who were to be positioned centrally on brightly lit sets (Carey, 1981, p.103). It was only with the appointment of Dore Schary in 1948 that this production policy altered. The exceptional total for United Artists reflects its role as a distribution agency for independent productions.

CHARACTERISTICS OF FEATURE FILM PRODUCTION DURING THE STUDIO SYSTEM

Hollywood feature film production had been stabilized in the 1930s by the 'Studio System' in which eight production companies, the 'majors', dominated the marketplace. Collectively they formed a 'mature oligopoly', which precluded head-to-head competition in favour of loose agreements that ensured sustained output during the Depression. The majors divided into the Big Five: Paramount, MGM, Twentieth Century-Fox, Warner Bros. and RKO; and the Little Three: Columbia, United Artists and Universal. The Big Five were vertically integrated companies owning production facilities in southern California, a worldwide distribution network and extensive cinema chains located on prime sites. The Little Three owned smaller production facilities and distribution units, but did not own their own cinema circuits. Although the majors put most of their energies into their first features or 'A' films, they all produced 'B' films/second features (also referred to more abrasively as 'quickies' or 'cheapies'), low-budget films made for the bottom half of the double bill that became the standard exhibition practice from 1935 onwards. As Brian Taves has shown, the 'B's were essential to the stability of the Studio System, a formulaic aspect of production sold for a flat fee, rather than the variable box-office percentage that the studios negotiated for their 'A' features (Taves, 1993, p.314). 'B' features were the staple of a group of much smaller production companies, known collectively as the 'B-Hive' or 'Poverty Row'. Republic and Monogram, which had limited distribution networks and averaged over thirty films a year, were the most important of these.

It was a system designed to ensure volume production – around 500 films per year on average – and consistent quality. This required an hierarchical labour force where the creative skills of directors, scriptwriters and cinematographers were subordinated to close control by the producer who used the carefully budgeted shooting script as the 'blueprint' for the film and viewed the daily rushes as a form of 'quality control' to ensure that the film was of sufficient technical quality ('production values') to maintain or enhance the studio's reputation. The producer was responsible to the studio executives who, in turn, had to respond to the directives of their New York offices, which measured production targets and budgets against box-office returns and the advice of their marketing staff. The vertically integrated majors supplied their own cinemas more-or-less continuously, but all the majors worked on the basis of block booking and blind buying to force independent cinemas to take their films in a package, sight unseen, thereby ensuring that they could 'hide' films which were thought to be of dubious quality or uncertain box-office appeal.

WARTIME PRODUCTION AND THE RISE OF FILM NOIR AS OPPOSITIONAL FILM-MAKING

The rise of film noir was connected with the destabilization of this smoothly running system, initially by the exigencies of wartime production. Robert Sklar argues that not only did the material restrictions imposed on the film industry – a 25 per cent reduction in the allocation of raw film stock to studios came into force in 1943, together with restrictions on the amount that could be spent on set design and decor – result in a general shift towards black and white thrillers that could be produced quite cheaply, but also promoted an ideological shift that embraced more 'difficult' and controversial issues (Sklar, 1978, pp.252–3). As Paul Kerr argues, these constraints spurred the production of films noirs starting with 'B' features whose personnel were adept at disguising indifferent or minimal sets through shooting from unusual angles or with low-level lighting. Noir's striking contrasts of light and shade partly stemmed from the night-for-night shooting of exterior scenes practised by the 'B' units which worked through the night after the 'A' units had gone home (Kerr, 1996, pp.107–27). Although these conditions of production imposed severe restrictions of time and money, they offered a marked degree of creative freedom, subject to very little intervention from the front office, provided they were on time and within budget (Flynn and McCarthy, 1975, pp.13–43). Some talented directors relished the scope this allowed them, notably Edgar Ulmer, who deliberately chose to work in these conditions, often acting as his own producer (Meisel, 1975, pp.147–52). Ulmer had worked as a set designer for both Max Reinhardt and F.W. Murnau and as an art director for MGM. He directed a number of low-budget films in the 1930s before moving to Producers Releasing Corporation in 1942. PRC, formed in 1940, was one rung down from Republic and Monogram, producing the same mixture of comedies, musicals, westerns and crime thrillers. Ulmer made a number of films at PRC, including the noirish *Strange Illusion* (1945), a rather static murder mystery, but *Detour* (1945), shot in six days, has now assumed legendary status as one of noir's masterpieces.

Al Roberts (Tom Neal) is a frustrated artist, a nightclub pianist who hitchhikes his way towards Los Angeles in the expectation of joining his girlfriend, a singer trying to get into the movies. The long sequences of the drive westwards, created by shots of two people in conversation against a rudimentary backdrop, only serve to intensify the existentialist gloom of Al's voice-over narration as his journey assumes the proportions of an extended nightmare in which he feels confused and guilt-ridden. When the man who offered him a lift mysteriously dies, Al immediately assumes he will be blamed. He feels trapped and persecuted by the hitchhiker he picks up, Vera (Ann Savage) whom he inadvertently kills. As the story returns to its starting place, a shabby diner, the final scene is his anticipation of the moment of his apprehension, a police car emerging out of an indeterminate gloom to arrest him. Once again the minimalism of the setting invests this moment with almost overwhelming force as Al intones grimly: 'No matter what you do, no matter where you turn, Fate sticks out its foot to trip you.' *Detour* finds a highly expressive visual register that compensates for its 'deficiencies' in conventional production values and its short running time, 68 minutes. Its grim, 'unAmerican' fatalism was characteristic of the emerging cycle of film noir that, as Kerr suggests, used the exigencies of wartime production to develop into an oppositional mode of film-making which challenged mainstream practices.

Although the early noirs were mainly second features, the retrospective romanticisation of noir as the 'poetry of Poverty Row' is fallacious. As James Naremore observes, most noirs 'belong to an ambiguous middle range of the industry' (Naremore, 1998, p.139). Many were 'programmers', intermediate productions that fell somewhere between first and second features, commanding reasonable budgets, but with far less market 'hype' on their launch than a full 'A' production. As Lea Jacobs has shown, the 'A'/'B' distinction was never as fixed as might first appear; there was considerable movement between categories because a film's status was often determined by distribution and exhibition arrangements. A particular feature could move up and down the spectrum depending on the box-office returns in its first run. The distinction between a first and second feature was often a fluid one with a considerable number of 'crossovers' (Jacobs, 1992, pp.1–13).

The group of films released in 1944–5, that, as has been mentioned, initiated the main noir cycle – *Double Indemnity, Laura, Murder, My Sweet* and *Mildred Pierce* – were all intermediates. They were not the most prestigious films released by their companies – Paramount, Twentieth Century-Fox, RKO and Warner Bros. respectively – in that year, but nevertheless boasted popular stars and reasonably high production values. *Laura*'s budget of over $1,000,000 was substantial, but a third of the $3 million that Twentieth Century-Fox spent on its patriotic Technicolor epic *Wilson* (1944) (Solomon, 1988, p.242). *Mildred Pierce* belonged to the 'mid tier' ($350,000–$500,000) of Warner's production slate, well below the $2 million spent on a prestige film such as *A Stolen Life* (1946), but well above the $100,000 spent on 'programmers' such as *Escape from Crime* (1942) or *Secret Enemies* (1943) (Glancy, 1995, p.64).

THE 'PARAMOUNT DECREE' AND POSTWAR PRODUCTION CHANGES

The federal government's efforts to regulate the film industry more closely and eliminate its oligopolistic practices culminated in the Supreme Court's ruling against the majors in May 1948, known as the Paramount Decree, because Paramount was the first major named in the case. The ruling ended the practice of block booking and terminated vertical integration: the majors had to separate, 'divorce', their exhibition from their distribution and production arms and were expected gradually to sell off their cinema circuits (Izod, 1988, pp.122–3). Each film now had to be rented on a separate basis and the majors cut back production, concentrating on a smaller number of better-produced films to woo exhibitors. The majors deployed more and more of their energies into the 'superproduction', the roadshowed epic that could exploit the introduction of costly technical developments, including Technicolor and CinemaScope, which proclaimed cinema's superiority to television (Maltby, 1983, pp.63–73). These 'prestige' films were often well over two hours long and therefore eliminated the need for a support feature. As Thomas Schatz argues, this shift towards fewer, more individualized and carefully marketed films signalled 'an emphatic end to the studio-based production system, with its contract personnel, steady cash flow, and regulated output' (Schatz, 1989, p.435). Production by the majors declined from 477 films released in 1940, to 187 in 1959, a fall of over 60 per cent.[2] This process was accelerated by audience decline and the rise of television, discussed later. All the majors experienced slumps in profit from the high of 1946, but only RKO ceased trading, in 1957.

Within the more fluid and unstable pattern of production that followed the Paramount Decree, and with the majors concentrating on prestige productions, a greater space opened up in the mid-bottom range of the market. Poverty Row companies such as Monogram and Republic were tempted into producing intermediates or 'ambitious "B"s', in a bid for critical and commercial prestige. *Gun Crazy* (1950) was just such a film, produced by the King Brothers who had made their money installing slot machines, then numerous 'cheapies' for Monogram, and were now making a bid for higher cultural status with United Artists acting as distributor. The King Brothers were prepared to employ the blacklisted Dalton Trumbo, credited under the pseudonym of Millard Kaufman, as they were anxious to secure the services of the man who had formerly been the highest-paid writer in Hollywood. However, their dubious reputation made front-line stars wary of taking parts and they were forced to use John Dall and Peggy Cummins, who were not big draws (Kitses, 1996, pp.12, 57, 73–5). The director, Joseph H. Lewis, had a $450,000 budget and the luxury of a thirty-day shoot which he used to construct several elaborate long takes including the celebrated sequence in which Annie and Bart rob the Armour meat-packing plant, shot with great ingenuity in a single take of three and a half minutes. Lewis cleverly uses a fog-bound setting for the dénouement where there is no need for a large cast or expensive panoramic shots, but which also contributes to the mood of moral confusion that makes *Gun Crazy* a celebrated film noir. Overall the film has the fast-paced 'furious' quality that was the hallmark of the 'B' feature 'actioner', overlaid with a subtlety of characterization and care in execution that were more characteristic of the 'A' film.

NOIR AND THE RISE OF INDEPENDENT PRODUCTION

Even before 1949 the majors were buckling under the weight of their enormous overheads – real estate, sound stages, technical and creative personnel – and in an effort to cut back drastically on their contracted staff, looked increasingly towards outside producers. By 1951 most of the majors had established the practice of renting out studio space to independents and investing in independent production where they took less financial risk than on their own in-house features. The shift towards independent production was, as Janet Staiger argues, gradual and uneven: it became a firm option by the mid-1950s and dominant by 1960 (Bordwell, Staiger and Thompson,

1985, p.10). Initially the change was more apparent than real as the new 'package system' had to offer a script, stars and a director, while the studios offered technical facilities, distribution and finance; independent producers were 'only as free as their production-distribution deal lets them be' (MacCann, 1962, p.59). However, despite these constraints, there was more flexibility and creative independence for key personnel. This was particularly true at United Artists, the only studio which Otto Preminger thought had 'a system of true independent production. They recognize that the independent has his own personality. After they agree on the basic property and are consulted on cast, they leave everything to the producer's discrimination. Most of the time, when the others make an independent contract, they want to be able to approve the shooting script and the final cut' (quoted in Balio, 1976, p.239). Thus although, as is customary, the 1949–60 period can best be described as one of transition rather than a radical break from past practices, it was a period which offered more scope and possibilities for ambitious producers and directors. As Richard Maltby comments, '[i]ndependent production was, by its nature, somewhat more amenable to experimentation and risk-taking than the entrenched studio system' (Maltby, 1983, p.75).

Many independent producers turned to film noir as a way of providing cost-effective but sophisticated entertainment. Enterprise Productions, founded by David Lowe, was an idealistic, left-liberal concern that tried to foster a communal ethos and encourage film-makers who were critical of the establishment. It was the home for Robert Rossen's *Body and Soul* (1947) and Abraham Polonsky's *Force of Evil* (1948) starring John Garfield, and Max Ophuls' *Caught* (1949), before folding through commercial pressures (Arnold and Miller, 1986, pp.9–12). Diana Productions was more individualistic, formed in 1945 through the coming together of Walter Wanger, already established as an independent producer, one of Hollywood's leading ladies, Joan Bennett, Wanger's wife, and émigré director Fritz Lang (Bernstein, 2000, pp.197–216). The company's major financier and distributor was Universal, looking to upgrade its product and attain Big Five status. Lang's artistic standing, Wanger's reputation as a producer of taste and distinction and Bennett's box-office clout were an attractive package for Universal to realize these ambitions, with the safeguard of the final cut. For Lang it offered the possibility of far greater artistic control similar to that which he had enjoyed at UFA, the chance to make and market 'Fritz Lang' films. For Wanger it was the opportunity to enhance his reputation as a creative producer; and to Bennett it gave greater control over her choice of roles (McGilligan, 1997, pp.344–64).

Diana's first film, *Scarlet Street* (1945), analysed in detail in Chapter 6, was sexually risqué and technically accomplished, an adroit merging of European and American cultural concerns that was highly successful (Bernstein, 2000, p.205). However, Diana's second film, *Secret Beyond the Door* (1948), which enjoyed a substantially higher budget after Universal had merged with International Pictures in 1946 in an effort to further upgrade its films, was riven by increasingly acrimonious relations between the principals (Dick, 1997, p.119). By the time of the film's release, Universal-International was experiencing financial difficulties which made the company cautious about the film's challenging style and subject matter. The film was recut after unfavourable responses from a preview audience, poorly distributed and performed badly at the box-office (Bernstein, 2000, pp.212–14). After this failure, Diana Productions was dissolved.

The failure of Enterprise and Diana Productions shows the volatility of filmmaking in postwar Hollywood, the limitations of the notion of 'independence' and the difficulties of achieving success. However, both companies' films demonstrate their makers' ambitions to produce sophisticated, demanding and adult entertainment and their use of film noir as the appropriate vehicle for these aspirations.

THE DECLINE OF FILM NOIR

Film noir may be said to be in decline from 1952 onwards, the result of the creative exhaustion of the cycle, further cut-backs in production and the majors' greater concentration on colour 'superproductions', spectacular epics which exploited the new widescreen technologies and were an attempt to woo back the family audience (Belton, 1992). As Arthur Lyons argues, by the mid-1950s films noirs were almost entirely 'B' features, produced either by small companies or the more cost-conscious majors: RKO, Columbia, Universal and United Artists acting as a distribution agency (Lyons, 2000, p.63). But the trend at the lower end of the market was to produce sci-fi and horror films aimed at the increasingly dominant youth market (Doherty, 1988, pp.115–39). A 1957 survey showed that 72.2 per cent of cinemagoers were under thirty and their taste was for more 'teenpics', specifically teen-orientated films (*Variety*, quoted in Conant, 1960, p.5). This competition further eroded noir's production base. The 'B' feature had been completely eliminated by 1960 as low-budget film-making was reorientated to television production; television, as a low-contrast form, was inimical to the rich chiaroscuro that characterised noir (Kerr, 1996, p.121).

However, cycles in the process of disintegration and fragmentation often throw up some of the most interesting examples and film noir was no exception. Two late noirs, Robert Aldrich's *Kiss Me Deadly* (1955) and Orson Welles's *Touch of Evil* (1958), are among the most highly valued and extensively discussed noirs. As the majors concentrated increasingly on their 'prestige' features, their own intermediate productions became less important to their economic welfare, which meant an extension of the creative space, free from front-office interference, that had previously only been enjoyed by 'B' productions. For an emerging director such as Samuel Fuller, who made a series of innovative noirs from *Pickup on South Street* (1953) through to *The Naked Kiss* (1964), the cycle retained its attraction. Others, including Stanley Kubrick with *Killer's Kiss* (1955) and Paul Wendkos with *The Burglar* (1957), saw noir as the chance to produce low-budget films that were stylistically ambitious, and both are attempts to graft avant-garde techniques onto mainstream film-making. *Killer's Kiss*, written, produced and directed by Kubrick with a cast of unknowns and a running time of only 67 minutes, was made for a mere $75,000 (Howard, 1999, p.38). But once again the constraints act as the spur for Kubrick to experiment creatively. The flashbacks are deliberately obtuse, expressionist lighting mingles with surreal nightmare sequences presented on negative film stock, and documentary-style hand-held hidden camerawork for crowd scenes contrast with a highly abstract sequence where the nightclub dancer's story unfolds in voice-over as a ballet dancer performs exercises against a black backdrop. However, these attempts to reach an audience that could support and sustain radical experimentation failed because the art house film circuit was insufficiently developed at this point to sustain noir as an avant-garde mode of film-making (Wilinsky, 2001).

CENSORSHIP

The restricted range of themes and issues broached by Hollywood feature films in the 1940–59 period was largely the result of censorship. The tight regulations that governed the film industry were the outgrowth of a long-standing concern, going back almost to the birth of cinema, about the susceptibility of audiences to the moving image. Because films were exhibited to such a broad public, including the 'unsophisticated and the impressionable', they were not allowed the same freedom of expression as literature, theatre or the press. Lacking this constitutional protection, the film industry lived in constant fear of the imposition of external regulation – either federal legislation or the judgements of the notoriously idiosyncratic and capricious state and municipal authority censorship boards or the lobbying of religious groups. In order to forestall outside intervention, the film industry attempted to take charge of its own regulation acting through the Production Code. This was drafted by two Catholics in the early 1930s in response to increased concerns about the effects of Hollywood films, including a sustained campaign by the Catholic Legion of Decency. Joseph Breen, a lay Catholic, was appointed as head of the Production Code Administration from 1934 to enforce the Code's guidelines. Breen was a virulently anti-Semitic conservative who believed he had to defend traditional morality against the commercial greed of a Jewish-dominated mass entertainment industry, the 'alien invasion' (Couvares, 1996, pp.129–58).

The Production Code's three General Principles attempted to ensure that films showed 'correct standards of life', including the injunction that crime must never go unpunished, while its numerous Particular Applications closely regulated the ways in which sex and violence might be depicted. 'Adultery and illicit sex' could not be explicitly treated nor justified, nor could 'lustful embraces' be shown and nudity was expressly forbidden. In addition to proscribing any sympathy for the criminal, the Code also refused to allow the detailed and explicit depiction of criminal methods. In sum, the Code was an attempt to make films promote home and family values and uphold American legal, political and religious institutions and acted as 'a determining force on the construction of narrative and the delineation of character in every studio-produced film after 1931' (Maltby, 1993, p.38).

The majors bound themselves to such a restrictive code because it allowed them to lay claim to being responsible providers of wholesome recreational entertainment with high moral standards. Adherence to the Code meant that the majors' films would have unrestricted access to all cinemas across the length and breadth of America without risk of local censorship or federal interference (Maltby, 1983, p.104). And, it must be said, the film industry itself was, on the whole, conservative and conformist, more interested in a film's profitability than its challenging or crusading subject matter. Studio executives themselves were often cautious and conservative figures, obsessed by the need not to alienate audiences or the spectre of external regulation.

However, as numerous commentators have pointed out, these restrictions began to loosen during the war as public attitudes became more progressive. The 'particular applications' of the Code, if not its overarching ideology, came to be seen as unduly restrictive and anachronistic. Noir film-makers became adept at circumventing the Code's regulations through ellipses and suggestive mise-en-scène. But the scale and range of film noir's challenge, its emphasis on crime, sex and violence, disturbed psychological states and illicit relationships, was such that the cycle became a significant part of the process through which the Code was questioned and eventually discarded (Maltby, 1993, pp.50–2).

The complexities of that shift can be examined through some representative instances. In September 1943 Breen sanctioned *Double Indemnity*, which he had banned in October 1935 because it violated the code's strictures about adulterous relationships and detailed murder plotting. He had warned then against the 'low tone and sordid flavor' of this tale of adultery and murder, and that he would be 'compelled to reject' any treatment if submitted, as it would harden young and impressionable audiences to the thought and fact of crime. These observations were contained in a letter to MGM, which had optioned the novel, but copies were sent to Paramount, Fox, Warner Bros. and Columbia, which had also shown interest. Billy Wilder's adaptation for Paramount was mindful of these issues and softened some of the elements: the main protagonist does not commit suicide, instead he kills his accomplice and dies after having confessed his crime into a dictaphone. This also removed the problem of the collusion of the senior insurance agent in his escape. Mollified, Breen passed the film with only minor quibbles about language and the way in which Barbara Stanwyck was dressed in certain scenes (Schumach, 1975, pp.63–6). However, *Double Indemnity*'s 'adult' treatment of sex and violence and the degree to which it creates sympathy for the adulterous, murdering couple, was seen by both audiences and the industry as a watershed that allowed further, even more explicit films to be developed (Leff and Simmons, 1990, p.127). These included MGM's *The Postman Always Rings Twice*, another Cain adaptation, which the studio had optioned in 1935, but felt unable to produce until 1944 after *Double Indemnity* had shown the way (ibid., p.132).

The majors' new-found boldness was also a signal to independents to handle more controversial material. Ernst Lubitsch had attempted to remake Renoir's *La Chienne* in the 1930s without success. However, a more tolerant Breen passed Diana's adaptation *Scarlet Street*, which clearly shows Kitty (Joan Bennett) is a prostitute living with her pimp, in 1944, only for a furore to be created in several local censorship boards; the film was initially banned outright in New York, Milwaukee and Atlanta. It was only after extensive mollification by Wanger and Universal's executives that these actions were dropped (Bernstein, 1999, pp.157–85). *Scarlet Street*'s success was another notable nail in the Code's coffin, but its rocky passage through state regulations was a powerful reminder of the strength of the forces that film noir was capable of stirring up.

These instances showed that film noir, like the gangster films of the early 1930s, pushed at the limits of what was permissible. Although Breen could posture in a general way, it was clear that the floodgates had been opened. More precisely, if Breen's attitude towards sex and adultery was in some disarray, noir's depiction of violence and psychopathology created even more problems, especially as audiences had been shown Nazis or the Japanese represented as sexually twisted psychopathic killers in patriotic war films (Leff and Simmons, 1990, p.128). In general terms this allowed noir criminals to display the same traits, for instance Richard Widmark's Tommy Udo in *Kiss of Death* (1947), but created problems if the figure was law-abiding. In his initial screenplay for *The Blue Dahlia* (1946), Raymond Chandler had Buzz (William Bendix) kill the unfaithful wife of his pal Johnny (Alan Ladd), 'under the

The clandestine couple: Alan Ladd and Veronica Lake in *The Blue Dahlia* (George Marshall, 1946)

stress of great and legitimate anger, then blanked out and forgot all about it'. However, because the Navy objected to representations of ratings or officers returning as compulsive and disturbed killers, this ending was dropped in favour of a contrived and old-fashioned dénouement where the least likely suspect, the house detective, is finally revealed to be the killer. The violence and brutality were toned down, reflections on police incompetence were dropped and the hero was promoted in rank and thus made more respectably middle-class (Phillips, 2000, pp.190–8).

These battles over what was permissible raged throughout the immediate post-war period, but became more sporadic in the 1950s, especially after the decision of the Supreme Court in May 1952 that films were a 'significant medium for the communication of ideas' and therefore subject to the same safeguards as the press under the First Amendment to the Constitution which guaranteed freedom. The Code was increasingly recognized as irrelevant and outmoded, no longer easily enforceable, nor a guide to what the general public would tolerate and it gradually became redundant. Astonishingly, it was not replaced by a ratings system until 1968.

AUDIENCES

During the 1930s Hollywood films played to an average weekly attendance of between 50 and 60 million. Admissions increased significantly during the war years, rising to a peak of 84 million in 1944. Thereafter there was a significant decline until 1950 when the prewar level of 55 million was reached. Attendances declined more sharply after this point, and, despite a brief upsurge in the mid-1950s, had fallen to 32 million admissions per week by 1959 (Finler, 1988, p.288). This desertion of the cinema by the 'habit audience' – those who went regularly, usually twice a week – was part and parcel of a wider change of lifestyle of a young, affluent and mobile, car-owning middle class, which moved from inner-city areas to rapidly expanding suburbs no longer within easy reach of a local cinema. Many small cinemas closed, the ones which had made the family film and the 'B' feature profitable, further accelerating their decline. This move to the suburbs was made by the former core audience, young adults, who began marrying and producing children at a younger age after the war. Their lifestyles, with guaranteed paid holidays, a shorter working week and rises in wages and disposable incomes, could accommodate more elaborate and time-consuming forms of entertainment: gardening, camping, golfing, fishing, boating and DIY. The popularity of DIY was a significant indicator of the increasing home orientation of most Americans who could now watch television. In 1950 3.9 million households owned a television set (9 per cent of the total), by 1959 this figure was 44 million representing 86 per cent of the total households (ibid., p.289). The decline of cinemagoing preceded the major expansion in the ownership of television sets, which was therefore a symptom rather than the cause of these more fundamental changes in lifestyles and patterns of consumption. Nevertheless, by the mid-1950s onwards television became '*the* mass entertainment for new baby boom families in their suburban homes' (Gomery, 1992, p.88 original emphasis). Television programming had become sufficiently varied and attractive, both during the week and over the weekend, to absorb the cinema's family audience.

In addition to these broad demographic trends, audience composition and taste also shifted significantly. Research conducted shortly after the war revealed that the conventional industry nostrum that women formed the majority of the film audience was misplaced: males and females attended at roughly equal rates. The research also revealed that the young attended more than the old, which had always been the case, but it also proved that the better educated and more affluent were the most frequent cinemagoers (Handel, 1950, pp.99–108). The average cinemagoer was also becoming more particular in his/her choice of film after 1947 (Wilinsky, 2001, p.96).

The consumption of film noir therefore took place within the context of these far-reaching changes, which initially worked in its favour. The 'adult' content and sophisticated pleasures that noir provided, together with its generally masculine orientation, were much more likely to succeed in this changed context of reception. Film noir flattered the more cosmopolitan, less parochial disposition of an emerging group of discerning cinemagoers which was looking for more 'adult' films (Sklar, 1999, pp.81–92). These discriminating patrons were primarily young adults who, unlike their parents, no longer wanted opulent settings, 'an exotic and make believe world', but films which allowed them to understand themselves and society (ibid., pp.86–7).

Studios were better able to target particular audience fractions through developments in market research pioneered by George Gallup who set up the Audience Research Institute in 1940, which conducted thousands of detailed surveys for the majors. (Ohmer, 1999, pp.61–80). The Motion Pictures Producers Association set up and funded the Motion Picture Research Bureau in 1946, which also helped film-makers to target their films more precisely. As more detailed information became available, it became easier to tailor a film for a select group rather than a mass audience. Films noirs need to be understood as a definite strategy by a range of production companies to provide a particular kind of adult entertainment. The scale of the noir cycle and the success of numerous films as documented in studio histories makes it possible to argue that noir played to younger, male-dominated audiences who enjoyed crime thrillers with an adult content. Hence the dominance of crime thrillers in the postwar period as opposed to the female-orientated Gothic noirs that were so popular in wartime. Of course, to claim that noir satisfied a particular taste is not to say that these were the only type of film to be enjoyed at this point. Indeed, with the exception of *The Postman Always Rings Twice*, no films noirs were popular enough to make the list of major box-office hits during the 1940–59 period. Of the 298 top-grossing films in the 1944–56 period, only 9 are films noirs, or 3 per cent.[3] Even at noir's height in the immediate postwar period, the most popular films were musicals (e.g. *Easter Parade*, 1948), biblical epics (e.g. *Samson and Delilah*, 1949) or sentimental melodramas such as *The Bells of St Mary's* (1945) (Finler, 1988, pp.276–7).

The ways in which films noirs were advertised reveals that the target audience was the same as hard-boiled pulp fiction: urban working-class males. The title card for *Murder, My Sweet* trumpeted the film as 'TWO-FISTED, HARDBOILED, TERRIFIC!' Between a two-shot of a tough, unshaven Dick Powell gazing into the brazen eyes of the *femme fatale* and another of him struggling with the hulking Moose Molloy, the copy continues: 'MEET the year's biggest movie surprise . . . Dick Powell playing a new kind of role . . . In a murder-mystery that packs as big a punch as the NEW Dick Powell!'[4] *Detour* may have been a particularly low-budget release, but its poster was highly typical: a montage of graphic scenes depicting sex and death next to the caption: 'He went searching for love . . . But Fate forced a DETOUR to Revelry . . . Violence . . . Mystery!' On the right-hand side of the poster, Ann Savage and Tom Neal lean on the same lamppost, he upright and wary, she cool, confident and suggestively pressed against the metal. The combination of sex and violence in these film posters, whose artwork and colours resemble the paperback fiction covers, continued throughout the cycle. *House of Bamboo* (1955) shows Robert Ryan gun in hand apparently warding off a blow; behind him is a scantily clad Shirley Yamaguchi in front of a montage of Japanese signifiers.

However, while such general inference may be made about noir audiences, more detailed information about the appeal of particular films is sadly lacking. As thoughtful a scholar as James Naremore only addresses the issue in broad terms: 'Even when [films noirs] were not among the industry's leading moneymakers, they were reasonably popular and widely distributed . . . most of them were favourably reviewed in the popular press' (Naremore, 1998, p.139). Studio production histories can be drawn upon in trying to establish patterns of film-making, but there are no comparable studies of distribution, marketing and exhibition practices, the specific contexts of consumption, where the impact of income, class, gender, age, sexual orientation and ethnicity may be appreciated (Maltby, 1999, p.4). Until such histories are conducted, along the lines of Mary Beth Haralovich's case study of the marketing of *Mildred Pierce* (Haralovich, 1997, pp.196–202), establishing the precise appeal of particular films is largely guesswork or inference from reviewers, particularly in popular newspapers, journals and the trade press, but even that level of detail is often lacking.[5]

There are two other aspects of reception to be considered which are extensively documented: critical reviewing and retrospective revaluations. Richard Maltby has argued that even if censorship regulations were loosening, there was a postwar 'climate of concern' about the effects of Hollywood films on audiences (Maltby, 1993, pp.39–48). Films noirs were often attacked in some quarters for their 'absolute lack of moral energy, their listless, fatalistic despair' (quoted in ibid., p.41). As discussed in Chapter 1, such films were deemed to be irresponsible and pernicious by a section of the intelligentsia. These anxious liberals deprecated film noir as 'a low-status product, playing predominantly to the bottom end of the urban market which reformers, liberal or otherwise, always worried about most' (ibid., p.46). Film noir, even if not named as such, was being polemically interpreted as the symptom of a sick society by an intelligentsia that was hostile to 'subversive' popular culture.

The reasonable popularity of many films noirs suggests that this critical animus was not widely shared and probably not very influential with the cinemagoing public. The film industry itself was more responsive to box-office success than critical respectability and could largely ignore such hostility. Occasionally films noirs attained respectability through their artistry: Robert Siodmak's *The Killers* (1946) was nominated for Academy Awards for direction and screenplay. The semi-documentaries were considered to be responsible film-making with the approval and co-operation of the authorities in their making. For instance *Crossfire* (1947), whose visual style and sense of alienation are as dark as any in the cycle, was lauded for its responsible handing of the issue of anti-Semitism.[6]

As discussed in the previous chapter, the championing of film noir began in France, culminating in Borde and Chaumeton's *Panorama du film noir américain* (1955). Since then the entire canon has been raked over and re-valued with several noirs – *The Big Heat, The Big Sleep, Double Indemnity, Gun Crazy, Night of the Hunter* and *In a Lonely Place* – the subject of monographs in the British Film Institute's 'Film Classics' series. The academic enthusiasm for film noir, including the present study, shows no signs of abating and it is ,bolstered by noir's secure place within more populist accounts. *The Big Combo* may have been dismissed on its release in 1955 by the *Monthly Film Bulletin*, but thirty-four years later *City Limits* placed it first in their 'top ten' noirs (Hugo, 1992, p.248). This retrospective revaluation is, like any other process of sorting and ranking, highly selective and ideologically charged, and needs itself to be the object of sceptical analysis.

Studios and directors may not have known or used the term film noir – though Robert Aldrich had a copy of Borde and Chaumeton's *Panorama* on the set of *Kiss Me Deadly* with him – but it is clear that the production of 'adult' thrillers exploring difficult psycho-sexual and social issues was a deliberate policy which gradually emerged in the early years of the war and expanded into an important cycle of films after the success of *Double Indemnity*. Although the noir canon contains many routine films, some noirs consciously exploited the, highly contested, spaces that opened up to explore controversial material in ways that challenged established conventions and they continue to speak powerfully to contemporary audiences. Films noirs, as Naremore argues, are 'best described as liminal products' which have 'come to occupy a borderland between generic thrillers and art movies' (Naremore, 1998, p.139).

NOTES

1. Technological developments, including faster film stock and deep-focus cinematography are discussed in the next chapter.
2. Calculations based on the figures given in Finler (1988, p.280).

3. The most successful films noirs according to the *Motion Picture Herald*, were *The House on 92nd Street, Mildred Pierce, Gilda, Notorious, Spellbound, Nora Prentiss, Key Largo* and *Detective Story*. With the exception of the first, all have major stars. See Nachbar (1988, p.70 and n.11, p.79).
4. My comments and further references are based on the selection of full-page reproductions in colour in Bassoff (1997). Silver and Ward (1993) include many posters in their survey, as does Muller (1998).
5. There is a selection of *New York Times* reviews, 1914–68 (1970: Arno Press, New York) and also Denby (ed.) (1977).
6. Even if this was a surrogate for the homophobia (taboo in 1947) that is the subject of the source novel, Richard Brooks's *The Brick Foxhole*.

CHAPTER THREE

Noir Style

Commentators on film noir have always stressed its arresting visual style; indeed, several have argued that film noir is best defined by its stylistic unity. Higham and Greenberg's celebrated description evokes an archetypal noir urban scene: 'A dark street in the early morning hours, splashed with a sudden downpour. Lamps form haloes in the murk. In a walk-up room, filled with intermittent flashing of a neon sign from across the street, a man is waiting to be murdered . . . shadow upon shadow upon shadow . . . every shot in glistening low-key' (Higham and Greenberg, 1968, p.19). Their emphasis on chiaroscuro lighting with its opposed patterns of light and dark as the quint-essential noir 'look' has come to dominate discussion of noir's style, but they do not exhaust its stylistic range which, as James Naremore remarks, is more heterogeneous than such accounts acknowledge (Naremore, 1998, p.168). In what follows I shall describe not one 'essential' noir style, but several, often overlapping, visual registers that show shifting and complex variations. Robert Porfirio argues that there were four distinct phases: an early period of experimentation, 1940–3; a studio-bound 'expressionist' period, 1944–7; a 'location' period dominated by semi-documentaries and social problem films, 1947–52; and a final period of 'fragmentation and decay', 1952–60 (Porfirio, 1979, pp.52–60). These phases coincide with the production ones identified in the previous chapter, but add the dimension of a distinct stylistic shift within the major phase: 1944–52. Part of noir's style, though rarely discussed, is its aural dimension, both its distinctive and innovative jazz scoring, and its dialogue and voice-overs with their quotable one-liners.[1]

Like any aesthetic innovation, film noir had to differentiate itself from the dominant conventions of what has been termed Hollywood's 'classical' style (Bordwell, Staiger and Thompson, 1985; Bordwell, 1985, pp.156–204). The classical style was an attempt to produce a cinema that was comprehensible to a wide audience. Its unambiguous clarity stemmed from the subordination of all devices of style to the motivations of the characters and the consequences of their actions. To achieve this clarity, Hollywood film-makers employed a systematic set of camerawork and editing practices which constructed viewers as 'ideal observers', able to see and hear events from the best possible vantage point, thereby ensuring that their concentration is always focused on the main characters, played by stars, and on the significant elements of the storyline in which they were involved. These devices included carefully centred frontal compositions with an harmonious balance and proportion; the famous 180 degree rule in which the camera never crosses an imaginary line that runs through the centre of the screen's main action, thus creating a semi-circular playing space that remains constant and where the viewer is never disorientated; and continuity editing which ensured that any spatial or temporal gaps are carefully smoothed over through a 'match-on-action' or through a dissolve, an unobtrusive blending of the fade-out and fade-in. The playing space is dissected for dramatic effect by a standard pattern of cutting: moving in from a panoramic 'establishing' shot through long shot to mid-shot to close-up of the main characters. Their actions or conversation are shown through a succession of shot-reverse shots, where the cut alternates between an angled shot from one end of the 180 degree line to another from the opposite direction at the other end which simply reverses the space. The characters' eyelines are matched to maintain continuity. In this way an 'objective' space is created, one that seems to exist independently of the characters and the viewer. Each scene has a neoclassical unity of time, space (a definable locale) and cause-effect action.

Part of what came to be known as the 'invisible' style is an unobtrusive use of lighting which places the characters in maximum focus through 'high-key' or 'glamour' lighting, where shadows cast by the hard, direct key light placed above the actors are eliminated by the extensive use of soft, diffused and indirect side or 'fill' lights that fill in these shadows and sculpt faces attractively, and back lights that carefully distinguish actors from the background. This evenly balanced three-point lighting was a deliberate aesthetic choice as it was more expensive to power and required greater detail of sets and decor. It also required a narrow range of camera angles and relatively small movements, together with highly predictable editing, in order to ensure that actors and sets were shown clearly. Lenses were used at maximum aperture, a technique that gave a shallow depth of field and a soft focus. This 'restrained style', employing a narrow range of stylistic options, became dominant in the later studio period, 1936–9, producing an American 'cinema of quality', glossy adaptations of middlebrow bestsellers aimed at middle-class taste (Cormack, 1994, p.84ff).

Janey Place and Lowel Peterson's seminal account of film noir style argues that its distinctive look comes from 'antitraditional' lighting and camerawork

(Place and Peterson, 1996, pp.65–76). Noir lighting is characteristically low-key where the use of fill lights is deliberately restricted, creating stark contrasts between the narrow areas that are harshly illuminated by the unsoftened key light, and surrounding areas obscured in deep black shadows. The fill lights were sometimes eliminated altogether, producing large areas of total darkness. Instead of using conventional lighting positions 'the *noir* cinematographers placed their key, fill and backlight in every conceivable variation to produce the most striking and offbeat schemes of light and dark' (ibid., p.66). Placing the key light below the actors, created gigantic shadows and garish facial expressions, while 'strange highlights' were frequently deployed on faces to show dementia. Close-ups of lead actresses, which were conventionally softened and glamorized by placing spun glass or gauze over the camera lens, were rarely used in noir, which photographed its heroines in hard, undiffused light, making them at once alluring and impenetrable. Interior sets in film noir are always dark, with 'foreboding shadow patterns lacing the walls', while exteriors are often shot night-for-night, i.e. actually shot at night, producing jet black skies as opposed to the grey skies of day for night. Film noir also uses deep focus and wide-angle lenses so that not only are all the objects shown in sharp focus, which creates a closed, 'unheeding' universe, but also a distorted one, where faces bulge outward in close-up, or buildings bend. Wide-angle lenses also draw the viewer into the picture, which makes dramatic events more immediate.

Place and Peterson also identify an 'antitraditional' mise-en-scène where the conventional balance and harmony of the classical style is intentionally disrupted in favour of 'bizarre, off-angle compositions of figures placed irregularly in the frame', creating an unstable world (ibid., p.68). There is a pervasive use of claustrophobic framing devices including doorways, windows, stairways and metal bed frames, that seem to invade the space of the characters, trapping them. Mirror images and various kinds of reflections are prevalent, suggesting deceptiveness, doubling, neurotic narcissism and disordered fantasy. Conventional establishing shots are often withheld, frustrating the viewers' desire to orientate themselves to the space in which the action takes place. Instead of conventional close-ups of head and shoulders, noir directors often use 'choker' close-ups shot right under the actor's chin, the harshly lit face dominating the screen. These excessive close-ups often alternate with extreme high-angle long shots, creating jarring juxtapositions that further unsettle the viewer, replacing the smooth tracking shots that were customarily used and breaching the established norms of continuity editing. It was a style that helped to create noir's distorted, morally ambiguous and confused universe.

Noir's sound tracks were also distinctive. The classical approach to film scoring was the idiom of late nineteenth-century European romanticism, particularly Wagner, Mahler and Richard Strauss, whose main features were full symphonic scoring, lush orchestration, the use of melodies as leitmotifs and the underscoring of dramatic action (Gorbman, 1987; Kalinak, 1992). Many noirs used variations of this model, including Miklos Rozsa's wonderful orchestration for Siodmak's *Criss Cross* or Max Steiner's for *Mildred Pierce*. However, a significant number also used a less conventional musical style. Bernard Herrmann's plays off the romantic score in John Brahm's *Hangover Square* (1945) against the discordant sounds used during the blackouts of the protagonist, composer George Harvey Bone (Laird Cregar), where he' transforms into a murderous psychopath. George's own piano concerto is characterized by its modernist atonality and dissonance (Gorbman, 1987, pp.152–3). In *Detour*, discussed in the previous chapter, Al's distracted play-ing of Brahms's 'Waltz in A Major', in which he replaces its classical har-monies with the far less stable rhythms of 'boogie-woogie', is an index of his psychic disintegration following his girlfriend's departure and the end of his dreams of becoming a concert pianist.[2]

In one of the few accounts of noir music, Robert Porfirio argues that noir is distinguished by its frequent use of jazz which derived from the American black *demi-monde*, and had associations with Weimar culture which pioneered the connections between Expressionism and jazz (Porfirio, 1999, pp.177–97). Unlike symphonic orchestration, jazz is improvizational, and noir tends to use its strident, dissonant aspects rather than its capacity for warmth and senti-mentality. Jazz is often used to signal disturbed mental states, disorientation or breakdown, and it was film noir, not the earlier gangster cycle, that made the connection between urban violence, drugs and aberrant sexuality, particu-larly in Robert Siodmak's films *Phantom Lady*, *The Killers* and *Criss Cross*, dis-cussed in Chapter 6. In Rudolph Maté's *D.O.A.* (1950), the jazz club is the dangerous, uncontrolled place where the hero's murder takes place. Vincent Minnelli's pastiche of the noir style in the 'Girl Hunt Ballet' sequence in *The Band Wagon* (1953) uses a jazz score.

Noir's unconventional visual style was made possible by technological developments, notably the widespread use of faster film stock with reduced graininess, allowing lower lighting levels. A new range of Fresnel lenses, assisted by new techniques of lens coating, which allowed light transmission to be improved, permitted wide diameter lenses to be placed close to a power-ful light source without loss of focus (Ogle, 1972, pp.59–60). Consequently it was possible to use a single light source placed in any position, thus creating the chiaroscuro effects already mentioned. This economical and labour-saving system was also attractively cheap for 'B' units (Kerr, 1996, p.123).

These lighting techniques and the increasing use of lightweight cameras with built-in noise dampening devices, allowed filming to take place in pre-viously inaccessible positions. Actions could be staged in very confined spaces with the actors at very close range, and the habitual use of low-angle cine-matography gave the figures an added sense of confinement, entrapment, distortion or menace, making the use of space disorientating and adding to the claustrophobia of cramped interior shooting. It also promoted the use of subjective effects in which a hand-held camera is positioned from the point-of-view of the protagonist. A famous example occurs near the opening of Delmer Daves's *Dark Passage* (1947), where escaped convict Vincent Parry (Humphrey Bogart) rolls down a hill in a rubbish bin before blundering through the undergrowth to make his escape. As Barry Salt notes, by 1946 the crab dolly had been introduced which could be steered by all four wheels and therefore turned instantaneously from a forward tracking movement to a 'crab' movement sideways at 90 degrees to the original path, permitting longer takes. This significantly increased the manoeuvrability of the camera, permitting more fluid or more disorientating effects in either interiors or ex-teriors (Salt, 1992, p.230). Finally, the 'Dutch tilt', where the frame is skewed from vertical, was occasionally used to create a further level of disorientation.

THE EVOLUTION OF THE NOIR STYLE – THE EXPERIMENTAL PERIOD: 1940–3

These general and formalist accounts of the noir style are useful starting points, but do not account for its evolution, nor its variations. As I argued in the background chapter, film noir was significantly influenced by the work of Orson Welles and Greg Toland on *Citizen Kane*, in many ways the start of the development of an alternative aesthetic tradition that ran counter to the glamorous style of the 'cinema of quality'. However, Boris Ingster's *Stranger on the Third Floor*, an RKO 'B' feature, released in September 1940 seven months before *Citizen Kane*, is usually identified as the first film noir.[3] Ingster, who had worked at UFA, drew freely on German Expressionism, particularly in the central sequence in which reporter Mike Ward (John McGuire) dreams that he is being tried for the murder of his irritating neighbour Meng, a nightmare clearly triggered by Ward's own sense of guilt that his earlier testimony has helped convict an innocent man of murder. At one point Ward is shown in a cavernous cell trapped by huge diagonal shadows, a direct reference to *Caligari* and typical of the abstract design and lighting of the whole sequence. In a final moment of terror Ward sees the shadowy figure of the trial judge transformed into a composite figure, scales of justice in one hand, scythe in the other, the paranoid conflation of the law with death. Ward wakes to find Meng's throat has been slashed and is torn between believing himself culp-able or that the murders are the work of the mysterious stranger played by Peter Lorre. Cinematographer Nicholas Musuraca's low-key lighting casts suggestive shadows as the stranger disappears down the staircase of Ward's boarding house. Through its innovative visual style, which borrowed heavily from Expressionism, *Stranger on the Third Floor* transforms a routine murder mystery into a powerfully Freudian study of paranoid guilt in which dream and reality become blurred.

A parallel development took place at Paramount, which always had a reputation for greater innovation than its rivals, with more independence given to close collaborations of directors, cinematographers and designers (Finler, 1988, p.162). Hans Dreier, who had been an influential art director at UFA, joined the studio in 1923 and was supervising art director from 1932 through to his retirement in 1950. Dreier evolved Paramount's 'European' look, which included his designs for Von Sternberg's *Underworld*, mentioned in Chapter 1. In October 1941 he outlined details for cutting production costs through greater emphasis on stylization (Biesen, 1998, pp.96–100). This influence was first felt in the second features including *Among the Living* (1941), a blending of Southern Gothic and noir with notably atmospheric direction by Stuart Heisler and photography by Theodore Sparkuhl, a veteran of both German Expressionism, and French Poetic Realism: he photographed *La Chienne*. It was followed by *Street of Chance* (1942), the first adaptation of Cornell Woolrich's fiction, which made a genuine attempt to recreate 'the atmosphere of Woolrich's universe: the hapless and desperate individual at loose in New York City; a sense of doom and foreboding; and the use of amnesia' (Silver and Ward, 1980, p.271). Sparkuhl's camerawork creates an oppressive, claustrophobic mise-en-scène with lowered ceilings shot from sunken angles, patterns of diagonal and vertical shadows, complemented by David Buttolph's disorientating jazz score.

Paramount's next noir, *This Gun for Hire* (1942), adapted from Graham Greene's novel, was an intermediate, but in his determination to cut costs, Dreier encouraged director Frank Tuttle and cameraman John Seitz to use mirrors, odd angles, low-key lighting and fog-bound exteriors to obscure the limited number of sets available. Tuttle adroitly alternates extreme long shots with tightly framed close-ups of the outlaw 'couple', Alan Ladd and Veronica Lake, to give greater dynamism to the protracted chase sequence, and Seitz's expressionist photography helps to create the sense of schizophrenia and entrapment in the psychologically damaged Raven (Ladd), often shot half in shadow half in light, or with shafts of light falling across his body. Seitz's rich chiaroscuro is well suited to Ladd's sculpted beauty and helps evoke sympathy for his character.

A third key development occurred in Warner Bros. *The Maltese Falcon* (1941), with screenplay and direction by John Huston. Huston's adaptation was much closer than previous versions to the cynical tone of Hammett's hard-boiled novel, retaining as much of Hammett's dialogue as possible, telescoped into crisply economical key scenes, where an audience is invited to relish the mordant wit of the verbal exchanges between the characters. Huston worked carefully with composer Adolph Deutsch to produce a minimalist, self-effacing score so that Hammett's words retain primacy (Marks, 2000, pp.179–80). The character interactions take place in carefully detailed interiors where each object contributes to the delineation of character. Huston's compositions are deliberately off-centre, either claustrophobic or unbalanced and shot from below eye-level. As befits the film's 'realistic' rather than Gothic mode, Arthur Edeson's low-key lighting has a subtle suggestiveness that avoids bold chiaroscuro (Naremore, 1973, pp.239–49). In essence, *The Maltese Falcon* was a variation on the contemporary crime thrillers that Warner Bros. had made in the 1930s, lean and fast-paced to ensure low costs, but with a subtle suggestiveness that was new.

The fourth influence on the initial evolution of film noir was Alfred Hitchcock who initiated the development of the modern Gothic romance-thriller with *Rebecca* (1940), his first American film. *Rebecca* was the outcome of the occasionally hostile but creative relationship between producer David O. Selznick, whose reputation for glossy melodramas with female protagonists adapted from middlebrow fiction had made him almost synonymous with the 'cinema of quality', and Hitchcock whose *métier* was the masculine thriller with dark, psychosexual overtones (Leff, 1987, pp.36–84; Schatz, 1989, pp.273–94). *Rebecca* uses a female voice-over, that of the unnamed heroine (Joan Fontaine), for the oneiric opening sequence in which she returns in her dreams to her former home, Manderley, now a burnt-out ruin wreathed in mists. As her story unfolds in flashback, Manderley is, in her neurotic perception, a labyrinthine and forbidding Gothic mansion, which contains dark secrets about her husband's former wife, Rebecca. In several crucial scenes Hitchcock uses low-key lighting and unbalanced compositions to evoke an atmosphere of fear and guilt. When her husband Maxim de Winter (Laurence Olivier) is interrupted as he shows a home movie of their blissful honeymoon, the scene darkens and a bright light from below starkly illuminates their anxious and separated faces in the gloom, as each begins to realize the overwhelming presence of the dead Rebecca falling like a deep shadow between them. As she is shown round Rebecca's bedroom by the housekeeper Mrs Danvers (Judith Anderson), the low-angle, claustrophobic camerawork converts a light and spacious room into an oppressive space, with shadows falling across Fontaine's body as she listens to Danvers' ardent recollections of her dead mistress and her exquisite underwear, suggesting both infatuation and sexual desire. In a later scene in the same room, Danvers occupies the deepening shadows as she tries to tempt the new Mrs de Winter to throw herself from the open window. As with all the Gothic noirs, *Rebecca* has lush orchestration, by Franz Waxman, that underlines the emotional climaxes.

Rebecca's combination of high production values and psychological depth was highly successful at the box office (Finler, 1992, pp.166–7). It enabled Selznick to loan out Hitchcock to RKO for *Suspicion* (1941), which explored comparable themes, and to make three other romance-thrillers: *Spellbound* (1945), *Notorious* (1946) and *The Paradine Case* (1947), as well as encouraging numerous other film-makers to produce similar films.

STUDIO EXPRESSIONISM: 1944–7

The early developments of film noir paved the way for the trio of films released in 1944 mentioned in the last chapter – *Double Indemnity, Laura* and *Murder, My Sweet* – whose success was crucial to the establishment of the cycle. All three were almost entirely studio-bound, a characteristic of this phase of noir's evolution. Each film rewards careful analysis, but Paramount's *Double Indemnity* is discussed in Chapter 5.

Twentieth Century-Fox's *Laura* had a talented and prestigious émigré director, Otto Preminger, and also the progressive Lyle Wheeler, the studio's supervising art director, who can be credited (together with Leland Fuller the unit art director) with the carefully designed and meticulously dressed sets that characterize the film.[4] Wheeler suggested the famous opening shot which travels slowly and minutely round the apartment of Waldo Lydecker (Clifton Webb), taking in every inch of the room as he had been inspired by a cut scene from Hitchcock's *Rebecca* that used a similar technique (Heisner, 1990, p.203). The shot initiates the film's critique of Lydecker as narcissistic and sexually ambivalent, Hollywood's customary portrayal of an aesthete intellectual, and inaugurates the fascinated if bemused contemplation of objects that characterizes detective Mark McPherson (Dana Andrews), the ordinary Joe trying to fathom an alien lifestyle. Laura herself (Gene Tierney) has an ambiguous status as the fantasized object of male possession: McPherson falls in love with her portrait before he ever meets her. *Laura* does not move out onto New York's 'mean streets', but instead remains in the rarefied world of expensive restaurants, luxurious apartments, modern offices and art galleries. As with Lydecker's apartment, 'each interior is conceived as a character study of the inhabitant's personality and circumstances' (ibid., p.204). Laura's own apartment, which McPherson repeatedly visits, is heterogeneous, expressive of her enigmatic nature and search for self-definition. It is in her apartment, lit in ambivalent patterns of shifting shadows, that he falls asleep and is woken by the appearance of Laura herself as if her portrait has come to life in another deliberate noir confusion of dream and reality which the film never fully resolves. David Raskin's score avoids the usual nineteenth-century romanticism for a more impressionistic effect in which Laura's theme deliberately suggests her spirit and independence working against what Raskin considered to be Preminger's overly judgemental conception of her character (Kalinak, 1992, pp.159–83). *Laura* is a Hitchcockian romance-thriller which explores sexuality in a complex and quite daring way through the suggestiveness of decor.

RKO's *Murder, My Sweet* (1944), an adaptation of Chandler's *Farewell My Lovely*, was more influenced by *The Maltese Falcon*. The studio owned the rights

The vulnerable private eye: Marlowe (Dick Powell) in a vertiginous setting in *Murder, My Sweet* (Edward Dmytryk, 1944)

to the Chandler novel, which had been made only two years before as *The Falcon Takes Over*, but the creative team of Adrian Scott, a writer newly turned producer, screenwriter John Paxton and director Edward Dmytryk was determined to make its mark through a radically different approach that would approximate much more closely to the novel's cynical, dispassionate take on American society.[5] However, unlike Huston, Dmytryk and his cinematographer Harry J. Wild developed the legacy of Welles's *Citizen Kane*: voice-over narration, expressionist lighting, distorting and disorientating reflections. *Murder, My Sweet* also uses subjective camerawork to approximate the drifting in and out of consciousness of its detective hero Philip Marlowe (Dick Powell) as he is drugged, choked, knocked senseless and shot. When Marlowe awakens from his drug-induced stupor in Dr Sonderborg's clinic and comments in voice-over on the smoke and the 'grey web woven by a thousand spiders' that clouds his vision, we see him through smoked glass that simulates his confusion. The visual style is complemented by Marlowe's voice-overs, which reproduce Chandler's descriptions of disorientation directly: 'I caught a black jack right behind my ear. A black pool opened up at my feet. I dived in. It had no bottom' (Phillips, 2000, p.36).

Throughout, Dmytryk emphasizes the deceptiveness of vision. In the first scene we see Marlowe under interrogation, his eyes bandaged and a glaring light shining on his face in an otherwise pitch-black room. As he begins his flashback, the scene cuts to Marlowe's workplace where he is absorbed watching the neon lights of the city. As each flash reveals the reflection of his brooding face in the windowpane, he muses upon 'the dead silence of an office building at night – not quite real' and 'the traffic down below was something that didn't have anything to do with me'. His reverie is interrupted when the next flash discovers the hulking presence of Moose Malloy (Mike Muzurki), his bulk all the more intimidating by being reflected in the same pane of glass, where he seems to loom over Marlowe like an evil force. In these deft opening scenes, an oneiric mood of uncertainty is economically created, establishing Marlowe as a vulnerable detective, very different from the shrewdly calculating Sam Spade, although their surface cynicism appears very similar. Marlowe may quip expertly in dialogue, but the voice-over narration, as in the above instance, often discloses an existential bewilderment at the seductive but disorientating city that stretches beneath his gaze.

MODIFIED EXPRESSIONISM: THE INFLUENCE OF VAL LEWTON

Robert Porfirio has suggested that 'RKO developed the quintessential noir style of the 1940s due to a unique synthesising of the expressionistic [*sic*] style of Welles and the moody, Gothic atmosphere of Lewton' (in Silver and Ward, 1980, p.40). Lewton's work was discussed in Chapter 1 and its influence on RKO's development of film noir is nowhere better demonstrated than in the seminal *Out of the Past* (UK title: *Build My Gallows High*, 1947), directed by Jacques Tourneur. Although clearly drawing on the hard-boiled tradition, the film avoids the tight plotting of *The Maltese Falcon* or *Murder, My Sweet*, in favour of an episodic, novelistic expansiveness as private eye Jeff Bailey (Robert Mitchum) recounts, in extended flashback, his infatuation with Kathie Moffat (Jane Greer), the girlfriend of gangster Whit Sterling (Kirk Douglas), whom he has been hired to bring back. Nicholas Musuraca's cinematography has great range and subtlety, beginning with his sharp evocation of the crisp, wholesome beauty of small-town America, filmed on location in the mountain resort of Bridgeport, California, a pastoral setting of lakes, rushing streams and pine forests. *Out of the Past* is a film of locales, not interiors: a black nightclub in Harlem, Sterling's mansion at Lake Tahoe, downtown San Francisco, a remote cabin in the mountains and Acapulco where the central scenes take place.

The locales are transfused by Jeff's emotional recollections. His memories of Kathie in Acapulco are so ravishing that he is seduced by them again even as he tries to expiate their effects through his 'confession' to his sensible girlfriend Ann (Virginia Huston). Kathie is first glimpsed entering the shabby bar where Jeff has been forlornly waiting. As she comes in from near invisibility on the bright plaza in a pale dress and matching straw hat, she seems to materialize out of the brightness itself, her silhouette framed in the entrance way before taking her place at a table near Jeff.[6] Kathie thus emerges as if out of a dream and her delicate ethereality makes her seem both innocent and overwhelmingly desirable. She only appears to him at night when she 'walked out of the moonlight smiling', Jeff recalls fondly as he recounts how they become lovers on the sandy beach with its delicately draped fishing nets, the bay behind picked out in shimmering moonlight by Musuraca's carefully contrastive photography. The suggestive cinematography evokes a trance-like landscape that seems to have no beginning and no end and which Jeff's voice-over reproduces: 'I don't know what we were waiting for – maybe we thought the world would end. Maybe we thought we were in a dream and would wake up with a hang-over in Niagara Falls.'

Their affair culminates in the rain-swept lushness of his first visit to her cabin where a solitary lamp, photographed from a low angle, throws up huge shadows behind them, creating an ominous sense of foreboding that the narrator seems blind to, even in recollection. As the lamp blows over, plunging the room into darkness, the rain still raging outside and the wind blowing through the open door, the camera makes a slow, delicate tracking movement out onto the veranda before returning to the room which is now lit by moonlight, implying time has passed during which they have made love. It preserves the romanticism of Jeff's memories and deftly circumvents censorship restrictions.

This subtle suggestiveness is Tourneur's imaginative development of Lewton's legacy. Here, as in *Nightfall* (1957), Tourneur's priority is to integrate all the scenes into an atmospheric whole. As Naremore argues, *Out of the Past* significantly modifies an Expressionist register, generally avoiding the distorting lenses, odd angles and deep-focus compositions that Place and Peterson argue are essential to the noir style (Naremore, 1998, p.175). It does this in order to create, through the careful tonal shadings of its black and white cinematography, a melancholy romanticism that shifts noir's axis away from the toughness of Powell's Marlowe to the desolate fatalism of Mitchum's Bailey. Mitchum's modulated baritone narration is capable of greater inflection than the dead-pan drawl of Bogart or Powell, and contributes powerfully to the mood of blighted hope in which the only 'solution' seems to be that they die together in a police roadblock that Bailey has engineered. *Out of the Past* is the masterpiece that many have celebrated because it has the confidence to modulate the noir style so that it becomes capable of evoking a genuinely tragic pathos.

THE LOCATION PERIOD AND
THE SEMI-DOCUMENTARY: 1947–52

Out of the Past was prepared to move out of the studio onto location and shows the influence of the counter-current towards a documentary-style realism that challenged the studio-bound expressionist style, which dominated the early period. This counter-current was, like expressionist techniques, inspired by wartime restrictions and technological changes. Moving out on location was another way in which the restrictions on set costs could be circumvented and shooting on location was made much easier through the use of lighter cameras and more portable lighting equipment (Salt, 1992, p.226). Location shooting was also the *sine qua non* of numerous wartime documentaries, which gathered praise for their sophisticated camerawork. After the war shooting on location became one way of relieving pressure on studio space, avoiding labour disputes that disrupted studio workings, saving costs and giving a greater degree of independence to directors (Lafferty, 1983, p.24).

Whereas Greg Toland's low-lit, deep-focus compositions were capable of expressionist uses, they were greeted in the trade as the move towards enhanced realism. The long-established and highly regarded cinematographer James Wong Howe argued that lower lighting levels enabled a cameraman to move towards 'the actual room-illumination levels whose effects we are trying to duplicate.' He traced this 'hard, undiffused' look to the influence of picture magazines such as *Life and Look*, and photographic journals such as *U.S. Camera* and *Popular Photography*: 'The public has seen the stark realism of the newspaper reporters . . . and wants something of that type of realism . . . in its movies' (quoted in Walker, 1992a, p.27). Hitchcock was again a pioneer with *Shadow of a Doubt* (1943) where he encouraged cameraman Joseph Valentine to film on location with 'everyday people' moving through the scenes as this created 'an atmosphere of actuality that couldn't be captured in any other way' (quoted in Richardson, 1992, pp.157–8). Immediately after the war these ideas were reinforced by the impact of Italian neo-realism. Rossellini's *Rome, Open City* (1945) with its location photography, use of non-professional actors, naturalistic lighting and observant camerawork that generated drama from the accumulation of small detail, its privileging of social concerns over psychosexual issues, was highly influential (Ray, 1985, pp.138–9). *Rome, Open City* was also popular on the pre-art house circuit in major cities, indicating a more sophisticated audience taste for 'adult' cinema which was now expected to deal with 'real life' (Wilinsky, 2001, pp.16, 19–21, 25–8).

These developments resulted in the semi-documentary, a topical 'true' story shot on location. It was pioneered by producer Louis de Rochemont, encouraged by Twentieth Century-Fox's production head Darryl Zanuck who was looking for relatively cheap features that would not interfere with the studio's more expensive and stage-bound literary adaptations (Solomon, 1988, p.68). De Rochemont's first semi-documentary was *The House on 92nd Street* (1945), directed by Henry Hathaway, which was a critical and popular success. De Rochemont, who had made the 'March of Time' newsreels, imported newsreel techniques: a stentorian voice-over narration, accompanied by stirring martial music, in the reconstruction of an 'actual case' thereby giving an apparent authenticity to the selection and presentation of the material. *The House on 92nd Street* tells how a Nazi spy ring that had infiltrated wartime America was smashed, 'photographed in the localities of the incidents depicted . . . Wherever possible in the actual places the original incidents occurred, using FBI employees, except for the principal players.' Although the semi-documentary was developed by Twentieth Century-Fox, all the majors produced similar films including Universal's *The Naked City* (1948), Paramount's *Union Station* (1950) and Columbia's *711 Ocean Drive* (1950).

With their conformist orientation, extolling the virtues of government law enforcement agencies, the efficient workings of the FBI or US Treasury Department, or, as in Hathaway's *Call Northside 777* (1948), the willingness of American democracy to learn from its mistakes, these semi-documentaries

Semi-documentary noir: *The Naked City* (Jules Dassin, 1948)

have often been regarded as antithetical to the subversive existentialism of film noir. However, their politics were more ambivalent than is usually recognized. *Call Northside 777* is centrally concerned with the plight of ethnic minorities and their lack of a 'voice' and justice only comes from the obsessive quest of the hero, played by James Stewart. Their style was also more hybrid and elastic than is often recognized, as demonstrated by Mann's *T-Men* analysed in Chapter 6, or Hathaway's *Kiss of Death* (1947), which uses a female narrator, Nettie (Coleen Gray), the supportive second wife of Nick Bianco (Victor Mature), a small-time criminal. Her narrative presents a man whose turn to crime is the result of poverty, and whose efforts to go straight are inevitably frustrated by employers' refusal to give a job to a jailbird. *Kiss of Death* was filmed entirely on location in New York's Chrysler Building, Tombs Prison, Criminal Courts Building, Marguery Hotel and also in the nearby Sing Sing Penitentiary and a New Jersey Orphanage.[7] A sense of confinement comes from the cramped or cluttered interiors rather than expressionist framing devices. When Nick learns of his first wife's suicide in the prison factory, Hathaway's camera tracks along the row upon row of machines with their dinning noise.

Kiss of Death, like other semi-documentaries, uses a 'relaxed', almost casual editing style and a loose progression of scenes, very different from the pared-down action and tightly economical editing of expressionist noir. As Jack Shadoian comments, 'a more coercive editing, and more studied compositions, would have worked against the documentary feel' (Shadoian, 1977, p.130). The exterior scenes have a harsh, raw quality, grey and subdued. The most memorable of these takes place on a cheerless, nondescript suburban station where Nick waits anxiously for the train that will take Nettie and his children to safety. A large black car pulls up, only for the driver to walk away, harmlessly; the children play too close to the track and Nick pulls them back. These small, apparently contingent, events both establish the documentary feel, yet are full of tension. The final half hour of the film (after Nettie and the children have departed) plunges into a more shadowy world as Nick, who has made a deal with Assistant District Attorney D'Angelo (Brian Donlevy) to gain his freedom, tries to trap the sadistic gangster, Tommy Udo (Richard Widmark). In the concluding scene, Nick waits in his darkened house for Udo's arrival, a confrontation that culminates in the final shoot-out on the dimly lit streets.

Kiss of Death's hybridity, its slippage between realism and Expressionism, is typical of the way the semi-documentary developed. An Expressionist register is used either to evoke a menacing underworld, or seedy ethnic areas of American cities, as in Elia Kazan's *Panic in the Streets* (1950), filmed primarily on the waterfront and French Quarter of New Orleans. Huston's *The Asphalt Jungle* (1950), made for MGM, carried this further in its story of a failed heist where the criminals emerge as rounded individuals. Their impoverished milieu is brilliantly evoked in the opening long shots of a run-down quarter of New York shot in the cold grey light of dawn as petty criminal Dix Handley (Sterling Hayden) ducks behind the pillars of a deserted marketplace dodging the police patrol car that climbs slowly up a steep hill. He crosses the empty, narrow street making for the peeling building that houses Gus's diner, his sanctuary. In the final sequence the mortally wounded Dix drives desperately out of the city towards the beloved farm in Kentucky where he was raised. Again in long shot he stumbles out into a field where he collapses, the grazing horses wandering over to lick this odd intrusion, as the camera tracks back to reveal the full beauty of this scene, which evokes, tragically, the pastoral myth of the innocent countryside as opposed to the corruption and degradation of the city.

FRAGMENTATION AND DECAY: 1952–8

The gritty realism of *The Asphalt Jungle* exerted more influence over the later films noirs than the earlier more expressionist works. The characteristic 1950s noir is the pared-down, tautly scripted crime thriller, which focuses on organized professional criminals in their battle with the authorities. Expressionist stylization is downplayed or avoided altogether in many 1950s noirs, which assault the viewer rather than evoking an atmosphere. Location shooting becomes more routine and flatly naturalistic, involving the reduction or elimination of supplementary lighting on daylight exteriors (Salt, 1992, p.243). A representative film is Budd Boetticher's *The Killer Is Loose* (1956) in which a myopic bank clerk, 'Foggy' Poole (Wendell Corey), breaks out of prison to seek revenge on Detective Sam Wegener (Joseph Cotten) who accidentally shot Poole's wife in a raid on their home after Poole had been identified as the inside man in an earlier robbery. It is Wegener's wife, Lila (Rhonda Fleming), who is Poole's real target and the film is a tense cat-and-mouse thriller shot in an uncomplicated, naturalistic style in and around small-town locations and suburban homes.

Jack Shadoian regards Phil Karlson as the most representative late noir director (Shadoian, 1977). *Kansas City Confidential* (1952) and *The Phenix City Story* (1955) are savagely naturalistic exposés of organized vice and corruption in American cities, shot in a flat documentary style. The intervening film, *99 River Street* (1953), is more stylized, but its grim, gruelling brutality shows the distance travelled from the romanticism of 1940s noirs. Karlson was an intelligent artist and his masterpiece, *The Brothers Rico* (1957), shows the noir style evolving into its replacement, 'postnoir', that creates menace and a sense of pervasive corruption whilst eliminating expressionist effects almost entirely (Carl Macek, in Silver and Ward, 1980, p.44).

Its central figure is Eddie Rico (Richard Conte) who has 'escaped' from the Italian ghetto in New York where he grew up and, he believes, the criminal syndicate he worked for as an accountant. He now runs a successful laundry business in Bay Shore, Florida, the image of the archetypal American middle-class, suburban man in his grey flannel suit (Cohan, 1997, pp.1–33). He has a modern open-plan house, a geometrically arranged spacious office and a plush convertible that gleams in the rich sunlight. *The Brothers Rico* evokes a clean, calm world that is haunted by the presence of the syndicate whose reach is global: 'The visual look of the film implies that the more evenly and fully you illuminate, without distorting the world through light and shadow and unusual angles and compositions, the more horrible it becomes' (Shadoian, 1977, p.250). Like the late noirs of Fritz Lang, analysed in Chapter 6, Karlson represents the organized, corporate world of 1950s America as a soulless mask covering over corruption. The hotel room of syndicate boss Sid Kubik (Larry Gates) is shot in high-key clarity. It is the shock cut that provides the comment: in another room Eddie's brother Gino is being savagely beaten. It is only when Eddie returns to New York that Karlson uses chiaroscuro compositions, including the spectral night-time assassination of Eddie's other brother Johnny.

The meaningless quest that Eddie undertakes and his inability to control events that lie at the heart of *The Brothers Rico* anticipates the modernist noirs analysed in Chapter 7. However, this chapter must end with an analysis of Orson Welles's *Touch of Evil* (1958), which, although atypical of the 1950s, exemplifies the high point of the expressionist style that Welles himself inaugurated with *Citizen Kane*.

Touch of Evil's exteriors were shot on location in Venice, southern California, with its ersatz veneer of European sophistication, decaying oil wells and sense of general decline. Venice becomes Los Robles, a border town, a liminal space between Mexico and the United States, filled with detritus of all kinds, where right and wrong is ambiguous, and the boundaries between dream and waking, sanity and madness are constantly blurred. This ambivalence encompasses the principal characters. The American police captain, Hank Quinlan (Welles), who proceeds through hunch and intuition, is a corrupt racist, haunted by the murder of his wife, seeking solace with the Mexican whore Tanya (Marlene Dietrich). Mike Vargas (Charlton Heston), the Mexican narcotics agent, is upright, incorruptible and rational, yet powerless to prevent the abuse of his young American wife Susan (Janet Leigh). The see-sawing battle between the two men provides the fulcrum for this shifting, restless exchange between two cultures, Latin and Protestant, between good and evil, civilization and libido.

Touch of Evil is a deliberately confusing, disorientating film and repeated viewings serve not to clarify the confusion, but to appreciate the systematic ways in which Welles deliberately frustrates a desire for lucidity. At the centre of the film is a calculated opacity as to whether or not Susan was actually raped by the teenage gang who descend on her isolated motel. In that terrifying scene we see, from her point of view, a group of glassy-eyed Latinos close in, including a fish-eye close-up of the leader Pancho who flicks his tongue like a serpent which embodies a WASP culture's worst nightmare (Naremore, 1989, p.164). Susan wakes to find herself in a seedy hotel room to see the pop-eyed, upside-down face of drug-dealer Grandi (Akim Tamiroff), strangled by Quinlan in another horrific encounter, which lolls hideously over the rail at the bottom of her bed.

This sense of a waking nightmare is present throughout the film. The fluidity of the famous continuous crane shot that occupies the opening three minutes does not establish a clear sense of space, but rather a swirling, confused sequence of disconnected actions (the actual explosion happens off camera) whose only logic seems to be that they are typical of a border town where people move restlessly between two countries. Welles uses an extreme wide-angle lens throughout which distorts faces, especially in close-up, and buildings, making them seem unreal. *Touch of Evil* is both intensely claustrophobic, as in the interrogation of Sanchez; and agoraphobic as in the final scene where the jarring combination of extreme low- and high-angle shots create a sense of limitless darkness (Orr, 1993, p.169). The deep-focus compositions often offer multiple objects of attention. At one point Vargas calls the motel to check on Susan's welfare. Not only is he placed off-centre in the frame dominated by the unseeing eyes of the blind woman who owns the shop where the telephone is located, but outside in the street a heated conversation between Grandi and Quinlan's loyal sidekick Menzies (Joseph Calleia) is clearly visible, an argument that could have important consequences, but which we never hear. Far from being 'ideal observers', Welles makes his audience part of the pervasive miasma and confusion. The camera avoids any stable middle ground, which usually functions as a point of balance and adjustment for the viewer. Welles dispenses with master shots, reaction shots and his camera is continually restive without any static framing. Welles's rapid camera movements with a wide-angle lens makes the objects in the foreground seem to detach from the background and 'swim' past. Dissolves are never used, replaced by jarring cross-cutting or rapid montage. Although the action takes place almost entirely at night and uses low-key lighting frequently, with Quinlan in particular casting vast shadows of himself, it deliberately avoids the glamorous romanticism that chiaroscuro can possess in favour of a dingy look that gives the actors sallow faces and enforces the mood of corruption and decay. In several scenes, including Quinlan's murder of Grandi, the town's glaring neon lights flash on and off throughout the action, giving the brutal violence an hallucinogenic quality.

The closing scene, the *mano-a-mano* confrontation of Vargas and Quinlan, is shot from almost every conceivable angle except eye-level (avoided throughout the film) and makes no spatial sense whatsoever, as if it is still part of a nightmare. After Quinlan has shot Menzies, but been wounded himself, his stumbling descent is shown in a tilted long-shot before a cut to an overhead medium shot when he falls backwards into the fetid, garbage-strewn waters that lie near the creaking derricks which keep pumping inexorably. As Vargas is reunited with Susan in a concession to bourgeois morality, the inscrutable, mystical Tanya utters Quinlan's enigmatic epitaph: 'He was some kind of a man . . . What does it matter what you say about people?' This scene, with its nebulous and discordant melodrama, its grim absurdity and dark ironies – Vargas's ally Blaine arrives to tell him that Quinlan had been right all along about Sanchez – was the fitting culmination to a world of bewildering moral relativity.

At the time of its release *Touch of Evil* was judged confusing and 'artsy'. Universal, already nervous about losses in the first half of 1958, gave the film little publicity or circuit bookings. Like film noir as a whole, its importance was first recognized in France – *Touch of Evil* enjoyed a two-year run in Paris in

1959–60 – but only gained recognition in America much more slowly. It has now become a cult masterpiece. A restored version of the longer 'director's cut' discovered in 1975, 12 minutes longer than the 95-minute version Universal distributed in 1958, has been re-released theatrically. Although, as I have demonstrated, *Touch of Evil* does not exhaust the varieties of the noir style, its baroque expressionism is the culmination of its most powerful version, the one through which the cycle is now remembered.

NOTES

1. For anthologies of 'great lines' see the two collections by Thompson and Usukawa, *The Little Black and White Book of Film Noir* (1992) and *Hard-Boiled: Great Lines from Classic Noir Films* (1995).
2. There is a detailed discussion of *Detour's* music in Flinn (1992, pp.118–32).
3. In a recent study, Arthur Lyons disputes this conventional claim. He argues that two Universal 'B's, *Let Us Live* and *Rio*, together with Columbia's *Blind Alley*, all released in 1939, were the first noirs (Lyons, 2000, p.35).
4. Both were nominated for an Academy Award for their work on this film.
5. See Dmytryk's autobiography, *It's a Hell of a Life but Not a Bad Living* (1978, pp.58–62). Dmytryk commented acerbically that since most of the novel had been jettisoned in the studio's previous adaptation, no one would spot that this new film was a remake (p.61).
6. I am indebted here to Naremore's detailed analysis, complete with stills (1998, pp.175–85).
7. The publicity for *Kiss of Death*, as with *Naked City* and other semi-documentaries, emphasized the actual locations that were used.

CHAPTER FOUR

Themes and Narrative Strategies

I have discussed in the background chapter the popular conception that film noir offers a 'dark mirror' to American society. In this view, film noir's central preoccupations are 'claustrophobia, paranoia, despair and nihilism'. Its alienated protagonists, trapped in dark cities, expose the underside of American life. These existentialist themes mingled with ones drawn from a popularized Freudianism: schizophrenia, psychosis and disturbed sexuality. This existentialist-Freudian thematic paradigm was dominant in the early period, as in *Detour* analysed in Chapter 2, but as the cycle developed noir's concerns were broadened by an important body of noirs whose themes were social or overtly political. This group of films was sharply divided between right- and left-wing agendas.

The second half of the chapter discusses the complexities of noir's narratives. If noir's visual style is 'anti-traditional', its narrative strategies are similarly unorthodox, particularly in the earlier period where voice-overs, flashback and dream sequences are common, as film-makers struggled to express noir's dark themes. As Christine Gledhill observes, noir tends to foreground the problematic processes of narration in which there is often 'a struggle between different voices for control over the telling of the story' (Gledhill, 1998, pp.29–30).

THEMES

Existentialism: Alienation and Paranoia

Noir's existentialism, its sense that life is absurd and meaningless, its paranoid protagonists at the mercy of chance or fate, is neatly summed up in *The Dark Corner* (1946) where the resonantly named private eye Bradford Galt (Mark Stevens), framed for reasons he cannot fathom, cries in anguish to his secretary: 'I feel all dead inside. I'm backed up in a dark corner and don't know who's hitting me.' Adaptations of Cornell Woolrich, the hard-boiled author most associated with existentialism, show paranoid protagonists adrift in cities that are monstrous, hallucinatory and actively malevolent (Reid and Walker, 1993, pp.57–96). *The Chase* (1946) has a typical Woolrich protagonist, Chuck Scott (Robert Cummings), a down-at-heel, drifting war veteran uncertain of himself, who becomes involved accidentally with a psychotic gangster, Eddie Roman (Steve Cochran). He falls in love with Roman's wife Lorna (Michele Morgan) and the couple flee to Havana. But their romantic haven turns into a paranoid nightmare in which Scott becomes accused of Lorna's murder. Escaping the police, he flounders around in the murky shadows of an alien, labyrinthine city, the only light a thin glint under a door or the faint glow of a telephone dial. He watches helplessly as Roman's henchman Gino (Peter Lorre) eradicates all the evidence that could prove his innocence including the murder of key witnesses. Finally, Scott, as if detached from his own body, sees himself pitched over the quayside into the dark waters below. Although Scott wakes to find the trip to Cuba was all a dream, the film's atmosphere of paranoia and fear linger long in the memory. In addition to *The Chase* and *Fear in the Night* (1947), analysed later, there were five other Woolrich adaptations around the end of the war that were suffused with existentialist angst: *Phantom Lady* (1944), *Black Angel* (1946), *Deadline at Dawn* (1946), *Fall Guy* (1947) and *The Guilty* (1947).

The Gangster (1947), adapted by Daniel Fuchs from his own hard-boiled novel *Low Company*, reworks the figure of the gangster. Its protagonist, small-time protection racketeer Shubunka (Barry Sullivan), is no longer an energetic entrepreneur, but a man trapped in paranoid fatalism whose voice-over expresses the sceptical existentialist's morbid drive for self-definition: 'I was no hypocrite. I knew everything I did was low and rotten. I knew what people thought of me. What difference did it make? What did I care?' But he cannot stabilize his sense of self nor cut himself off from the society he loathes. His love for Nancy (Belita) the nightclub singer, has twisted into an insatiably possessive jealousy that drives her from him and only fuels his corrosive self-contempt, confirming the meaninglessness of his existence. He hangs around disconsolately in an ice cream parlour in Neptune Beach, a cheap resort for day-trippers whom Shubunka despises, while his rival, Cornell, takes over his patch. His death – gunned down by Cornell's men on the rainswept streets – is an ironic reprise of the 1930s paradigm. As he dies, Shubunka murmurs scornfully: 'My sins are that I wasn't tough enough. I should have trusted no one; never loved a girl. I should have smashed them first. That's the way the world is.'

Rudolph Maté's *D.O.A.* (1950), inspired by the Weimar film directed by Robert Siodmak, *Der Mann, Der Seinen Mörder Sucht* (*The Man Who Searched for His Own Murderer*, 1931), developed an existentialist scenario most fully. It is narrated by a man already dead. In its striking opening sequence shot from the character's subjective point-of-view, Frank Bigelow (Edmond O'Brien) blunders through what seems like a never-ending procession of corridors and double doors in a police station to announce that he has been fatally poisoned. Bigelow is the archetypal small-town ordinary Joe – a modern Everyman – a certified accountant from Banning, California, who takes a pleasure trip to San Francisco.[1] He is poisoned in a sleazy waterfront night-club where a jazz band play because, by chance, as he learns later, a shipment of iridium which he had notorized fell into criminal hands. When Bigelow learns the following day that he has less than forty-eight hours to live, he goes berserk, running furiously out onto the sunlit streets. The high-angle location shooting captures the indifferent crowds of everyday citizens as the camera follows Bigelow's breakneck dash towards he knows not where, fleeing from a nameless but deadly retribution for what was no crime but a routine part of his professional life. At midday, in the heart of a bustling metropolis, he is trapped and doomed. He comes to rest against a newsstand where *Life* magazine is prominently displayed. As he stares open-mouthed at a little girl playing with a ball, a few bars of a romantic Viennese waltz swirl through his mind (Turner, 1988, p.39). When Bigelow meets his girlfriend Paula (Pamela Britton) for the last time, a neon 'Bank of America' sign glares brightly above them. *D.O.A.*'s malign logic offers no retreat back into small-town life where the hero might be redeemed. When Bigelow collapses at the end of his story, his case is labelled Dead On Arrival by a bemused police captain who knows there is now no case to investigate, thereby rendering Bigelow's story pointless.

Urban Angst: the Noir City

Bigelow is a man adrift in the big city and the alienation and paranoia that noir's protagonists experience is partly a product of urban angst. Noir's preoccupation with city life, derived as has been shown from the Weimar 'Street' films, 1930s gangster films and hard-boiled fiction, is signalled in the archetypal opening aerial shot of the neon-lit city and its recurring use in titles: *The Naked City, Dark City, Cry of the City, City Across the River, While the City Sleeps* and *Captive City*. Raymond Chandler's famous description of Philip Marlowe walking down the 'mean streets' of Los Angeles was a metaphor for the whole encounter with the sinister modern city. Film noir's sense of the city was also influenced by the 'Blood on the Pavement' artists whose canvasses emphasized the underside of modern urban life and the lonely desperation of the night-time city. The most influential of these artists was Edward Hopper whose *Drug Store* (1927) and *Nighthawks* (1942) depicted bleak moments of urban living (Silver and Ursini, 1999b, pp.22–6). Hopper, who was an avid fan of the pictures and designed many movie posters, crops his paintings aggressively, as if they were frozen stills from a film. Noir directors were also influenced by the sensationalist photojournalism of Arthur H. Fellig, known as Weegee, but they borrowed from hundreds of accounts – in fiction, written journalism and sociological studies – where the city is presented as at once all-enveloping and unreal. The noir city has a fundamental ambivalence, dangerous, violent, squalid and corrupt but also exciting and sophisticated, the place of opportunity and conspicuous consumption (Krutnik, 1997, pp.83–109). Films noirs present a city of contrasts sharply divided by wealth. Noir protagonists may occupy dingy rooming-houses, grimy diners and run-down smoke-filled bars, but they are drawn to the world of smart money – to bright garish nightclubs, spacious, over-decorated luxury apartments and imposing mansions – like moths to a flame.

The noir city is symbolically homeless, its denizens act out their lives in public spaces: in diners, bars, nightclubs, automobiles, streets, alleyways, impersonal luxurious hotel suites or cheerless, uncomfortable apartments. There is a concentration on transient spaces – bus terminals, train stations, markets, sports arenas, hotels and motels – or ones that are precarious: rooftops, walkways, bridges, high window ledges, unlit alleys, railroad tracks, moving trains and cars (Christopher, 1997, p.17). Protagonists often find themselves in deserted industrial or commercial locations, whose factories are abandoned or seem to be falling into disuse. In *D.O.A.* Bigelow drives to a nondescript, scruffy, run-down area of San Francisco where a seedy photographic studio is located. After he is shot at, he dives into an abandoned factory building, dodging bullets amongst the rusting pipes, tanks and rickety metal staircases shot in deep focus to give these evocative objects exaggerated prominence.

Film noir's existentialism places great emphasis on the city as a trap. Interiors are often cramped, awkward and claustrophobic: train compartments, tiny hotel rooms, the back seats of cars, lifts and telephone booths which often become 'upright coffins' (Arthur, 1985, p.209). Externally, the city is a labyrinth, dark, confusing and hostile, filled with dead-ends, and above all threatening. Noir's victim heroes are shown descending into an underworld city, a nether city or necropolis that exists below the surface or after dark (Christopher, 1997, p.45). Here the locales are emblematic: subway tunnels, underground car parks, the storm drains of *He Walked by Night* discussed in Chapter 6, or the Viennese sewers of *The Third Man* (1949), discussed in Chapter 9.

Edward Dimendberg has identified a major shift in noir's representation of the city, moving from an existential concern with the centripetal metropolitan inner city – densely populated, cramped and built vertically – in the

1940s, to a concern with the centrifugal town with its spread-out, ribbon development in the 1950s (Dimendberg, 1996, pp.56–66). The cycle of city exposé films beginning with *Kansas City Confidential* (1952), which were fuelled by the Senate hearings on municipal corruption chaired by Senator Kefauver, exemplified this trend. They replaced a concern for the lost individual with a generalized attention to organized vice and corruption (Straw, 1997, pp.110–28). Noirs of the 1950s such as *Desperate Hours* (1955) or *The Killer Is Loose* (1956), locate their action in the suburbs and concentrate on the threat to families and the community rather than the angst-ridden loner.

Freudianism

I argued in the background chapter that a simplified version of Freudianism had entered into American popular consciousness during the interwar period. In an early noir *This Gun for Hire* (1942) discussed in Chapter 2, the warped killer Raven (Alan Ladd), physically maimed and psychologically crippled by childhood abuse, wonders if he can turn to psychoanalysis for help: 'Every night I dream. I read somewhere about a kind of a doctor, a psych-something. You tell your dream, you don't have to dream it any more.' Hitchcock's *Spellbound* (1945), analysed below, was also explicitly concerned with mental trauma and psychoanalysis and was praised for its detailed and sensitive treatment of the topical theme of psychological readjustment after the war, discussed further in the next chapter (Leff, 1987, p.159). The escaped killer Al Walker (William Holden) in Rudolph Maté's *The Dark Past* (1948) suffers from a childhood trauma, witnessing the death of his father, gunned down by the police, whose blood drips down through the cracks in the table under which Al was hiding. Dr Andrew Collins (Lee J. Cobb), the avuncular police psychiatrist Al is holding hostage, gradually unravels the causes of Al's psychotic behaviour through interpreting his dream in which he holds a ragged umbrella over his head in a vain attempt to protect himself. The rain symbolizes his father's blood and the hand in which Al imagines he is holding the umbrella has become paralysed through guilt and impotence.

The explicitness of *Spellbound*, *The Dark Past* or Fritz Lang's *The Woman in the Window* (1946) where the protagonist lectures on Freud, is only one aspect of noir's use of Freudianism. Noir's preoccupation with fantasies, dream states, schizophrenia, unconscious and repressed desires, concealment, displacement and condensation, its whole concern with psychological states is, like existentialism, part of the fabric from which noir is woven (Krutnik, 1997, pp.45–55). This rich texture of Freudian motifs distinguishes noir from earlier crime fiction and informs the sexual melodramas of Gothic noir such as *Rebecca* and other romance-thrillers such as *Leave Her to Heaven* (1946) where the narrative wavers between condemnation of the actions of the over-possessive wife Ellen (Gene Tierney) which culminate in her deliberate suicide designed to destroy the happiness of her husband and her adopted sister, and an understanding of its roots in her obsessive devotion to her father, an incestuous longing that has left her psychologically crippled.

Like existentialism, Freudianism formed part of noir's initial preoccupation with individual pathology and becomes less important as the cycle moved into an exploration of more social themes in the 1950s. There are exceptions: *The Big Combo* (1955), whose ostensible subject is criminal corporations, is deeply imbued with a psychopathology that unites criminal and policeman. *Vertigo* (1958), discussed later, was the most profound of noir's exploration of psycho-sexual dislocation.

Social Themes

If social themes came to dominate later noirs, they were also present in early examples. It is possible to identify both right- and left-wing responses to an 'age of anxiety': the upheavals of the Second World War and the transition from service to civilian life. As discussed in Chapter 1, this mutated into the threat of the atomic bomb and the Cold War's preoccupation with the Communist menace abroad and its subversion of the 'American way of life' at home.

(1) Law and Order   In the conservative version, the overriding theme is the enforcement of law and order where government agents or policemen root out and destroy 'the enemy'. The semi-documentaries were, as has been noted, usually informed by a right-wing ideology that celebrated the vigilance, hard work and courage of American institutions. The early examples – *The House on 92nd Street* (1945) and *13 Rue Madeleine* (1946) – are still preoccupied with fascism; but, as Nazis operate like gangsters, this shifts seamlessly into a concern with crime lords. Joseph H. Lewis' *The Undercover Man* (1949) was a re-run of the Capone indictment. Frank Warren (Glenn Ford) is the tireless Internal Revenue agent who uncovers a web of intimidation, murder, fraud and tax evasion organized by the shadowy 'big fellow'. He finally persuades a judge that the assembled jurors have been suborned and, granted a fresh jury, is able to punish those responsible for the graft and corruption that have infected every level of American society.

Law and order films in the 1950s are obsessed with corporate crime, with takeovers by ever more powerful and well-organized syndicates. *The Racket* (1951), set in an anonymous Midwestern city, looked back to the prohibition era (an earlier version had been released in 1928), but its struggle between honest cop Captain McQuigg (Robert Mitchum) and mobster Scanlon (Robert Ryan) is framed within an overarching corruption which reaches the highest levels of government: it is clearly hinted that the real crime lord is the state governor. Both Scanlon and McQuigg are old-fashioned individualists in an age of dishonest corporatism. *The Enforcer* (UK title: *Murder INC.*, 1951) was a more paranoid film in which the tireless DA Martin Ferguson (Humphrey Bogart) battles a murder syndicate run by Mendoza (Everett Sloane) which is both ruthlessly efficient and the sinister creation of a deranged 'evil genius'. The opening scene, in which the key witness Rico is so frightened, even in the confines of the police station, that he throws himself from a window, captures the intensity of the paranoia that is sustained throughout in what is a peculiarly dark and claustrophobic film even by noir's standards. This visual style, as noted in the previous chapter, often undercuts the right-wing ideology as the paranoia and fear it evokes are often much more memorable than the efforts of the law enforcers.

The early 1950s generated a sub-cycle of noirs that was explicit about the Communist threat. *Walk East on Beacon* (1952) was Louis de Rochemont's anti-Communist equivalent to *The House on 92nd Street*. *I Was A Communist for the F.B.I.* (1951), in which an ordinary citizen (Frank Lovejoy) is recruited to infiltrate the Communist Party, and *The Thief* (1952), a film entirely without dialogue, where Dr Allan Fields (Ray Milland) plays an Atomic Energy Commission scientist who is stealing secrets but finally gives himself up, show different aspects of the Communist threat together with its defeat by the vigour of American democracy. *Suddenly* (1954) is a deeply paranoid film where even in a tiny, sleepy town like Suddenly, the President's life is vulnerable. John Baron (Frank Sinatra), a disaffected veteran who found his true identity in the war because he was good at 'chopping', killing repeatedly and with relish, now makes his livelihood as an assassin. He never discloses who his paymasters are, but the inference is obvious.

Samuel Fuller's *Pickup on South Street* (1953) is more complex because its right-wing premise is complicated by Fuller's sympathies with the 'low-life' protagonists: the ageing tie-seller Moe (Thelma Ritter) who supplements her meagre living by selling information; Candy (Jean Peters), the fundamentally decent 'good-time girl'; and the central figure, pickpocket Skip McCoy (Richard Widmark), who inadvertently discovers a secret microfilm during one of his routine 'dips'. The three form a strange, shifting alliance which ultimately brings down the Communist spy ring, in which each discovers a basic patriotism even if, as Skip avers, they do not care to have the flag waved in their faces.[2] It is Moe's death and her subsequent funeral that are the film's most poignant moments. The latter is photographed in a stationary long shot, which gives the scene a quiet dignity after the violence of her killing. These aspects shift attention away from the defeat of Communism towards sympathy for the detritus of the modern city, the outcasts from the American dream, a concern which is at the heart of the left-wing films.

The outsider as patriotic hero? Skip McCoy (Richard Widmark) in *Pickup on South Street* (Samuel Fuller, 1953) interrogating Candy (Jean Peters)

(2) Corruption and Outsiders Although the important presence of conservative films noirs within the cycle must be denied, a more powerful group of films was informed by a left-liberal critique of American democracy as sick and corrupt. These films attempted to keep alive the spirit of the 1930s New Deal – and its cultural image, the Popular Front, a broad alliance of left-wing activists – in which the inequalities of capitalism require welfarist intervention and amelioration (Denning, 1997). Orson Welles was the most significant Popular Front figure. His disparate films noirs in a career frustrated by studio intransigence and enforced exile – *Journey into Fear* (1943), *The Stranger* (1946) and *Mr Arkadin* (1955), as well as *The Lady from Shanghai* (1948) and *Touch of Evil* (1958) – are informed by an existentialist Marxism that characterizes a generation of film-makers whose radicalism was forged in New York's political theatre of the 1930s: Jules Dassin, Edward Dymtryk, John Huston, Elia Kazan, Joseph Losey, Abraham Polonsky, Nicholas Ray and Robert Rossen whose collective contribution to film noir was substantial (Neve, 1992).

Dassin's *Brute Force* (1947) uses the prison film to mount a critique of totalitarian institutions. Its allegory is both social and existential, the prisoners' bid for freedom, which their leader Joe Collins (Burt Lancaster) knows is doomed, is a generalized revolt against entrapment and persecution. To the left, crime was either the cry of the dispossessed and the marginalized, or a message about the greed engendered by the capitalist system in which crime is an inverted form of the spirit of American enterprise. *Body and Soul* (1947) – written by Polonsky, directed by Rossen and starring John Garfield, an actor known for his left-wing sympathies – was the paradigm story of the slum kid who becomes a successful boxer, but who is corrupted by material success.

Garfield also starred in Polonsky's *Force of Evil* (1948) as Joe Morse, a gambling syndicate lawyer employed to turn the 'numbers racket' into a legal lottery, who misrecognizes ruthless exploitation as enterprise and which leads to the death of his innocent brother Leo (Thomas Gomez), who had sacrificed his own ambitions to send Joe through law school. Polonsky expressed the attraction of film noir to left-wing writers when he observed, 'the intellectual content is absorbed into what people think is a dark, criminal type of picture anyhow and so there's an acceptance of it' (quoted in Neve, 1992, p.150). In a memorable final scene, shot on location in the cold, raw light of dawn, Joe slowly descends the steep banks underneath Manhattan Bridge: 'I just kept going down and down. It was like going to the bottom of the world, to find my brother.' When Joe discovers Leo's body he reflects: 'They had thrown it away on the rocks by the river, like an old dirty rag nobody wants. He was dead and I felt I had killed him.' The studied cadences of Polonsky's prose and George Barnes's limpid photography, which retains the soaring arch of the bridge in frame throughout, create an allegorical scene which symbolizes Joe's moral awakening and elevates the conventional plotting of a commercial crime film into an expressive tableau about the price of success.

Philip Kemp argues that this attack on capitalist greed was not solely the property of the left, as many films noirs that have no discernible connection with left-wing sympathizers mount a powerful critique of amoral *laissez-faire* capitalism. Therefore the attacks on the left were made against 'known sympathisers' of Communism rather than against the content of particular films (Kemp, 1986, pp.266–70). These attacks had immensely destructive effects. The careers of both Polonsky and Dmytryk were blighted when they were blacklisted as part of the 'Hollywood Ten'. Even the liberal head of production at RKO, Dore Schary, despite his objections, was forced to abandon both his blacklisted personnel and his 'message pictures' as the majors capitulated to right-wing pressure (Neve, 1992, pp.198–202). This severely damaged the careers of nearly everyone in this group and put a very effective brake on left-wing films noirs.

Those who survived direct indictment, including John Huston and Joseph Losey, made a few further films before moving to Europe. Huston's *The Asphalt Jungle* (1950) contrasts the band of sympathetic outcasts engaged in robbery with the corrupt lawyer Alonzo Emmerich (Louis Calhern), who rationalizes crime as 'only a left-handed form of human endeavour', and the self-righteous police commissioner. Losey's *The Prowler* (1951), scripted by the blacklisted Dalton Trumbo who had to remain uncredited, was a powerful allegory about the 'false values' that capitalism induced, the desire for '100,000 bucks, a Cadillac and a blonde', which corrupt the personable young police officer Webb Garwood (Van Heflin) (Losey, quoted in Ciment, 1985, p.100). In Losey's remake of Fritz Lang's *M* (1951), the police and gangsters are equally corrupt corporate entities, which makes the child murderer a sympathetic outsider turned into a scapegoat. Losey argued that whereas Lang had shown a pitiful monster, his own 'point of view was that society was responsible for him and he was sick . . . a product of a mother-dominated and materialistic society of lower middle-class America, where everyone has to be a big he-man otherwise they were sissies' (ibid., pp.110,114).

Kiss Me Deadly

Robert Aldrich's *Kiss Me Deadly* (1955), though late in the cycle, is often cited as one of noir's masterpieces precisely because it explores so many of the key themes. *Kiss Me Deadly* was adapted from a right-wing source, one of Mickey Spillane's 'Mike Hammer' novels, which celebrated a commie-bashing, xenophobic private eye with a relish for violence. Spillane's novels were extremely successful, the most popular crime fiction of the 1950s (Cawelti, 1976, pp.183–91). Aldrich, who had worked as assistant director on *Body and Soul* and *The Prowler* but was too young and too lowly to be implicated in the blacklisting, loathed Spillane and regarded his creation Mike Hammer as 'cynical and fascistic' (Arnold and Miller, 1986, pp.13–14). His co-screenwriter, A.I. Bezzerides, had written the screenplay for Dassin's *Thieves Highway* (1949) based on his own novel, which showed the abuse of decent farm workers by greedy wholesalers, another metaphor for capitalist exploitation.

Kiss Me Deadly continues a left-liberal critique of capitalism by turning the self-righteousness and brutal pragmatism of Hammer's world inside out, but it broadens this into a wider allegory of a society that seems about to self-destruct. In a brilliant move, Spillane's prosaic search for a cache of Mafia drugs becomes the film's quest for the 'great whatzit', the atomic bomb: 'There was a lot of talk about nuclear war at the time, and it was the foremost fear in people's minds' (Bezzerides quoted in Server *et al.* (eds) 1998, p.121). The opening of the box containing the bomb parallels Pandora's mythical unleashing of sin into the world. It is a quest that provides a logical goal for a society shown as violent and thoroughly corrupt.

From the outset, Aldrich depicts a dissonant world. A young woman, clad only in a trench coat, runs in terror along a pitch black road, the silence broken only by her gasps and panting. She makes a frenzied cruciform gesture, the first of several in the film, to flag down a speeding sports car. As she and the driver, a disgruntled Hammer, drive off, the title credits unroll in reverse as if to suggest a looking-glass world, one which is supposedly speeding forward, but actually running backwards towards oblivion. Moments later a huge, partially obscured limousine blocks the road and in a confusing scene we glimpse only shoes and disembodied voices, drowned by the woman's screams as she is tortured and then killed. We witness the twitchings of her naked, dangling legs while an off-screen voice remarks that to wake her would be to perform a resurrection.

This disorientating, terrifyingly violent and sadistic scene is in excess of anything so far depicted in noir's dark universe and acts as a prelude to a film that depicts a world at once recognizable and demented. Although much of the film is shot on location, Aldrich's use of Los Angeles 'is the opposite of the documentarist's and bears little relation to the goals of a fictional verisimilitude. The film's look is surreal; the world is carefully and fastidiously distorted' (Shadoian, 1977, p.268). *Kiss Me Deadly's* Los Angeles is the city of the future, a postmodern centrifugal sprawl with no centre, its inhabitants lost by the sides of the endless freeways like Wilshire Boulevard, a four-lane highway on which Hammer's ultramodern, sparely furnished flat with its impersonal ansaphone is situated (Arthur, 1996a, p.23). Hammer moves around this amorphous city in his souped-up Chevrolet Corvette, which takes him from the fading tenement apartments of Bunker Hill to the mansions of Bel Air, where the gangsters relax by their swimming pools, and to the fashionable beach house in Malibu where the final explosion takes place.

Hammer is a creature of this dislocated, postmodern world, miraculously surviving the encounter in which the young woman was killed and he was pushed over the cliff in his car, to return, like Lazarus, from his grave, and with his body unmarked as if he might not be real. He is a man without culture, lacking any knowledge of art, music and literature. Yet the most cultivated, urbane and philosophical character, Dr Soberin, is also the most dangerous and the most transient, more a world-weary aesthete than scientist, always moving to some new place, otherwise, 'it would be impossible to be sad and melancholy again'. The race that everyone is engaged in, to find the 'great whatzit', ends only in destruction and death. This modern apocalypse renders what preceded it meaningless: the great secret of the modern world is its ability to annihilate itself, the ultimate 'va-va-voom' of the dimwitted Nick. There is no escape for the detective even if he is stumbling with his secretary Velma in the surf at the end: both are far too close to the nuclear explosion to have any chance of surviving (Arnold and Miller, 1986, p.14 and n.37, p.245).

NARRATIVE STRATEGIES

Film noir's unorthodox narrative patterns often depart significantly from classical Hollywood's mode of storytelling, which, like its 'invisible style' was governed by the desire for self-effacing craftsmanship and an apparent objectivity. As David Bordwell observes, classical narration derives from the dominant conventions of the nineteenth-century novel and is based on a tight causality in which each action leads swiftly and logically on to the next, creating a self-contained, consistent and credible world where everything is completely comprehensible. To achieve this clarity, Hollywood film-makers favoured linear narratives with a very definite time-frame which allowed the film to progress smoothly with no apparent redundancies or gaps. This leads to a strong resolution or closure in which all the loose ends are tied up and where all the elements of the story, all the questions, enigmas and disruptions raised during the course of the narrative, have been answered, order and harmony are restored and no questions or ambiguities remain (Bordwell, 1985, pp.156–204). This fundamental paradigm holds true even for the crime fiction genre from which film noir often derives, which customarily uses a 'suppressive' or 'restricted' narration where the viewer is kept deliberately in the dark about the clues or secrets that constitute the mystery that the text unravels.

As discussed in Chapter 1, film noir derived its complex narrative strategies from German Expressionism and French Poetic Realism which subverted or problematized several of the classical paradigm's fundamental features and produced the ambiguous and inconclusive endings that characterize the cycle. In the most detailed consideration of noir narration, J.P. Telotte argues that film noir shows a 'remarkable pattern of narrative experimentation', unique for a particular body of films within Hollywood cinema (Telotte, 1989, p.3). Telotte argues that this experimentation took place along three distinct modes: extensive use of voice-over/flashback, or multiple narration which interrupts, interprets or rearranges the time frame; the use of dream sequences and subjective camerawork that frequently attempt to render psychological disturbance; and the attempt at an objective narration in the semi-documentaries which has already been covered in the previous chapter. Although many noirs, for example *Dead Reckoning* (1947), combine two or three of these modes, Telotte's categories provide a sound analytical framework; but, following Maureen Turim, I shall split the voice-over/flashback narratives into two basic types, the investigative and the confessional (Turim, 1989, pp.170–89).

Voice-Over/Flashback Narration 1: Confessional

At a straightforward level, the voice-over was an attempt to replicate the first person narration of the pulp fiction sources from which many noirs were adapted. Julio Moreno argued that the device was merely 'second-grade objectivism', where one character's experience is presented to us from an impersonal viewpoint, because the films place the spectator in the presence of the facts narrated directly without intermediaries and lose the distance that written narration can supply through its insistent use of the past tense (Moreno, 1953, pp.341–58). However, flashbacks can undermine the apparent objectivity of the images as they can question the reliability of the narrator whose flashbacks try to make sense of a past that is rendered as strange, threatening and unfinished, as in *Detour* and *Out of the Past* analysed in previous chapters. *Sunset Boulevard* (1950), like *D.O.A.*, uses the flashback narrative of a man already dead. Although the protagonist appears to be in control of the retelling of the story, it is really the past events that are still controlling him, which he would love to alter if he could. The use of the masculine pronoun is warranted here because, although there are notable examples of female narrators – *Rebecca* (1940), *Mildred Pierce* (1945) or *Raw Deal* (1948), analysed in Chapter 6 – the confessional narrative is dominated by the male protagonist's retrospective examination of the ways in which he was seduced and betrayed by a duplicitous *femme fatale* (Hollinger, 1996, pp.243–59). The compulsive need to understand her motivations and to justify his own helplessness prompt his retelling of a story, which becomes a plea for understanding or sympathy.

Double Indemnity's (1944) confessional flashback, coming at the beginning of the cycle, was highly influential (Telotte, 1989, p.39). Writer-director Billy Wilder and his co-screenwriter Raymond Chandler use an intermittent flashback, which creates a counterpoint between the confession itself and the confessor's present situation. *Double Indemnity*'s celebrated opening scene – the car speeding recklessly through the night-time streets, the bedraggled man blundering through the soulless passageways of the Pacific All Risk Insurance Company – is both dramatic and disturbing, providing an ominous context for the narrative which follows as Walter Neff (Fred MacMurray), near death, discloses all into the office dictaphone. Although made to a mechanical recording instrument whose function is usually mundane, the dictaphone has a symbolic significance as it is the 'property' of his boss, Senior Claims Investigator Barton Keyes (Edward G. Robinson), the only person, Neff now realizes, he cares about. Neff needs to 'put the record straight' for the man beneath whose waistcoat 'beats a heart as big as a house'. Thus Neff's flashbacks have a double purpose: to try to exorcise the malign influence of the *femme fatale* Phyllis Dietrichson (Barbara Stanwyck), and to renew a bond of loyalty with Keyes which offers some form of redemption.

This is important in establishing audience sympathy, as Neff is no innocent but a smart young professional who has 'explored all the angles' before he met Phyllis; it is Neff who decides on the double indemnity stratagem. His recollections have a curious mixture of self-congratulation in which he details the brilliance of the scheme, self-pity at his manipulation by a

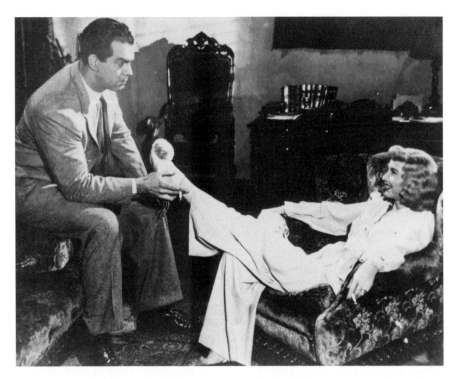

Walter Neff (Fred MacMurray) 'exploring all the angles' with Phyllis Dietrichson (Barbara Stanwyck) in *Double Indemnity* (Billy Wilder, 1944)

practised seductress-cum-murderer and the characteristic noir fatalism that he has compulsively carried out what anyone would do given the circumstances: 'You're like the guy behind the roulette wheel, watching the customers to make sure they don't crook the house. And then one night you get to thinking how you could crook the house yourself and do it smart, because you've got the wheel right smack under your hands.'

As Neff's confession concludes, Keyes has arrived on the scene. Begging for a chance to make a dash for the border, Neff cannot even make it to the lift, but slumps in the doorway with Keyes bending over him. Keyes lights a match for Neff, a reversal of the gesture that has symbolized their close relationship all along, and a clear indication of the homoerotic subtext that has under-pinned Neff's overwhelming desire to tell all to Keyes, whom he knows is openly contemptuous of women. The film's ending is strikingly different from the novel's where Walter is preparing to commit suicide with Phyllis. Wilder uses the counterpoint of past and present to produce a narrative of female seduction that becomes, as he said himself, 'a love story between the two men' (quoted in Allyn, 1978, p.120).

The Lady from Shanghai (1948) is a world away from the hard-boiled tradition, its story adapted by Orson Welles from Sherwood King's novel *Before I Die*, which makes repeated references to dreams. It has a detached, bemused, almost whimsical narration provided by Welles himself as the jobbing sailor Michael O'Hara who acknowledges his stupidity in ever becoming entangled with a *femme fatale* – 'If I'd known where it would end, I'd have never have let anything start . . . If I'd been in my right mind . . . But once I'd seen her I was not in my right mind for some time.' In this case the flashback is uninterrupted as Welles attempts to create an oneiric narrative which is also a moral fable, the traditional function of the mariner's tale. O'Hara's story, summed up in his tale of the crazed sharks eating themselves off the hump of Brazil, is a fable of irrational predatoriness. Arthur Bannister (Everett Sloane), the successful but crippled lawyer, and his beautiful wife Elsa (Rita Hayworth), the exotic and inscrutable woman from the Orient, seem to exist for no other purpose than to consume each other. In the famous dénouement in the amusement park's hall of mirrors where Elsa and Bannister shoot each other, the bewildering variety of confusing and distorted images doubled and redoubled offers a visual image that symbolizes the ultimate opacity of the pair's motivations. The narrative seems not so much to progress towards a resolution, as compulsively double back; its present retelling is just one more effort to extract the meaning of the story (Graham, 1981, pp.21–37). As O'Hara himself concludes: 'Maybe I'll live so long I'll forget her. Maybe I'll die trying.'

Voice-Over/Flashback 2: Investigative

Investigative narratives often have enigmatic central characters – for instance *Citizen Kane* (1940) or *The Mask of Dimitrios* (1944) – but the narration itself is multiple. Anthony Veiller's screenplay for *The Killers* (1946) expands its source, a cryptic Hemingway short story that only directly provides the material of the opening scene, into a complex succession of eleven disconnected and overlapping flashbacks.[3] The object of the narrative is the Swede (Burt Lancaster), a man who has lost his desire to live, making no attempt to run or hide from two hired killers. As David Bordwell points out, none of the flashbacks are revealed to be hallucinatory, oneiric or duplicitous, but are scrupulously restricted to what the successive narrators know; each consists only of the events which the character was present to witness (Bordwell, 1985, p.196). The Swede himself is not permitted a voice but remains, like Charles Foster Kane, the enigmatic absent centre. Although Insurance Investigator Riordan (Edmond O'Brien) gradually pieces together what happened, the investigation is ultimately irrelevant; all that may happen as the result of its outcome is that 'the basic rate at the Atlantic Casualty Company, as of 1947, will probably drop one tenth of a cent'. What is revealed is 'a chaotic world in which people are doomed to exist at cross-purposes' (Shadoian, 1977, p.86). The Swede could not have avoided his death, which is one of innumerable such casualties in an arbitrary and malign universe. The obscure, clouded motivations of the protagonists weave together a tale of crime and erotic attraction – the Swede's infatuation for *femme fatale* Kitty Collins (Ava Gardner) – that is as powerful as it is inexplicable, opaque to rational investigation.

The radical modernism of *The Killers* was different from the explicit Freudianism of John Brahm's *The Locket* (1947), which uses a complex series of flashbacks within flashbacks to 'explain' the mental instability of Nancy Blair (Laraine Day) who collapses on the day of her wedding. Her former husband, Dr Harry Blair (Brian Aherne) interrupts her wedding by warning husband-to-be John Willis (Gene Raymond) about her past. Blair's extended flashback contains within it the recollections of her first husband, the painter Norman Clyde (Robert Mitchum) who went to see Blair for the same reason, to warn him about Nancy. Within Clyde's reminiscences is embedded Nancy's own recollections of the 'primal scene', the traumatic accusation by her mother's employer, Mrs Willis, that she stole a locket and the brutal extraction of a confession for a crime she did not commit. The accusation exposes the heartlessness of upper middle-class society and its contempt for the servant class, but also that Nancy's desires for beautiful possessions and with that her entry into the privileged classes, must be forever denied. This leads to the compulsive kleptomania and lying that have ruined the lives of her two previous husbands. The moment of Nancy's triumph, her marriage to the son of that hateful mother who gives her the locket as a wedding present, is forestalled by Blair's arrival.

The Locket is a radically ambivalent film. On the one hand it can be read as a misogynist warning to prospective husbands – never trust your bride – which the male narrators, one of whom is a trained psychiatrist, are keen to organize. On the other, the Freudian scenario of Nancy's narration and her collapse are the most graphic sections of the film and suggest that her subsequent behaviour is to be understood as the inevitable consequence of this psychological trauma for which she is to be pitied. In Nancy's slow descent towards her bridegroom she upsets a music box whose tune recalls the traumatic childhood scene of the stolen locket. The tune displaces the wedding march and precipitates a series of recollected images, figures and scenes from her past, which swirl in front of her causing her collapse. *The Locket*'s oscillation between condemnation and sympathy for its central protagonist, draws attention to the processes of narration and to the attempt of male narrators to control the 'problem' of femininity.

Subjective Camerawork and Dream States

The most radical attempt at subjective narration was Robert Montgomery's *Lady in the Lake* (1947) where the camera becomes the eyes of detective Philip Marlowe.[4] However, as several commentators noted at the time, there is never the sense that we are entering a subjective consciousness, simply that the private eye's vision replicates the impersonal as far as possible.[5] The much more frequent use of subjective camerawork and point-of-view narration derives from German Expressionism's attempts to provide a visual correlative for disturbed psychological states. Two films directed by émigré Curtis Bernhardt, *Possessed* and *High Wall* (both 1947), use this technique to convey the mental conflicts of their amnesiac protagonists.

Possessed begins with an extended sequence shot from the point-of-view of Louise Howell (Joan Crawford) to capture the distracted, catatonic state in which she wanders through the Los Angeles streets asking for 'David'. Her perspective is sustained during her hospitalization and interrogation by psychiatrists, who use narcosynthesis to induce her to recount the causes of her condition. Although associational dissolves are used to suggest a confused mental state, her flashback settles into a conventional narration of events, which the audience is invited to accept as true.

High Wall concerns a war veteran, ex-army pilot Steve Kenet (Robert Taylor), who has a blood clot pressing on his brain that results in violent headaches and amnesia. He appears to have killed his wife, but has no recollection of the circumstances of her death. Through the sympathetic ministration of Dr Ann Lorrison (Audrey Totter), he relives those events under narcosynthesis. His recollections are shown subjectively, partly through his eyes as he advances murderously towards the terrified face of his faithless wife, and partly through hers as she gazes at the fixed expression of hate looming towards her. Bernhardt then cuts to a medium close-up as Kenet tries to strangle her, his grip loosening when he clutches his head and falls down. His collapse into unconsciousness is conveyed by a whirlpool dissolve in which a carousel is spinning round. Only when he revisits the place – the house of his wife's lover Willard Whitcombe (Herbert Marshall) – does he recall that the carousel image was prompted by the music box that had fallen on the floor during the struggle and he understands Willard is the real killer.

Noir's use of dream sequences to express psychological disturbance also derives from Expressionism, as in *Stranger on the Third Floor* discussed in Chapter 2. However, the most ambitious example occurs in Hitchcock's *Spellbound* (1945), the story of a traumatized amnesiac war veteran John Ballantine (Gregory Peck), who believes himself guilty of the murder of Doctor Edwards whom he is impersonating. *Spellbound*'s dream sequence, designed by the Surrealist Salvador Dali, was used by Hitchcock because he 'wanted to convey the dreams with great visual sharpness and clarity, sharper than the film itself' (Leff, 1987, pp.138–9). The disorientating spatial and temporal illogicality and apparent randomness of Surrealism's sharply etched images would create an entirely different world from the main narrative and perhaps more accurately convey mental processes. The dream set is dominated by the huge eyes that were a Dali trademark, steeply sloping roofs and a strange landscape of converging lines that suggested 'the infinity of distance'. Selznick, who thought the experiment too radical for American audiences, drastically pruned the sequence, which muted Hitchcock's intentions (ibid.).

A Cornell Woolrich adaptation, *Fear in the Night* (1947), uses a dream sequence to help convey the protagonist's paranoia and confusion. *Fear in the Night* has a wonderful surreal opening in which Vince Grayson (DeForest Kelly) experiences a nightmare in which he murders a man in a mirrored room from which he cannot escape. He falls into what seems like an endless tunnel before waking, only to find the evidence – cuts on his arm, two thumb prints on his neck, a button torn off in the struggle and the key to the mirror cupboard – that proves the dream was true. Doubting his sanity and convinced he is a murderer, Grayson becomes estranged from his elder sister and his girlfriend and attempts suicide. He is saved by his detective brother-in-law, who gradually uncovers the clues that reveal he was hypnotized.

These subjective devices were film noir's attempt to objectify internal states, but Hollywood film-makers, unlike their Expressionist forebears or Surrealist painters, were operating within a conservative commercial regime in which audience understanding and acceptance, as interpreted by the producer or the studio, counted for more than artistic innovation and experimentation. As with noir style, there is a fundamental tension between the radical experimentation inspired by European modernism and the demands of generic conventions. In the 1950s where there is less concern with individual pathology, these experiments with subjective camerawork, flashbacks or voiceovers die away in favour of more conventional narration. However, there was one magnificent exception that, like *Touch of Evil*, was the furthest a commercial film-maker could go, Alfred Hitchcock's *Vertigo* (1958).

Vertigo's preoccupation with the nature of perception and deceptive appearances is signalled in the opening credits with their giant eyes. Although it is narrated in the present, *Vertigo* is a tale that is obsessed with the past, with the European remnants of nineteenth-century San Francisco. Its investigator-hero, 'Scottie' Ferguson (James Stewart), is a man with a fatal weakness, fear of heights, which in the opening scene of a roof-top chase, results in the death of a fellow policeman. Hitchcock uses subjective shots of Scottie's petrified gaze down at the horrifying drop to the street below to create a scene of psychological trauma. Bernard Herrmann, who worked with Hitchcock several times beginning with *The Trouble with Harry* (1955), contributed an unnerving score which deliberately avoids a conventional melody, denying the usual pleasures of identification with characters through their individual melodies. Herrmann's score is insistent, but harmonically ambiguous with a shifting, unpredictable rhythm and tempo, which reinforce the ambiguity in the film's themes and visual effects (Kalinak, 1992, pp.3–19).

At its centre is a false enigma. The woman whom Scottie takes to be the suicidal Madeleine Elster (Kim Novak) obsessed with Carlotta Valdes her great-grandmother, is a fake, engaged by Madeleine's husband Gavin Elster (Tom Helmore) in order to falsify his wife's death and gain possession of her fortune. Scottie has been employed by Elster, his old college friend, in order to fail, his vertigo making him powerless to prevent what seems to be Madeleine's suicide from the tower. That second failure is even more emotionally damaging for Scottie because he has fallen in love with the woman he takes to be Madeleine, whom he apparently saved from drowning and who has become the woman of his dreams.

After the inquest, in which the coroner blames Scottie for weakness and lack of foresight, Hitchcock inserts an explicitly subjective sequence in which Scottie is possessed by his own death wish. As he lies restlessly in bed, Scottie experiences a nightmare in which an intense red light pulsates across the screen as he relives in sharp but dissociated images what has happened: the bouquet of flowers in Carlotta's portrait that he had seen Madeleine copy burst into his anguished face; her jewelled necklace flashes in front of him and a new portrait of Elster, Carlotta and Madeleine appears, their scornful expressions seeming to mock him. As the pulsating light intensifies, Scottie advances towards the open grave that he thinks is Carlotta/Madeleine's but which becomes his own, gaping to receive him. As he falls, the void becomes a revolving tunnel round his disembodied head, then the dark silhouette of a male figure falling through endless space first towards the roof where Madeleine died, then dissolving into nothingness, symbolized by a blank white screen. After this intense sequence, Hitchcock cuts to an institutionalized Scottie who has retreated into wordless catatonia: a living death beyond the reach of his friend Midge (Barbara Bel Geddes) or his doctors.

In his distracted state, Scottie wanders the streets of San Francisco in the search for a woman he knows to be dead, which, as Hitchcock witheringly remarked, is an act of necrophilia (Truffaut, 1986, p.370). In a grim irony he catches a glimpse of the woman, Judy, who impersonated Madeleine, and, unaware of the truth, obsessively recreates this gauche working-class girl from Kansas as the 'real' Madeleine, dressing her in exactly the same clothes and with exactly the same hairstyle. The switch to Judy's perception at this point where she composes a confessional letter she eventually discards, and the truth of Madeleine's death, which is revealed in her flashback, was often criticised, but it creates sympathy for a woman who loves Scottie and hopes she can cure him. That is impossible as Scottie is not interested in Judy herself, but in her impersonation. When her makeover is complete, she seems to materialize out of the green light of her hotel bedroom as Madeleine, the woman of his dreams. The green light 'gives her the same subtle, ghostlike quality' that recalls Scottie's earlier pursuit of Madeleine to the cemetery where Carlotta lay buried (Hitchcock, in ibid, p.371).

That illusion is shattered when Judy puts on Carlotta's necklace as they prepare to go out, which allows Scottie to grasp what has taken place. In a desperate act of exorcism he takes her back to the mission tower where Madeleine's 'death' was staged. In his eyes it is not so much her part in the crime that must be confronted, but what he sees as her act of betrayal towards him – 'I loved you so' – now bound up with his determination to redeem his weakness and be 'free of the past'. Judy, fleeing from the dark figure she mistakes for Madeleine/Carlotta, throws herself from the tower in a 'true' re-enactment of the faked death. The final image is of the dark, spectral shape of Stewart's outstretched, etiolated body gazing down at her body, seemingly poised for final plunge into the abyss of death. It was a striking, haunting image, the culmination of *Vertigo*'s radical narrative strategies and dark exploration of psychic trauma.

Both *Vertigo* and *Kiss Me Deadly* pushed at the very limits of what was possible within the generic structures of the crime thriller, but both were in advance of popular taste and relatively unsuccessful at the box-office.[6] In their very different ways, both offer a profound critique of the American Dream, presenting a society which is wracked by psychological and social trauma. Their central protagonists are men who seem to have returned from the grave and who are haunted by a past which they can neither acknowledge nor escape from.

NOTES

1. For a detailed analysis to which the following is indebted, see Shadoian (1977), pp.174–90.
2. The film's publicity poster strapline read: 'Meet the Rogue's Gallery of the Underworld Who Joined the Fight Against Espionage . . . On the Side of the *USA*'.
3. The screenplay was co-written by an uncredited John Huston.
4. Orson Welles intended to make a version of Joseph Conrad's *Heart of Darkness* where the camera assumed the perspective of the narrator, Marlow; see Carringer (1985, pp.3–15).
5. See Joseph P. Brinton III (1947, pp.359–66). For further general discussion of subjectivity and point-of-view in films see Branigan (1984) and Mitry (1998).
6. For *Kiss Me* Deadly's reception see Arnold and Miller (1986, pp.42–5); for *Vertigo*'s see Kapsis (1992, pp.39, 49–54, 121–2, 149).

CHAPTER FIVE

Gender in Film Noir

Character Types and Performers

Film noir's construction of gender is one of its most distinctive features. Instead of the strong, heroic males and supportive females that populate classical Hollywood's films, film noir is littered with weak, confused and powerless males, the victims of duplicitous *femmes fatales*. In addition to these central archetypes, film noir depicts several other male types, including psychopaths and damaged men, aspects of what Frank Krutnik in his study of masculinity in film noir calls its 'pervasive problematising of masculine identity' (Krutnik, 1991, p.99). As would be expected in a patriarchal culture and in such a male-dominated form as film noir, there is a greater range of male types than female ones, but even within a more restricted compass, female roles are not exhausted by the *femme fatale* and her opposite, the supportive homebuilder, as Elizabeth Cowie has shown (Cowie, 1993, pp.121–66). This chapter will analyse the variety of the principal male and female character types in film noir, which are complex constructions of gender that condense a range of social meanings. These character types are both embodied and extended by the stars who play them, consequently their performances become central to the meaning of the types.[1] Building on the very limited discussion of stardom and performance in relation to film noir, the second part of the chapter will analyse the roles of the most important actors.

THE MALE VICTIM

The male victim is the most pervasive character type in film noir, showing what Krutnik describes as noir's fascination with the spectacle of the passive or emasculated man (Krutnik, 1991, p.127). The main type of male victim is the dupe of the *femme fatale*, which derives from the two James M. Cain adaptations, *Double Indemnity* and *The Postman Always Rings Twice*, middle-class professional and working-class drifter respectively. This figure is not admirable or innocent but morally weak, apparently helpless in the throes of desire and attempting to escape the frustrations of his existing life. As has been shown, Cain's victims have a compulsion to tell their stories, to explain if not excuse their actions, and there is a powerful element of masochism, of self-loathing in their make-up along with their passivity. Billy Wilder took this trait further in *Sunset Boulevard* (1950) where Joe Gillis (William Holden) plumbs the depths of abjection in becoming the grinning gigolo for the increasingly possessive and unstable silent film star Norma Desmond (Gloria Swanson). Several commentators at the time related the victim hero's para-noias and persecutory fantasies to the fear of passive homosexuality, which they were convinced was an important element in the psychological make-up of postwar American males (Buchsbaum, 1992, pp.88–97).

The more innocent male victim is the one framed for a crime he did not commit – Alan Curtis' young businessman in *Phantom Lady* (1944), Pat O'Brien's art expert George Steele in *Crack-Up* (1946) or Ray Milland's journalist in *The Big Clock* (1948) – who are all respectable middle-class professionals. But working-class characters are also often victims simply by being in the wrong place at the wrong moment: Bill Williams's hick sailor in *Deadline at Dawn* (1946) or John Payne's ex-fighter turned delivery man in *99 River Street* (1953). Often the victim will battle his way out of adversity, displaying heroic qualities of energy, resilience and courage, or he may need help to do so. But the figure also frequently falls prey to doubts about his own sanity, as often happens in stories of amnesiac war veterans discussed in the next section, or noirs that have been adapted from stories by Cornell Woolrich, already discussed.

The weakness, confusion and need for others' help of the victim hero can create a sympathetic Everyman, as in Jacques Tourneur's *Nightfall* (1957), adapted from a David Goodis novel, another hard-boiled writer whose work features displaced victims with unstable identities.[2] Jim Vanning (Aldo Ray), is a mild-mannered commercial artist who has changed his identity and is suffering bouts of amnesia because of a chance encounter with gangsters whilst on a camping trip where his friend Gurston was shot, but the stolen money left behind. Vanning is on the run from the thieves who want to regain the money, and from the police who believe he killed Gurston. Ray's subtle, beautifully judged performance creates a vulnerable, appealing figure, desper-ate to regain control of his life but unable to do it, who feels betrayed by the model, Marie (Anne Bancroft), but finally learns to trust her and use her support. Unlike Jeff Bailey, Vanning has no sordid past that he can never be free from and eventually wins through.

DAMAGED MEN: MALADJUSTED VETERANS AND ROGUE COPS

Richard Maltby has suggested that the returning veteran is the key noir pro-tagonist of the immediate postwar period, 1946–8, either explicitly identified as such or metaphorically: someone who has to account for a missing period in his life (Maltby, 1992, p.46). These veterans brought with them a range of social and psychological problems, as discussed in the background chapter, and their amnesia can easily turn them into victim heroes as in *Deadline at Dawn* (1946), *Somewhere in the Night* (1946), *High Wall* (1947), *The Crooked Way* (1949) and *The Clay Pigeon* (1949). They may also be unpredictably violent: Robert Taylor's Steven Kenet in *High Wall* or Johnny Morrison (Alan Ladd) in *The Blue Dahlia*. Both men are resentful, prickly and turbulent, still psychologically organized for war, and therefore obvious suspects for the murder of their faithless wives. Bill Saunders (Burt Lancaster) in *Kiss the Blood off My Hands* (1948) is even more unstable, as his long incarceration as a POW has left him embittered, with shattered nerves and a furious temper. After he accidentally kills a man in a pub in a fit of rage, Saunders becomes the prey to blackmailers and the denizens of a nocturnal London of outcasts and criminals.

Edward Dmytryk's *Crossfire* (1947) contained the widest range of malad-justed veterans, from the sensitive and vulnerable falsely accused victim, Mitchell (George Cooper), to the psychotic Montgomery (Robert Ryan) whose murderous anti-Semitism gives the film its social problem gloss. In a memorable scene Mitchell encounters 'the man' (Paul Kelly) who may be the husband of Ginny (Gloria Grahame), the dancer who has befriended Mitchell and lent him her apartment. He emerges out of the shadows, talks enigmat-ically about the meaningless posturings of his life, and later vanishes again from view. A spectral presence or 'lost soul', Kelly's deracinated Everyman embodies the film's pervasive sense of a restless, dislocated society, which cannot be mended simply by the capture of Montgomery.

The maladjusted veteran ceased to be a topical figure by the end of the 1940s, replaced by the rogue cop, another figure trained to kill, skilled in covering up his tracks, and a similarly destabilizing social force. The figure overshadows the many exemplary law enforcement agents in film noir, show-ing the pervasive corruption and instability that is at the heart of the noir world (Krutnik, 1991, pp.191–3). The rogue cop may have a basic decency which means he tries to reform: Robert Taylor in *The Bribe* (1949) and *Rogue Cop* (1954), and Gig Young in *City that Never Sleeps* (1953); or he may be corrupted too far: Van Heflin in *The Prowler* (1951), Lee J. Cobb in *The Man Who Cheated Himself* (1951), Fred MacMurray in *Pushover* (1954), Steve Cochran in *Private Hell 36* (1954), or Orson Welles in *Touch of Evil* (1958).

A third group, the most interesting, become violently unstable through their contact with criminals whom they loathe uncontrollably: Dana Andrews in *Where the Sidewalk Ends* (1950), Kirk Douglas in *Detective Story* (1951) and Glenn Ford in *The Big Heat* (1953). Robert Ryan's Jim Wilson in *On Dangerous Ground* (1952) was the most powerful embodiment. Wilson is the archetypal loner, wolfing down a spartan meal in his dreary rooms whilst examining mugshots of cop-killers before joining his two colleagues in the patrol car. Wilson is permanently edgy and the shadowy mise-en-scène as he pursues his prey along dark, cramped alleyways suggests that he carries the city's filth and depravity within him. As he mauls the prostitute Myrna, she recognizes his similarity to her hoodlum boyfriend; when he beats a confession out of the hapless Bernie, the violence and his anguished questions escalate together: 'Why do you make me do it? You know you're gonna talk. I'm gonna make you talk. I always make you punks talk. Why do you make me do it? Why? Why?' Only in the upstate snow-bound countryside does he begin to cleanse himself of the city, finding love and redemption through the love of Mary (Ida Lupino), the blind sister of the disturbed teenage boy he has to track down.

THE PRIVATE EYE

The private eye with his belted trench coat, fedora and dangling cigarette is one of the most popular images of film noir and the closest of the noir male types to the conventional hero, the courageous 'tough guy' who demonstrates exceptional physical endurance, loyalty to his male partner and healthily heterosexual desire for beautiful women (Cohan, 1997, p.42). The first fully-fledged noir private eye, Humphrey Bogart's Sam Spade in *The Maltese Falcon* (1941), was a decisive break from the 1930s tradition of debonair amateur sleuths. Spade is an egotistical competitor, hard, sarcastic and motivated largely by a determination to win out over everybody rather than a commitment to truth or justice. He displays no grief at the loss of his partner, evades the grieving widow with whom he has had an affair and now discards, and hands Brigid O'Shaughnessy (Mary Astor) over to the police not so much because it is 'bad business to let the killer get away with it', but because he knows that she cannot be trusted and to love her would turn him into the weak 'sap' he so despises (Maxfield, 1996, p.23).

By contrast, Dick Powell's Philip Marlowe in *Murder, My Sweet* (1944) embodied Raymond Chandler's conception of the modern knight, an outsider in the corrupted city, who, if cynical, clings to some ideal of justice and retains a hope that things can be made better even as he realizes that such a hope is illusory. Powell was asked by the director Edward Dmytryk to play Marlowe, 'as I believed Chandler visualized him – really an Eagle scout, a do-gooder, with a patina of toughness, only skin deep' (Dmytryk, 1978, p.60). Marlowe has some feeling for the lumbering Moose Malloy and his cynicism never blinds him to the need to try to protect the weak. Unlike Spade he is emotionally vulnerable, and his prolonged physical and mental torturing, his confusion and symbolic blinding, make him a compromised tough guy. Humphrey Bogart's incarnation of Marlowe in Howard Hawks' *The Big Sleep* (1946) places him somewhere between the earlier two. Bogart's Marlowe is shrewd, wary and tough, armed with a carapace of cool one-liners and seemingly always in control, one step ahead of the opposition, but with enough sentiment to fall in love with Vivian Sternwood (Lauren Bacall) even if that may not be in his best interests.

It was the police officer rather than the private eye who dominates the 1950s, but Aldrich's *Kiss Me Deadly* (1955), analysed in the last chapter, subjected the figure to a thoroughgoing critique, beginning with the young woman's withering attack on his narcissistic chauvinism as they drive off in his car. Ralph Meeker plays Hammer as rudderless modern man, emotionally and sexually repressed, and without the leavening dead-pan humour of his predecessors and their worldly knowledgeability. The police despise him as a 'bedroom dick' gaining a living from blackmailing his clients. When his detective acquaintance Pat (Wesley Addy) tells him that he has become involved with atomic weapons and he replies apologetically, 'I didn't know', Pat replies caustically, 'You think you would have done any different if you had known?', an indictment of Hammer's whole 'what's in it for me?' philosophy. He has the tough guy's muscles and quick reflexes, but is oddly uninvolved even in the violence of his trade. He has become an empty, catatonic icon in a self-destructive world.

THE NOIR CRIMINAL AND PSYCHOPATH

The other quasi-heroic tough guy in film noir is the gangster. However, as many commentators have noticed, the noir gangster is no longer the dynamic, brash, confident entrepreneur of the prewar cycle, but riddled with existential neuroses exemplified by Barry Sullivan's Shubunka in *The Gangster* (1947). In Raoul Walsh's *White Heat* (1948), James Cagney turned his explosive tough guys from *The Public Enemy* (1931) or *The Roaring Twenties* (1939) into Cody Jarret, racked by unbearable headaches coupled with convulsive seizures, and fixated with his mother on whose lap he collapses. He seems to incarnate the unstable, explosive energies set loose by atomic fission and, in the famous final scene, he stands on top of a gas tank at the chemical plant – 'Made it, Ma! Top of the world!' – and blows himself up (Henriksen, 1997, pp.21–4). Lucy Fischer identifies Jarret as a representative figure of postwar anxieties about masculinity: the violent, psychologically damaged veteran, the feminized, hysterical 'mummy's boy' and the asocial psychotic (Fischer, 1993, pp.70–84).

Jarret's instability and random violence showed the gangster metamorphosing into its replacement, the psychopath, which Wayne Douglass identifies as American culture's response to boredom and conformity. The psychopath can cope with the complex, bureaucratized postwar environment through the pure pleasure of destruction itself, the delight in inflicting pain (Douglass, 1981, pp.30–9). As a composite folk devil, the psychopath became interchangeable with 'sex criminal', 'pervert' and 'homosexual' (Cohan, 1997, pp.114–21). Richard Widmark's Tommy Udo in *Kiss of Death* (1947) analysed later, was the template. Bogart's Glenn Griffin in *The Desperate Hours* (1955), terrorizing the archetypal all-American family in their suburban home, showed how the tough guy had degenerated into a monstrous figure. In *The Night Holds Terror*, released in the same year, the figure becomes interchangeable with the delinquent in Robert Batsford (John Cassavetes), head of a marauding gang, which is holding to ransom a young professional and his family. By pathologizing both the tough guy and the delinquent as psychopathic, Steven Cohan argues that American culture in the 1950s was actively engaged in the expulsion of working-class male violence, replacing these types by more middle-class figures (ibid, pp.120–1).

THE *HOMME FATAL*

The *homme fatal*, enigmatic, duplicitous and destructive, is the male counterpart to the deadly female and the opposite of the male victim. He appears most frequently as the ostensibly caring husband or protector who is trying either to murder his wife or drive her mad. The *homme fatal*, an exciting mixture of cunning, cool calculation, manipulative charm and deep-rooted sexual sadism, is a version of the aristocratic Byronic male and therefore frequently found in the Gothic noirs, for example *Gaslight* (1944), *Experiment Perilous* (1944) and *My Name Is Julia Ross* (1945). In *Suspicion* (1941), which is vaguely contemporary, the figure is played by Cary Grant as debonair Johnnie Aysgarth, charming, devastatingly attractive but enigmatic and possibly sinister. Hitchcock cast Grant in the role because he wanted audiences, whom he knew would always believe in Grant's innocence, to be shocked when it was finally revealed that he had indeed intended to murder his wife (Joan Fontaine) all along. The studio vetoed this strategy but, as Graham McCann argues, this only makes Grant's performance all the more unnerving because he becomes a disturbingly flawed, unfathomable figure rather than an black-hearted fiend (McCann, 1996, pp.119–20). Grant's ambiguous figure is more unsettling than the clearly villainous Robert Taylor in *Undercurrent* (1946) or Humphrey Bogart in *The Two Mrs Carrolls* (1947).

The *homme fatal* could also have connotations of sexual perversity as well as sadism: Laird Cregar's egregious Lieutenant Ed Cornell in *I Wake Up Screaming* (1941), the dapper Claude Rains in *The Unsuspected* (1947) and Clifton Webb's corrupt aesthete Waldo Lydecker in *Laura* (1944). At the beginning of *Laura*, Lydecker is the film's voice and consciousness, secure in the tasteful luxury of his apartment and confidently assuming a privileged position as the connoisseur who has groomed Laura's career and 'the only one who really knew her'. But as the film unfolds Lydecker is gradually revealed as a man gripped by an overwhelming sexual obsession with the woman he has 'created' but cannot control or understand. He turns out to have been Laura's murderer, or rather of the woman he mistakenly assumed was Laura, a secret kept hidden from the audience until the dénouement. It was, perhaps, not that unexpected, as Lydecker's dandified effeminacy would always mark him, in a Hollywood film, as impotent, sexually repressed or deviant (Dyer, 1993, pp.60–71).

THE *FEMME FATALE*

The figure of the deadly female – *femme fatale*/spider woman/vamp – emerged as a central figure in the nineteenth century and became one of the most persistent incarnations of modern femininity, the woman who 'never really is what she seems to be' and is therefore, in a patriarchal culture, ungovernable and threatening.[3] The *femme fatale* was a frequent character in 1940s films noirs, but all but vanishes in the 1950s, another indication of noir's shift in direction (Arthur, 2001, p.159). Rita Hayworth as *The Lady from Shanghai* (1948) – film noir's most enigmatic example – embodies the Orientalism that Mary Ann Doane notes as part of a type whose appearance 'marks the confluence of modernity, urbanization, Freudian psychoanalysis and new technologies of production and reproduction (photography, the cinema)' (Doane, 1991, p.1). As overpoweringly desirable, duplicitous and sexually insatiable, the *femme fatale* has been interpreted as a symptom of male anxieties about women, a creature who threatens to castrate and devour her male victim (Maxfield, 1996). Janey Place sees the figure as the male protagonist's *Doppelgänger* which emerges at night to destroy him: 'The sexual, dangerous woman lives in this darkness, and she is the psychological expression of his own internal fears of sexuality, and his need to control and repress it' (Place, 1998, p.53). Her appearance is always explicitly sexual with long dark or blonde hair worn loose, long, sensuous legs, heavy make-up, jewellery that sparkles, and revealing costumes (Gledhill, 1998, p.32). Noir's *femme fatale* as prefigured in Murnau's *Sunrise* (1927), is the 'woman of the city', incarnating the sexual pleasures of modern urban life. As Molly Haskell observes, as an American copy of a European original, noir's *femme fatale* is 'allied not with the dark forces of nature, but with the green forces of the capitalist economy' (Haskell, 1987, p.197). She represents an explicit challenge to the postwar consensus that women should be fulfilled by the roles of wife and mother.

In addition to her European lineage, the *femme fatale* was a stock type from hard-boiled fiction and two of the most powerful screen incarnations derived from Cain's novels: Barbara Stanwyck's Phyllis Dietrichson in *Double Indemnity* (1944) and Lana Turner's Cora Smith in *The Postman Always Rings Twice* (1946), both frustrated wives married to dull and older men. The *femme fatale*'s most characteristic role is as a nightclub singer on the fringes of the underworld. A modern Circe, she traps her victim through performing her seductive torch song whose erotic spectacle is the most explicit display of the figure's sexual threat. In *The Killers* (1946), Ava Gardner's Kitty Collins is first glimpsed by her victim, the Swede (Burt Lancaster) singing 'The More I Know of Love'. Gardner's siren has a dreamlike sensuality, the apotheosis of a mythical femininity, sexy and feline, with her sloe-shaped eyes, curvaceous, high cheekbones, cleft chin, full, upturned mouth, all an open sexual invitation. Even during the mundanities of planning a robbery, she is reclining suggestively on a bed, shot from a high angle and attractively lit to accentuate the lines of her body. This iconography is complemented by the proliferation of mirror shots, which signal her narcissism and duplicity. The *femme fatale* exists in the shadow world of film noir, often emerging from darkness into harsh light, or bisected by both to indicate instability. The figure's enigmatic qualities stimulate the central narrative drive, which comes from the desire to understand her motivations and thereby to reassert the rational control of the male ego, an impossible project.

THE NURTURER/HOMEBUILDER: THE GIRL-NEXT-DOOR

The antithesis of the *femme fatale*, often appearing in the same film, is the figure of the innocent almost asexual homebuilder, the wife or sweetheart who sees her role as support and solace for the man. In *Out of the Past* (1947), the wholesome sweetness of Ann (Virginia Huston) is contrasted with the duplicitous Kathie or the venal Meta (Rhonda Fleming). As befits her role, Ann is often static, framed as the eternal, understanding listener, offering forgiveness and the promise of a stable world of loyalty, faithfulness and loving security. She is associated with daylight, nature and open spaces and is photographed in conventional high-key lighting (Place, 1998, pp.60–1). Jane Wyatt in *The Pitfall* (1948), Cathy O'Donnell in *Side Street* (1950), Coleen

Gray in *Kiss of Death* (1947) or Teresa Wright in *The Steel Trap* (1952) are further examples, but they too are placed on the narrative margins, indicating the difficulties that film noir had in portraying a virtuous and stable family life. Indeed, Jans B. Wager has argued that film noir tends to portray the wife or sweetheart as the *femme attrapée* or domestic drudge (Wager, 1999).

One way out of this narrow confine was to make the figure more active as the beleaguered hero's helpmate. Ann Sheridan plays a wife determined to help clear her husband's name in *Woman on the Run* (1950), while Ingrid Bergman and Audrey Totter play psychiatrists who help cure the hero's trauma and assist his capture of the real murderer in *Spellbound* (1945) and *High Wall* (1947) respectively. Lucille Ball in *The Dark Corner* (1946) and Ella Raines in *Phantom Lady* (1944) are secretaries who assume the driving force in the investigation to clear their bosses' name. In the latter, 'Kansas' (Raines) assumes the male role when she stalks a sweating bartender through the dimly lit and deserted streets and he becomes so terrified that he dashes into the path of an approaching car. Later she transforms herself into a *femme fatale* in a provocatively tight black dress in order to seduce the hapless Cliff Milburn (Elisha Cook Jr). This gender role reversal is typical of noirs adapted from Woolrich novels (Williams, 1996, pp.129–44).

THE GOOD-BAD GIRL

The figure of the 'good-bad girl' combines the sexual stimulation of the *femme fatale* with the fundamental decency of the homebuilder and constitutes a central modern American type (Wolfenstein and Leites, 1950, pp.25–46). Her importance to the noir cycle is difficult to overestimate. She can appear to be cynical, wilful and obsessed with money, but this stems from disillusionment with men and the frustrations of a circumscribed life. Susan Hayward played the type as June, a dance hostess in *Deadline at Dawn* (1946). June, jaded by the sleazy corruption of city life, is mistrustful and cynical, reluctant to help the amnesiac veteran Alex (Bill Williams) whom she regards as a hick – 'Who were you at home, Boob McNut?' But her gradual involvement with this gentle, innocent and trusting man reawakens her fundamental faith in humanity. Joan Bennett's world-weary secretary in *Hollow Triumph* (1948) was a less successful, more compromised version.

Veronica Lake in *The Blue Dahlia* (1946) and Lauren Bacall in *The Big Sleep* (1946) are good examples of the type: cool, laconic, sexually assured and independent, yet on the hero's side. They offered the male protagonist a 'provocative, slightly mocking image of himself' which allowed him to feel at home with her as he might with a male companion (ibid., p.33). The good-bad girl has both masculine and feminine qualities and although appearing to be duplicitous, like the *femme fatale*, proves herself to be loyal. If she cannot actively help the hero, she can support him and believe in his innocence, or his ability to solve the problems. In *The Big Sleep*, Bacall's sultry, smoky-voiced contemporary good-bad girl was the perfect foil for Bogart's laconic private eye and audiences enjoyed their 'leisurely mating duels' in which the pair exchange provocative and witty wisecracks which masked tenderness and the capacity for genuine affection. The best and most complex example of the type is Rita Hayworth in *Gilda* (1946), analysed at the end of the chapter.

THE FEMALE VICTIM

The most obvious female victims are those whose terror, paranoia and neuroses are induced through the strange, baffling or malevolent behaviour of the *homme fatal* in the Gothic noirs already mentioned, including Joan Fontaine's insecure heroines in *Rebecca* (1940) and *Suspicion* (1941), or Ingrid Bergman's in *Gaslight* (1944). In a contemporary setting, there tends to be a greater degree of ambivalence in the behaviour of the type, which is expressed through the use of voice-over. *The Arnelo Affair* (1947) concentrates on a suburban wife and mother, Anne Parkson (Frances Gifford), who allows her frustrations and boredom – her husband is a workaholic lawyer, kind but dull and neglectful – to sanction her flirtation with Tony Arnelo (John Hodiak) a nightclub owner. Her reluctant, guilty excitement is conveyed by the voice-over where her feelings can be made explicit. Arnelo, an *homme fatal*, frames her for the murder of his former girlfriend and she is gripped by mounting terror. Her decision that suicide is the only solution is forestalled through his deathbed confession.

PERFORMERS

The analysis of stars and performance is underrepresented in film studies and accounts of film noir often tend to neglect this dimension.[4] They have taken little cognisance of an early study by Mitchell Cohen who argues: 'The faces, voices, and bodies that inhabit its physical and psychical terrain are as indelible as the impressions of smoky nightclubs, neon signs against a black sky, and cars hurtling around dark corners' (Cohen, 1974, p.27). Cohen observes that film noir needed a different kind of male actor, men of reaction not action, as self-confident heroism turned into paranoia. This led to a significant recasting of established performers – Robert Cummings, Fred MacMurray and Dick Powell – and to the rise of a new group of actors who came to film noir 'fresh and brought to the screen a new, largely beneath-the-surface acting style that combined force and vulnerability' (ibid.); this constituted a break with prewar styles and a decisive influence on succeeding generations of male performers. However, Mitchell neglects to survey the role of female stars whose performances are also crucial to the meaning of the noir cycle.

MALE PERFORMERS

The most important male star in film noir was Humphrey Bogart whose noir roles were a complex development of his vicious tough-guy persona built up by Warner Bros. in the 1930s (Sklar, 1992, pp.76–103). The key change occurred in *High Sierra* (1941) where Huston's script gave Bogart the opportunity to make the ageing gangster Roy Earle a sympathetic figure, beneath whose toughness lurk self-doubt, fallibility and the need for love. *The Maltese Falcon* (1941) allowed him to add a cynical wise-cracking humour, while *Casablanca* (1943) fashioned the image of the romantic idealist underneath the outward hard crust. He stayed among the 'top moneymakers' in the *Motion Picture Herald*'s yearly polls until 1950 playing a series of 'reluctant heroes', tough, laconic, world-weary but incurably romantic (Schatz, 1997, pp.217–21). His success was augmented by his partnership with Lauren Bacall – whom he had married amidst much publicity in May 1945 – in *To Have and Have Not* (1945), *The Big Sleep* (1946), *Dark Passage* (1947) and *Key Largo* (1948). Their partnership eclipsed that of Alan Ladd and Veronica Lake in *This Gun for Hire* (1942), *The Glass Key* (1942) and *The Blue Dahlia* (1946).

Bogart's nondescript even slightly puny physique – the object of jokes in *The Big Sleep* – and homely, 'lived-in' face, were expressive of the shrunken, introverted world of noir. He exemplified the new minimalist, pared-down acting technique in which his stiff face, perpetually tense, wary, tight-lipped and frowning, is only allowed an occasional smile; it is the eyes, knowing and sad, that express the sentiment that gave depth to his tough guys. His rasping voice, with the famous lisp, could convey scornful cynicism and bemused irony rather than overt sentiment, but in *Dead Reckoning* (1947) in particular, it could convey confused feelings churning inside. He developed his trademark mannerisms: linking his thumbs in his belt, putting his hands in his trouser pockets, pulling back his upper lip to reveal his teeth, tugging on his right earlobe. But these tics never obscured his ability to project opposing attitudes that gave depth to his characterizations, including perhaps his finest performance as the failing, psychotic writer of *In a Lonely Place* (1950). Bogart's range of performances in film noir have been overshadowed by his iconic status as the private eye, hunched in a trench coat, under a wide-brimmed fedora and with cigarette dangling from his mouth, the incarnation of sophisticated masculine 'cool' whom Jean-Paul Belmondo wants to imitate in *À bout de souffle* (1959).

John Garfield, another contract player for Warner Bros., also reworked the image of the tough guy beginning with his emotionally and psychologically scarred veteran of the Spanish Civil War in *The Fallen Sparrow* (1943). His working-class drifter Frank Chambers in *The Postman Always Rings Twice* (1946), was very popular and the first of a succession of postwar roles as the vulnerable loser. As a tough gangster in *Nobody Lives Forever* (1946), reluctantly resuming where he had left off before the war, a prizefighter in *Body and Soul* (1947), a syndicate accountant in *Force of Evil* (1948), and charter boat skipper in *The Breaking Point* (1950), he is adrift in a world populated by figures more corrupt than himself. Because Garfield always projects an inherent decency, his characters are allowed to find a moral redemption in defeat, including his petty thug Nick Robey, who terrorizes an ordinary working-class family in *He Ran All the Way* (1951). Garfield conveys Nick's longing for the family life he never had and can only enjoy at gunpoint. To the police he is simply a criminal to be gunned down and he dies wordlessly

The working-class loser meets his fate: John Garfield in *He Ran All the Way* (John Berry, 1951)

on the dark, wet, windswept streets. It was an evocative image of Garfield's man-of-the-people persona, which embodied New Deal populism and social tolerance that were now in retreat. Garfield, who first performed in New York's Group Theatre, was an active left-wing idealist who was badly damaged emotionally by the HUAC hearings, which may have contributed to his fatal heart attack in 1952 at the age of 39. In his noir roles, Garfield's performance style is subdued, almost immobile, hands loose at sides, mouth taut, only his eyes moving. It is, as Robert Sklar observes, not emotionless, but emotionally imploded, suggestive of a suppressed violence ready to erupt (Sklar, 1992, pp.180, 183–7). His style was expressive of a doomed, despairing, misunder-stood and thwarted persona which anticipated the angst-ridden 1950s stars: Montgomery Clift, James Dean, and Marlon Brando to whom he lost out for the lead in *A Streetcar Named Desire* (1951) (ibid., pp.204, 213).

Bogart and Garfield were established stars before the advent of film noir, but Robert Mitchum and Burt Lancaster achieved stardom through their noir roles. Big, burly and beautiful, their powerful physiques lent to the passivity and futility of their victim roles a sense of tragic waste. Mitchum's stardom came with *Out of the Past* and his incarnation of the flawed private eye Jeff Bailey has become one of the most celebrated noir performances. Like Bogart, Mitchum was a minimalist – with somnolent movements and hooded, lazy eyes – almost to the point, as reviewers commented, of catatonia. But it was a performance style that lent meaning to the smallest gesture: the flicker of the eyes when Kathie kills his partner in *Out of the Past* (1947) that acknowledges her corruption. It is his measured yet evocative narration, intoned in the gruff voice summoned as if by an act of great will, that convey his romantic longings, making Bailey one of the quintessential noir victims. Mitchum never surpassed this performance in his subsequent similar roles in *Where Danger Lives* (1950) and *Angel Face* (1952). Only Charles Laughton's *Night of the Hunter* (1955) allowed him to expand his range into a dominating performance as the psychotic fundamentalist preacher, preying on his victims across Bible-Belt America.

Lancaster, who had trained as an acrobat, was a more histrionic actor than Mitchum. But in his early roles in film noir he too played close to his body, rarely flashing what was to become the famous toothy grin, fear and fury kept under tight control. With the look and heroic build of an all-American boy, he embodied noir's other beautiful loser. His victims, especially the Swede in *The Killers* (1946) who waits passively for his killers and who utters a silent scream as he slides to the floor grasping the bedrail, are 'voluptuous masochists, yearning for defeat and death' (Fishgall, 1995, p.165). Where Mitchum is knowing, even in his misperceptions, Lancaster exudes a child-like vulner-ability, his voice surprisingly soft and gentle, his magnificent body held as if it were a burden to him, or an instrument to be broken in the folly of the attempted escape as in *Brute Force* (1947). His criminals are ordinary guys, curiously unsure of themselves, always adrift and powerless, as in his scheming husband in *Sorry, Wrong Number* (1948) or *Criss Cross* (1949), analysed in Chapter 6, his most poignant performance.

A number of actors – Dana Andrews, Wendell Corey, Glenn Ford, Edmond O'Brien, John Payne – could play the ordinary Everyman who, in film noir, is always enmeshed in circumstances beyond his control which expose flaws and weaknesses in his character. Dana Andrews was the most effective, precisely because his good looks and gruff, straightforward manner always suggest that he represents the all-American Good Joe, yet his outwardly sober professionals are never what they seem.

Andrews was the ultimate minimalist who 'brought many subtleties to his screen roles. Always under-playing, he used his eyes better than most actors and could convey the inner, tortured self-doubt of the *noir* protagonist with great skill' (Crowther, 1988, p.90). That sense of 'tortured self-doubt' comes through strongly in Preminger's *Where the Sidewalk Ends* (1950) in Andrews's performance as a rogue cop whose brutal methods lead to the death of a suspect, but whose behaviour is linked to a neurotic desire to exorcise the memory of his father, a small-time crook. However, it was most subtly present in *Laura* (1944) in his hard-bitten, philistine working-class cop Mark McPherson. In answer to Lydecker's question if he had ever been in love McPherson replies: 'A dame in Washington Heights got a fox fur out of me once.' As the film unfolds he loses that misogyny, taking up residence in Laura's apartment, gazing at her portrait, listening to her records and moving amongst her things: 'it gives us an enactment of the birth of an obsession rare for its tact and understatement. No histrionics, just immobility and silent invasion' (O'Brien, 2000, p.40). Andrews was chosen by Fritz Lang for two late noirs – *While The City Sleeps* (1955) and *Beyond a Reasonable Doubt* (1958) – analysed in Chapter 6, which are the culmination of Andrews's post-heroic persona, the man without qualities, beneath whose solidity lurk criminal desires that he cannot articulate.

If the psychosis of Andrews's characters lie buried deep within them, those of Robert Ryan are closer to the surface. Ryan's craggy good looks, imposing height and slim but muscular build made him a cross between leading man and heavy which gave a richness to his consistent portrayals of sensitive but violent loners who can explode at any moment. Ryan holds his lean body stiff and tense, never relaxing, always wary and on guard lest some gesture might betray weakness or vulnerability, a brooding intensity that suggests coiled depths. He played unstable damaged veterans in *Crossfire* (1947) and *Act of Violence* (1949), and a rogue cop in *On Dangerous Ground* (1952), already analysed. Ryan's tortured characters covered the class spectrum: a millionaire industrialist in *Caught* (1949), an ordinary Joe in *Clash by Night* (1952) and a psychotic handyman whose murderous rages are obliterated by amnesia in *Beware, My Lovely* (1952). His gangsters in *The Racket* (1951), *House of Bamboo* (1955) and *Odds Against Tomorrow* (1959) are all typically noir, angst-ridden and unstable, unsure of their true purposes. It is the suggestion of troubled depths, of the struggle between violence and tenderness that informs Ryan's most moving performances: as another damaged veteran in Jean Renoir's *Woman on the Beach* (1947) who falls in love with the wife (Joan Bennett) of a blind, obsessively jealous painter; or as the broken prizefighter dreaming of a last break in *The Set-Up* (1949).

If Ryan's neurotics are fundamentally decent, Richard Widmark's psychotics are creatures from the lower depths of humanity. Highly-strung, taut and blond, Widmark's hysteria was conveyed through his stabbing voice, clipped delivery, mirthless laughter, all the nervous pent-up energy of the lean body and hard, angular face; a cruel handsomeness that suggested corruption. Widmark, an experienced theatre actor, attracted great attention with his performance as the sadistic, giggling hit-man Tommy Udo in *Kiss of Death* (1947). In an infamous scene he pushes an old woman in a wheelchair down a flight of stairs, hissing with crazy laughter, having already told her his plans for her son, 'You know what I do with squealers? I let 'em have it in the belly so they can roll around a long time, thinking it over.' James Agee noticed this 'rather frail fellow with maniacal eyes, who uses a sinister kind of baby talk laced with tittering laughs. It is clear that murder is one of the kindest things he is capable of' (quoted in Buckley, 1986, p.222). In *The Street with No Name* (1948), Widmark played a similar figure, gang boss Alec Stiles, overwrought, neurotic and sexually ambivalent. Bosley Crowther observed: 'His timing and tension are perfect and the timber of his voice is that of filthy water going down a sewer' (quoted in ibid., p.259). Through these performances, and as the cheap, racist crook Ray Biddle in *No Way Out* (1950), Widmark exemplified the modern criminal, the conscienceless psychotic.

In *Night and the City* (1950) he deepened this characterization into a tragic figure as Harry Fabian, the small time spiv, an 'artist without art', who longs for that 'big break' which will give him the lifestyle and admiration he craves. He relies on his wits, imagination and daring, an immense, unstable, neurotic energy. But as the overreacher, Fabian constantly finds himself out of his depth in a nightmarish London underworld. In the dénouement he pounds through the labyrinthine streets towards the fog-bound Thames waterfront. 'I just wanna be somebody . . . I was so close to being on top . . . so close', he murmurs to his fellow outcast Molly, before being dumped into the dark waters. In Fuller's *Pickup on South Street* (1953) Widmark's Skip McCoy, the dregs of the city, has a fundamental decency which can respond to Moe's death and begin a new life with Candy (Jean Peters) even if his status as a permanent outsider is preserved.

The other actor who specialized in low-lifes was Dan Duryea, whose flaccid handsomeness combined old-world decadence with modern criminality. He played the charming aristocratic cad in *Lady on a Train* (1945) and a louche, scheming pimp in *Scarlet Street* (1945). His professionals – a journalist in *The Underworld Story* (1950) or private eye in *Manhandled* (1950) – were affable chislers out for the quick buck. His gangster in *Criss Cross* (1949) was a darker version. Like Widmark, Duryea could play figures whose mean, venal lives had a suggestion of greater potential. His alcoholic nightclub pianist in *Black Angel* (1946) and his washed-up private eye adrift in the Singapore under-world in *World for Ransom* (1954) cling to vestiges of romantic chivalry. Duryea's most complex role came in *The Burglar* (1957), adapted from a Goodis novel, in which his cheap crook Nat Harbin is a tragic, brooding figure. Harbin is haunted by his promise that he will look after Gladden (Jayne Mansfield), which was the dying wish of his mentor and surrogate father. The seriousness of his role as her guardian is at odds with the squalid world he forces her to inhabit and his own sexual desires. In the end he dies protecting Gladden from the corrupt cop Charlie.

FEMALE PERFORMERS

The most important female star in film noir was Joan Crawford whose film career stretched back to 1925. Her key film, for which she won an Academy Award, was *Mildred Pierce* (1945), another Cain adaptation which many commentators see as crossing the 'woman's picture' with film noir (Cook, 1998, p.77). Mildred's independence, drive, ambition and success as a busi-nesswoman are not celebrated but seen as corrosive of ordered family life and the instrument through which her daughter Veda (Ann Blyth) is corrupted by wealth and luxury. Veda becomes Mildred's dark double, embodying the glamour and active sexuality that Mildred has denied herself. In the end that dark self must be repudiated and Mildred returned to the safety and security of her loyal, long-suffering but dull husband Bert. *The Damned Don't Cry* (1950) played out a similar story. Crawford's Ethel Whitehead is another strong mother who refuses to be shackled by a drab marriage and lack of funds, leaving home after her only son is killed in an accident. Here the moral paradigm is more clear-cut as she becomes the mistress of a ruthless gangster who uses her in a power struggle with his rival. On the way she tramples on the loyal and loving Martin (Kent Smith) who cannot prevent her from meeting her fate back in the factory town from which she had tried to escape.

In *Possessed* (1947) and *Sudden Fear* (1952) Crawford plays more sympa-thetic women whose struggle for independence creates psychological torment when their lovers prove to be false and manipulative. In *Possessed*, as already discussed, this drives her into a complete mental breakdown; in *Sudden Fear* she concocts a clever plot to destroy her husband and pin his murder on her rival, relenting too late to save either. It seems that Crawford's characters must always be destroyed or humiliated, the price they have to pay for their independence, sexual attractiveness and ambition.

Both Barbara Stanwyck and Joan Bennett were also highly experienced Hollywood actresses by the time that film noir started and their independent women are variations around their central persona as archetypal *femmes fatales*, blonde and brunette respectively. Bennett is considered in some detail in Chapter 6 as her best roles were for Fritz Lang. Stanwyck has attained iconic status on the strength of her performance as Phyllis Dietrichson in *Double Indemnity* (1944). Dietrichson is signalled in the novel as explicitly vampiric, the woman of death with her silver blonde hair, pale complexion and sheath-like dresses (Dijkstra, 1996, p.29). Stanwyck's performance retains elements of this conception, in her pallor, the hard, insistent, almost hypnotic voice, rigid body postures, steely smile and the unmoving blonde hair like a metallic hood. Stanwyck's siren is erotic and also implacable; only in the moment of her death does she display any tenderness towards Walter or a fleeting regret. Her *femme fatale* in *The Strange Love of Martha Ivers* (1946) is more clearly motivated as Martha's ruthless ambition stems from childhood bullying by her aunt. But the dark secret of her aunt's murder hardens this drive into a need to dominate not only her weak husband Walter (Kirk Douglas) but a whole Midwestern town. When her security is threatened by the return twenty years later of Sam Masterman (Van Heflin), whom she believes was a witness to her aunt's death, her instinct is to seduce him into murdering her despised husband, seeing in Sam a fit mate, strong and ruthless. When he refuses and leaves, she aids Walter's attempt to kill her, pulling the gun deeper into her stomach as if relishing death as the sexual ecstasy and release that she has been denied in her life. She played another heiress, Leona Stephenson in *Sorry, Wrong Number* (1948) who again pays for her domineering destruction of a weak man by death. Stanwyck had more sympathetic roles in Siodmak's *The File on Thelma Jordon* (1949), discussed in the next chapter, Lang's *Clash by Night* (1952) and *Witness to Murder* (1954), but she remained the archetypal *femme fatale* through to her final noir role in *Crime of Passion* (1957) as another ruthlessly ambitious woman, Kathy Ferguson, who after regretting giving up her career as a columnist, seduces and kills the boss of her husband, a dull policeman, in order to further his career.

The other archetypal vamp was Claire Trevor whose career shows the evolution from gangster's moll – a part she reprised brilliantly in *Key Largo* (1948) – into the noir spider woman. She played brassy blonde temptresses in *Crossroads* (1942) and *Street of Chance* (1942), but her key role was as Velma/Mrs Grayle in *Murder, My Sweet* (1944) which, along with Stanwyck's

Dietrichson, established the *femme fatale* paradigm. Trevor had a more complex role in *Born to Kill* (UK title: *Deadlier Than the Male*, aka *Lady of Deceit*, 1947) as Helen Trent, a capable, independent woman who has a macabre relish for violence and ruthlessness and is therefore attracted to the psychopathic Sam Wyld (Lawrence Tierney). He admires her cool calculation and each displays a sadistic relish in the credulity of those weaker than themselves, but their mutual mistrust and ambition lead to destruction. Only in *Raw Deal* (1948), analysed in the next chapter, was Trevor given a more sympathetic role.

The two younger actresses who played an important role in the noir cycle are Lizabeth Scott and Gloria Grahame, performing variations of the *femme fatale*. Scott with her sultry, fragile beauty, the heavy dark eyebrows set against the long blonde hair complemented by a low and husky voice, played the archetypal siren in *Dead Reckoning* (1947). She played another seductress in *The Pitfall* (1948), luring the archetypal suburbanite, Dick Powell, away from home and family. In *Too Late for Tears* (1949) Scott played a particularly avaricious version of the *femme fatale*, whose justification for killing her weak-willed husband and keeping the bag of money is that she wanted 'to move out of the ranks of the middle-class poor'. She is, of course, punished. As she falls from a balcony in her efforts to elude the police, the bag bursts open and the dollars flutter down onto her prostrate body. Scott's roles also showed the vamp's evolution into the good-bad girl in *The Strange Love of Martha Ivers* (1946), *I Walk Alone* (1948) and *Dark City* (1950), where she played women on the fringe of the criminal world but not evil.

Gloria Grahame's sex appeal was rather different. She had a timorous thin-lipped, little-girl quality, squeaky-voiced and pumpkin-faced, always slightly playful. She played the duplicitous archetype in *Sudden Fear* (1952) and *Human Desire* (1954), but *In a Lonely Place* (1950) offered her the chance to play a modern woman, sensuous, independent, happy but also drawn into a masochistic relationship with the *homme fatal* Dix Steele (Humphrey Bogart), whom she defends, mistrusts and ultimately betrays emotionally. Grahame's most memorable role came as Debby Marsh in *The Big Heat* (1953) where she plays the archetypal moll with an intelligence, wit and irony – 'Hup, Debby, hup' she cries as she does the bidding of the gangster Vince Stone (Lee Marvin) – that transform it from stereotype into complex creation. She tells the avenging cop Bannion (Glenn Ford) that she knows both wealth and poverty, 'And believe me, being rich is better.' After Vince scars her with scalding coffee, Debbie becomes a sympathetic, tragic figure who gradually humanizes Bannion, and has the courage to kill the dead cop's wife Bertha Duncan – 'sisters under the mink' – which exposes the corrupt syndicate. Her death is the most poignant moment in the film, expiring with the scarred side of her face buried in the folds of her mink coat, the symbol of her acceptance of the gangster's values, but with the unblemished side signifying her basic decency and courage. This martyrdom was perhaps the most that film noir could offer women. In *Odds Against Tomorrow* (1959), at the end of the cycle, Grahame is again the *femme fatale* who begs Robert Ryan to add excitement to their lovemaking by describing how it feels to kill someone.

GILDA

The complexities and fluidity of gender roles in film noir may be appreciated through a case study of *Gilda* (1946), which explores one of the sexual triangles that are quite frequent in film noir. *Gilda*'s license comes from its invocation of place – Buenos Aires, a libidinal space which is decadent and where the normal rules do not apply – and time: it takes place at the moment the war ends, which also allows the release of repressed social and sexual energies. As Linda Dittmar argues, this space is one in which elements of the 'fantastic' can emerge (Dittmar, 1988, pp.5–18). All three protagonists, Ballin Mundson (George Macready), Johnny Farrell (Glenn Ford), the drifter-victim, and Gilda (Rita Hayworth) the good-bad girl, are creatures of wartime displacement and dislocation, recreating themselves in the cash economy of Argentina, figures who have 'no past and all future'. Mundson, the man from the 'old world', Europe, whose German accent and business connections strongly suggest his Nazi background, is another corrupt dandy-aesthete, elegant and sophisticated, who picks up the young American gambler Johnny, washed up on the docks and about to be mugged. From the first, their relationship has a curious perversity as Mundson compares Johnny to the cane with the phallic steel tip which he used to rescue him: 'You're almost as sharp as my other friend, but he'd kill for me.' Johnny replies, 'That's what friends are for.' Johnny becomes both Mundson's instrument and his pupil, in awe of the older man's charm, refinement and power. The implicit homoeroticism was evident at the time the film was made (Kobal, 1972, p.17) and made explicit the implications of intense male comradeship, fostered by war, that was largely repressed in such films as *The Blue Dahlia*, *Crossfire* and *Dead Reckoning*.[5]

It is the beautiful Gilda, brought back from one of Mundson's business trips and Johnny's former lover, who destroys their relationship. A complex *menage à trois* develops in which Johnny, given the job of being Gilda's protector and guardian, is torn between his loyalty to Mundson and his desire for Gilda, a voyeuristic sexual frustration that threatens to overwhelm him: 'I wanted to go back and see them together without me watching.' The three become locked into a dark triangle of suspicion and hate which stimulates Mundson: 'hate can be a very exciting emotion, very . . . Hate is the only thing that has ever warmed me.' Mundson is clearly vampiric, feeding off others' emotions and a 'fantastic' character, hardly human. Even after Mundson's apparent death, he controls Johnny, who marries Gilda so that he can imprison and humiliate her for her disloyalty to his friend. The pleasure he takes from this is as perverse as it is masochistic, his own erotic feelings sublimating into a protracted punishment.

Although Rita Hayworth is often regarded as an iconic *femme fatale* in *Gilda*, her role is much better defined as the good-bad girl, caught in an intense love-hate relationship between two males. Her frequently tantalizing and provocative behaviour, including her gaucho costume at the Mardi Gras, complete with whip, is a response to the male discourse that insists that women are the cause of all the trouble in the world, satirized in her song 'Put the Blame on Mame'. Unlike the *femme fatale*'s torch song, Gilda uses 'Put the Blame on Mame' as part of a strip tease designed to humiliate Johnny, a public and parodic enactment of the promiscuous, worthless tramp he has decided she always was. It is preceded by a private rendition sung to the men's room attendant who 'understands' her and functions as a kind of choric sage in the film. That earlier scene mobilizes the wholesome aspects of Hayworth's star persona, which are resistant to demonizing as a *femme fatale* (Dyer, 1998, pp.115–22). The tensions and instabilities of her role in the film are eloquent testimony to the ambiguities of the 'good-bad girl'.

Richard Dyer has observed that '[w]hat *Gilda* seems to point to is something that most noirs try to keep at bay – that all sexuality or all male sexuality is sick' (Dyer, 1993, p.71). As he suggests, this is often implied by other noirs, but never presented with such force. These dark and disturbing sadomasochistic sexual currents make the film's happy ending seem all the more contrived. It was made at the insistence of the film's producer, Virginia Van Upp, who was keen to have an upbeat ending in which both Gilda and Johnny can go 'home' to begin a new life in America (Martin, 1998, pp.214–15). Perhaps it was the only way of 'rescuing' the film from the disapproval of the censors or even suppressing the film's disturbing resonance by pretending that once on native soil these two young Americans can be wholesome and happy.

Film noir's construction of gender forms an important component of its subversive questioning of the American Dream. The sheer numbers of its weak, tormented male protagonists beset with psychosexual problems suggest a possible 'crisis' in masculine identity that intensified after the war. Noir was able to explore this issue in a richly complex manner as its generic space licensed the depiction of aberrant males in ways that were impossible in more realistic social problem films. It offered male stars roles which allowed them to develop a critical take on American manhood; several actors, notably Robert Ryan, gave their finest performances in noir films. Although noir offered more space for women than is sometimes allowed, its main drive was to demonize women's sexuality and to question the whole notion of the independent woman with an enhanced role in the postwar world.

NOTES

1. For discussions of stars as types see Dyer, *Stars* (1998, pp.47–59); see also Cavell (1979, pp.29–67). Alloway describes stars as 'maximised types' (1971, p.12). For a discussion of the function of cultural types see Spicer (2001, pp.1–5).
2. For Goodis, see Haut (1995, pp.21–34) and for a book-length study of Tourneur, Fujiwara (1998).
3. The seminal account remains Mario Praz, *The Romantic Agony* (1970 [1933]), pp.199–300; see also Patrick Bade, *Femmes Fatales* (1979).
4. Bruce Crowther (1988, pp.69–158) devotes three informative chapters to noir performers, including discussion of 'minor icons' and supporting players.
5. For further discussion of this point see Krutnik (1991, pp.164–81); Cohan (1997, pp.85–96).

CHAPTER SIX

The Noir *Auteur*

The concepts of genre and the *auteur* are often thought to be antithetical, the former emphasizing the recurrent patterns of popular culture, the latter celebrating the unique 'signature' of the individual artist able to 'transcend' generic formulae. However, this study has argued already for the importance of the authorial presence – Hitchcock's *Vertigo*, Welles' *Touch of Evil* – where the director's genius lies in the ways in which generic elements are used so as to yield their most profound meanings. Analysis of an *auteur*'s films noirs therefore provides another way of understanding the noir 'phenomenon'. Although a number of directors – Jules Dassin, Samuel Fuller, Fritz Lang, Joseph H. Lewis, Anthony Mann, Otto Preminger, Nicholas Ray, Robert Siodmak, Jacques Tourneur, Edgar Ulmer, Orson Welles and Billy Wilder – have some claim to *auteur* status, this chapter attempts to make the case for three: Mann, Siodmak and Lang. Each produced a substantial body of films noirs – over half-a-dozen – and all three were closely associated with the development of film noir, dual criteria which distinguish them from the other names on the list above, except Hitchcock who has been excluded for reasons of space and because his work has received such voluminous interpretation in recent years.[1] No justification is necessary for the choice of the émigrés Lang and Siodmak whose contribution to the noir cycle was immense; and while it is true that Mann was first critically rehabilitated on the strength of his Westerns, his seven noirs have also come to be seen as an important body of work, the efforts of an indigenous American director working creatively with an evolving form.[2]

ANTHONY MANN

Anthony Mann's early professional life was spent as a theatre director, moving to Hollywood as a talent scout for David O. Selznick in 1938, before joining

Paramount as an assistant director in 1939. He directed his first feature *Dr Broadway* in 1942 (Basinger, 1979, pp.20–2). Mann's third film *The Great Flamarion* (1945) had a noir plot. Eric Von Stroheim played the title role, a top-line variety star, trapped by a three-timing *femme fatale* (Mary Beth Hughes) whom he finally murders. His deathbed flashback narration, introspection and lingering ruination by a hopeless passion are archetypal noir, but *The Great Flamarion* is conventionally shot, with few unusual camera angles or effects of lighting.

Strange Impersonation (1946), also made for Republic, has a convoluted plot and much less accomplished acting, but shows an evolving noir style. In the scene where the heroine Nora Goodrich (Brenda Marshall) visits the seedy bedsit of the blackmailing broad Jane Karaski (Ruth Ford), the garish neon sign of 'Joe's Bar and Grill' flashes across their acrimonious conversation. In a vividly expressionist moment, a montage of looming heads interrogates the hapless Nora for causing her own murder, her enlarged shadow cast on the wall behind her. *Desperate* (1947) made for RKO, was a more accomplished work. Its story is conventional, an innocent young man Steve Randall (Steve Brodie) is framed for a crime he did not commit, but it contains the first of Mann's trademark scenes of brutal violence as the henchmen of Walt Radak (Raymond Burr) beat Randall viciously in a dank basement hideout, given a grotesque expressiveness by the fluctuating illumination of the single light bulb as it swings wildly from the force of the blows. Radak looks on, shot from an extreme low angle to emphasize his unnatural bulk.

These noir elements were developed through Mann's association with a talented screenwriter John C. Higgins (five films: *Railroaded, T-Men, Raw Deal, He Walked by Night* and *Border Incident*) and gifted cinematographer John Alton (five films: *T-Men, Raw Deal, He Walked by Night, Border Incident* and *The Black Book*). Their input was crucial to the evolution of Mann's distinctive noir oeuvre which combined clear, effective and generally fast-moving storylines with a baroque visual style that uses unusual camera angles and high-contrast, chiaroscuro lighting. Alton, as is clear from his 1949 'manual' *Painting with Light,* was well versed in the techniques of 'mystery lighting', used to 'heighten the atmosphere' and move away from the 'chocolate-coated photography of yesterday' (Alton, 1995, p.45). Alton noted the striking effects of 'passing automobile headlights on the ceiling of a dark interior', 'fluctuating neon or other electrical signs', as well as the play of light on 'shiny, wet surfaces' (ibid., pp.47–8, 59).

Mann's first film with Higgins, *Railroaded* (1947), was limited by PRC's (Producers Releasing Corporation) restricted budget, which only allowed a ten-day shooting schedule leading to underdeveloped characterization. *Railroaded* hints at the disturbing relationship that is beginning to grow between Sheila Ryan (Rosa Ryan) trying to clear the name of her innocent brother, the victim of a frame-up, and the sadistic gunman Duke Martin (John Ireland), but fails to enlarge this into an important focus. Guy Roe's rather uniform low-level lighting also inhibits depth of interest in the frame.

T-Men (1948) not only benefited from Alton's high-contrast photography, but also from an enhanced budget provided by Eagle-Lion, the company formed as the result of the merger between PRC and Rank. Eagle-Lion was attempting to upgrade the 'B' feature in ways that were characteristic of this period (Miller, 1978, pp.27–39). Mann commented in interview that *T-Men* was the first film on which he was able to work with a degree of creative freedom where the script could be developed from scratch and the actors properly rehearsed (Wicking and Pattison, 1969, p.35).

T-Men, as has been noted, is one of the group of 'semi-documentary' noirs which used actual locations wherever possible and celebrated the vigilance and efficiency of American institutions, in this case the US Treasury Department. However, although the narrative is interspersed with actuality footage of the department at work, the body of the film plunges into the noir world through its story of two agents – O'Brien (Dennis O'Keefe) and Genaro (Alfred Ryder) – engaged on a dangerous undercover mission to infiltrate the Vantucci counterfeiters in Detroit. Mann's creative compositions powerfully insinuate the ways in which both men become part of the world they seek to expose. In particular, the burly O'Brien is often indistinguishable from the criminals he mingles with. His beating of the low-life, Schemer (Wallace Ford), is as brutal as anything administered by Vantucci's hoods. However, he lacks their sadism. After Schemer's betrayal is exposed, he is trapped in a steam room, the heat turned up full blast. We see his contorted face emerge from the gloom and bang frantically on the glass as outside an impassive hood (Charles McGraw) sits with his arms folded. Schemer's gruesome demise is contrasted with Genaro's death that has the particular Mann quality of poignant brutality. As he feverishly ransacks a hotel room for the vital clue, Genaro looks up to see Vantucci's hoods enter with O'Brien in tow, reflected in the cheap mirror of the dressing table. There is a resonant exchange of glances between the two agents before O'Brien watches Genaro killed, his death shown in the involuntary twitchings of O'Brien's face in close-up while the shots are fired.

In its graphic depiction of violence and the price of justice, *T-Men* was a distinctive contribution to the short cycle of noir semi-documentaries as was *He Walked by Night* (1948) also made for Eagle-Lion. Mann is uncredited on this film, but he is known to have shot the majority of the scenes, including all the exteriors and the memorable final chase sequence. As Janine Basinger observes in her book length study of Mann, the studio scenes directed by Alfred Werker are flat and generally uninteresting, in contrast to Mann's contributions (Basinger, 1979, p.30). *He Walked by Night* has a factual basis in the murder of two policemen in Pasadena, California, by a young staff member of the police fingerprinting department. Higgins's screenplay converts Ray Morgan (Richard Basehart) into an unspecified electronics expert who has become a psychopathic loner. Rather than concentrate on Morgan's psychology – he seems to be motivated by a general resentment and alienation – Mann constructs a fast-moving cat and mouse thriller reminiscent of Lang's *M*, which charts the police's systematic efforts to capture Morgan and his brilliant evasions. The chase culminates in a bravura final sequence when Martin seeks refuge in Los Angeles' cavernous storm drains. Alton's extensive back lighting and rich deep blacks make the tunnels both eerie and strangely futuristic, lending the surfaces a metallic quality to suggest that Morgan is a creature from another world.

The most distinctive quality of Mann's next noir for Eagle-Lion, *Raw Deal* (1948), is its highly creative use of a female voice-over (Cowie, 1993, pp.138–45). The subjective narration is provided by Pat (Claire Trevor) the loyal and long-suffering girlfriend of petty criminal Joe Sullivan (Dennis O'Keefe), who is taking the rap for gangster boss Rick Coyle (Raymond Burr). As Pat visits the prison on the day Joe will be sprung, her voice-over explores her feelings of excitement, longing and fear as the corridors echo to the sound of her high heels. As Pat leaves she glimpses her rival Ann (Marsha Hunt) arrive, the middle-class lawyer who has fallen in love with Joe in the hope that he can redeem himself. The women's class position and background is carefully contrasted in their looks, make-up and dress, the one a gentrified, educated professional, the other a gangster's moll from the same slum, Corkscrew Alley, where Joe was born. However, *Raw Deal* refuses a simple good-bad moral distinction: both are strong and courageous, both in love with Joe, and both are prepared to kill for him.

Their struggle forms the main focus of the action and the burden of Pat's commentary. Pat's voice-overs are brief, intermittent and always accompanied by a haunting musical motif and slightly distorted photography that give them an oneiric quality. Her tone is deadpan and fatalistic, always sensing that a way out, a happy ending, is beyond her grasp. Ann is always in the way, physically separating her from Joe as in the station wagon that they steal, 'sitting next to Joe where I should be. Where I would be if she wasn't there.' Later, after a deliberate separation, she witnesses Joe shoving Ann aside to rejoin her: 'I suppose I should feel some kind of victory, but I don't. Walking past her this way . . . She too is just a dame in love with Joe.' As Basinger notes, the ambiguity of this poignant moment make it seem like a scene from European art cinema as the two women pass each other on the barren highway (Basinger, 1979, p.65). What Pat is fighting against is Joe's aspiration that he can be something better than his upbringing, a longing that is symbolized by Ann. He dies saving Ann from Coyle, after Pat has told him that Ann is in danger, a gesture that wrecks their plans to escape by sea. As she watches Joe die, Pat intones bleakly, 'In my heart, I know this is right for Joe. This is what he wanted.' Pat is that rare figure in film noir, a genuinely tragic working-class woman, and *Raw Deal* a moving elegy to her blighted hopes.

The complexity of the central relationships and the depth of feeling displayed mark *Raw Deal* as a mature work. Raymond Burr's Coyle, consistently photographed from extreme low-angle, as in *Desperate*, to exaggerate his bulk, is a more developed characterization. His brutality has a calculating sadism absent from the earlier film. Coyle takes enormous pleasure in burning the hapless Spider's ear with his expensive lighter and throws lighted brandy in the face of his girlfriend merely because she has accidentally bumped into him. In keeping with the greater depth of characterization, Alton's rich, dramatic photography is more nuanced and varied, closer to the modified expressionism of Musuraca, ranging from the delicate lighting of the numerous exterior scenes, to the grotesque gun-fight in the fog-bound alley that concludes the action. As Robert Smith has noted, *Raw Deal* is 'resplendent with velvety blacks, mists, netting and other expressive accessories of poetic *noir* decor and lighting' (Smith, 1996, p.197). The camerawork and the characterization give depth to a sordid tale, which, like *Out of the Past*, represents one of the high spots of noir romanticism.

By contrast, *The Black Book* (UK title: *Reign of Terror*, 1948) is a deeply political film, expressive of the forces that were at work in both Hollywood and in American society at a time when the Cold War was intensifying. Set in post-revolutionary France – the stentorian voice-over barks out: 'France July 26th 1794. Anarchy, misery, murder, arson, fear, these are the weapons of dictatorship' – *The Black Book* was an allegory designed, in producer Walter Wanger's words, 'to stop all kinds of totalitarianism' (Bernstein, 2000, p.231). The black book in which Robespierre (Richard Basehart) – 'a fanatic with powdered wig and a twisted mind' – keeps a secret list of those who are to be brought to trial, has obvious parallels to HUAC. This overt interventionism probably stemmed more from Wanger than Mann, but the ways in which that anti-totalitarian message is conveyed owed almost everything to Mann's close collaboration with Alton. *The Black Book* deserves to be installed in the noir canon despite, or rather because of, its extraordinarily bold mixture of genres, part costume drama, part action adventure, part gangster film and urban crime thriller with Paris doubling for Los Angeles or New York (Maltby, 1983, pp.142–4).

Mann sets the opening voice-over amidst a montage of fanatical figures, their faces shot in distorted close-up against a background of raging flames and the swish of the guillotine. It sets the tone for a bold plunge into a nightmare world in which virtually no frame is conventionally composed. Every conversation is framed either in tight, claustrophobic close-up, or from an odd angle, with bands or shafts of light penetrating the perpetual murk that invades every setting. The cutting is consistently jagged and unsettling, pitching the viewer between scenes, or juxtaposing shots from extreme angles to create a vertiginous sense of space that is thoroughly disorientating. The infrequent exterior shots take place on poorly illuminated, wet cobblestone streets where assassins lurk in every doorway.

As in *T-Men*, the basic plot device is of an undercover agent Charles D'Aubigny (Robert Cummings) posing as a villain, Duvall the 'butcher of Strasbourg', summoned by Robespierre to ensure that the citizens will vote him in as dictator. The film's violence is even more visceral and brutal than in Mann's previous noirs, often directed at or from the camera to involve the audience directly. As D'Aubigny rides in a carriage with the head of the secret police Fouché (Arnold Moss), a blazing torch is thrown in the carriage window seemingly at the viewer. A hideous face appears in the window of the carriage before Fouché blows a hole in his head right in front of our eyes. Near the end, the fastidious Robespierre, staring directly towards the camera, is shot in the mouth as he makes his final attempt to control 'my creation, the mob'.

The Black Book evokes a paranoid and terrified world in which all appearances, even the hero's, are deceptive and nobody can be trusted. The differences between hero and villain lie not in their tactics – both are willing to murder (the first action we see D'Aubigny perform is to kill the real Duvall), to lie, dissemble and manipulate – but in their purposes. D'Aubigny's former lover Madeleine (Arlene Dahl), appears to be on the side of justice, but also behaves as a *femme fatale* whose motives are ambiguous. Both she and D'Aubigny are corrupted by the world they have entered. *The Black Book's* stress on the ambivalence of taking action and the ways in which morality becomes blurred in the brutal clash of forces, focused in its driven and divided hero, make it a typical Mann noir. The almost overwhelming tension is dissipated by the elements of an action adventure film where the pair escape in disguise to a country farm, the only conventionally shot scenes in the film, and then make their way back to Paris to foil Robespierre's actions. But in the final scene Fouché, the great survivor, greets a figure with his back to the camera who gives his name as Napoleon Bonaparte, a reminder that the forces that threaten democracy are always present.

In the following year, Mann joined MGM where he enjoyed longer shooting schedules and higher budgets. As his contract was based on the success of *T-Men*, Mann's first film for MGM was another semi-documentary, *Border Incident* (1949), closely modelled on the earlier film, again featuring two undercover agents – the Mexican Pablo Rodriguez (Ricardo Montalban) and the American Jack Bearnes (George Murphy). They are on the trail of crooked rancher Owen Parkson (Howard da Silva) who smuggles Mexican peasant workers (*bracero*/'wetbacks') over the border into California with phoney work permits. In the opening scene, where the returning *braceros* are robbed of their money, Mann deliberately withholds establishing shots, using jarring cuts, from intense close-ups of individual faces to long shots of the group fleeing for cover, to create a tense and disorientating atmosphere where the viewer is never sure of the location of the action. As in *T-Men*, the most powerful moment occurs when one of the agents becomes a powerless witness to the other's death. Bearnes, whose cover has been blown, is threatened by the circular shaped blades of a discing machine, which moves forward with appalling slowness towards him across the ploughed field. Mann cuts between the blades, the desperate efforts of the injured Bearnes to dig down into the soft soil as protection, and the agonized face of Rodriguez gazing from the edges of the field. The force of Bearnes's death comes not only from its prolonged and graphic horror, but from the ethnic reversal: it is the Mexican who survives, not the WASP American. *Border Incident*'s setting and its dramatic use of landscape point forward to Mann's important sequence of Westerns beginning with *Winchester '73* in 1951.

Mann's final film noir, *Side Street* (1950) also for MGM, seems to have been an attempt to capitalize on the success of Nicholas Ray's *They Live by Night*,

The noir victim: Joe Norson (Farley Granger) at the mercy of gangster Georgie Garsell (James Craig) in *Side Street* (Anthony Mann, 1950)

released five months earlier by RKO, with Farley Granger and Cathy O'Donnell playing very similar roles. However, the similarity of the two films demonstrates the profound differences in sensibility between the two directors. Mann's film lacks Ray's romanticism and his invocation of the redeeming power of love, concentrating on an existentialist sense of individuals trapped in a hostile and overwhelming environment. *Side Street* retains a semi-documentary style, opening with an impersonal voice-over about the myriad inhabitants of New York City. Joe Norson (Granger) is the archetypal 'little man', who takes to crime in the hope of providing his pregnant wife Ellen (O'Donnell) with a better life. His one weak act, taking money that does not belong to him, plunges Norson into a nether world of sleazy nightclubs, criminal hangouts and shabby apartments. Joseph Ruttenberg's photography lacks Alton's rich, deep blacks, but successfully creates a grey, mournful, desolate world in which everyone has a price. In the dénouement, where Joe is forced at gunpoint to drive at high speed through the deserted Sunday morning streets, Mann alternates claustrophobic close-ups shot from below with long shots that show the car pursued by the police through narrow streets dominated by immense skyscrapers. Both function as metaphors of the entrapment and alienation of modern city life.

Mann's noirs may lack the sophistication and cultural range of the great émigré directors, but they construct a thoroughly American landscape that is perpetually dark and menacing, illuminated only by single sources of light – bare light bulbs, isolated street lamps, flashlights, candles and matches. The objects in cluttered rooms seem to press in upon the protagonists and shock cuts or swish pans, with their blurred images rushing past, unsettle the viewer. Mann's noirs achieve their economy through the deft use of composition rather than dialogue or exposition (Basinger, 1979, p.26). The typical Mann protagonist, anticipating his Westerns, is divided and unsettled, either hiding a dark secret, or a clandestine figure who has to penetrate a sordid world. Mann's films are distinguished by the brutality of their violence, leading one critic to call him a 'tin-can de Sade'. However, that violence is never gratuitous but the consequence of a ruthlessly competitive society where individuals struggle to succeed against the odds. Mann's noir universe, with the wonderful exception of *Raw Deal*, is a highly masculine one where the emotional climaxes occur between the two male protagonists.

ROBERT SIODMAK

Robert Siodmak had a successful career in Weimar cinema and several films, notably *Stürme der Leidenschaft* (*Storms of Passion*, 1931), contain noir elements in both style and subject matter.[3] Siodmak became one of a number of Jewish film-makers who fled from Nazi persecution, working in Paris from 1933 until his move to Hollywood when France was occupied in 1940. Siodmak's European films were little known in America and he took work as a journeyman director of 'B' features for various studios before gaining a long-term contract with Universal where his brother Curt was an established screenwriter.[4] Siodmak directed *Son of Dracula* (1943), one of the Gothic horror films in which the studio specialized, before making *Phantom Lady* (1944) Universal's first film noir, adapted from a 1942 Cornell Woolrich story. He was offered the direction by Joan Harrison, a former assistant to Hitchcock (whose *Shadow of a Doubt* was made for Universal), now an independent producer who found that Siodmak shared her interest in psychological disturbance and sexual pathology (Alpi, 1998, pp.118–19).

Phantom Lady's gender reversal has already been noted, but not its interest in male psychological problems. Its nominal hero Scott Henderson (Alan Curtis) is weak, passive and lachrymose, assailed by doubts about his memory and his identity and almost wishing his own destruction. These morbid traits link him with his wife's actual murderer, Marlowe (Franchot Tone), who has framed Henderson. Marlowe's dandified dress, his 'hysterical' headaches and profession as a modernist sculptor mark him as both homosexual and an *homme fatal*. Tone's mannered performance, compulsively rubbing his hands and staring fixedly at his reflection, was an early attempt to embody the type with its neurotic volatility, delight in destruction and unstable identity.

Phantom Lady's visual style, 'as much as any other film, defines the studio noir' (Porfirio in Silver and Ward, 1980, p.226). The studio sets with their glistening night-time streets are given a claustrophobic intensity through the use of heavy chiaroscuro lighting. When 'Kansas' visits Henderson in jail, the intense light from the window throws the pair into gloomy darkness, casting thick shadows on the floor. The starkness of this moment contrasts with cameraman Woody Bredell's frequent use of coloured backlights which softened and 'warmed' the blacks in several scenes, giving a silken texture (Alpi, 1998, p.124). The famous scene in the jazz club is lit in this rich and subtle fashion, given dramatic intensity by the increasingly frantic pace of the editing. With its innovative characterization and modulated expressionism, *Phantom Lady* was influential in the early development of film noir, with Siodmak drawing upon his European experience, including his ambitious French noir *Pièges* (*Traps*, 1939) to find a filmic equivalent to Woolrich's expressionist novel (Elsaesser, 2000, p.434).

Siodmak's second film for Universal, *Christmas Holiday* (1944), was even bolder in its exploration of sexual pathology. Screenwriter Herman J. Mankiewicz transposes the *fin-de-siècle* Paris of the Somerset Maugham novel from which the film was adapted, to New Orleans, with its connotations of a Frenchified decadence and corrupt Southern Gothic. These are personified by Robert Mannette (Gene Kelly), the scion of an important family gone to seed, who is both homosexual and entwined in an unhealthy, incestuous relationship with his mother, Mrs Mannette (Gale Sondergaard). Kelly, cast against type, invests this figure with a boyish enthusiasm and an energetic, outgoing charisma that disguise his depravity and captivate Abigail (Deanna Durbin). His mother colludes in his deception, dreaming of the son who could revive the family fortunes. Although Mrs Mannette alludes to 'certain traits' after her son has married Abigail, she comments, 'between us we will make him strong', thereby placing the young woman under a huge emotional burden that cannot be fulfilled. Unlike Abigail, Mrs Mannette claims that she 'really' loves Robert because 'I knew all about him and kept on loving'. After the trial in which he is convicted of murder, she slaps Abigail crying 'You killed him!'

Abigail's appearance as a nightclub singer, the guise in which we first see her, is her dark form of atonement for this 'failure'. Whereas 'Kansas' flirted with her dark other when she disguised herself as a *femme fatale* in *Phantom Lady*, Abigail's existence as Jackie Lamont at Maison Lafitte is a profoundly masochistic sexual degradation in which she attempts to share Robert's shame. Bredell's atmospheric photography creates a sleazy ambience, full of sinister shadows. Durbin, also cast against type, sings her trademark ballads sheathed in a tight black dress, suggesting that she has become the fallen woman of Maugham's novel. This dark, very unAmerican tale, is only partly compromised by its redemptive dénouement. After Robert is shot by the police following a prison breakout, he exclaims, 'You can let go now Abby' and as she gazes upwards, the storm clouds part.

Siodmak reflected in retrospect that his reputation was now tied to crime films: 'I was under contract to Universal International, and as is usual in the film city, if you are successful at making a certain type of picture then you are given more of them to make. You have to be one of the boys!' (Siodmak, 1959, p.10). However, he believed that crime films dealt with 'major emotions' and could achieve depth of characterization through exploring motivation and creating sympathy for the protagonist, which he judged the key difference from the 1930s gangster films (ibid.). This sympathy is a strong feature of his next two films for Universal, *The Suspect* (1944) and *The Strange Affair of Uncle Harry* (aka *Uncle Harry* and *Guilty of Murder*, 1945) whose central male protagonists, Philip Marshall (Charles Laughton) and Harry Quincey (George Sanders) respectively, are archetypal middle-aged suburbanites, who, in these subtle films noirs, seethe with repressed desires and reveal Siodmak's continued concern with duality, masochism and perverse relationships.

The Suspect's Edwardian England and *Uncle Harry*'s contemporary New England are petrified by gentility where the sympathetic protagonists try to break free from their constraints through their love for a wholesome young woman, played by Ella Raines. Their chance of happiness is threatened by the destructive, castrating women who dominate their lives. In Philip's case it is his shrewish wife Cora (Rosalind Ivan), who refuses him a divorce and threatens to ruin Mary (Raines). For Harry it is the incestuous longings of his younger sister Lettie (Geraldine Fitzgerald), whose 'luscious eroticism . . . in her negligee draped sensuously over a settee in a solarium filled with tropical plants', gives an incongruous Southern decadence to the Quincey home (Alpi, 1998, p.138). Lettie contrives to forestall Harry's romance with a young woman from the city, Deborah (Raines).

For both men, the frustration of their long-suppressed sexual desires releases their dark, murderous suppressed selves, which display unexpected resourcefulness. In *Suspect*, Philip eventually confesses to his murder of Cora and a suspicious neighbour, but in the darker *Uncle Harry*, when Harry confesses to the murder of his elder sister Hester, who drank the poisoned milk meant for Lettie, Lettie, charged with Hester's murder, denounces his spinelessness. In order to avoid a clash with the censors by depicting a hero whose crime remains unpunished, Universal insisted Siodmak remove the film's flashback narrative and substitute a fantasy structure in which the poisoning was all Harry's dream, causing producer Joan Harrison to resign in protest. As Michael Walker comments, the studio's strategy is actually effective because Harry's dream becomes expressive of his contradictory desires, wanting both to be rid of Lettie and to surrender masochistically to her stronger will when the scheme goes wrong (Walker, 1992b, p.122). Unfortunately, this effect is undermined, unlike in Lang's *The Woman in the Window* (1944), by the happy ending where Harry and Deborah are reunited.

The Dark Mirror (1946) had higher production values, as it was the first film made by the newly merged Universal-International whose production head William Goetz was determined to make 'quality product' (Dick, 1997, p.141). Writer-producer Nunally Johnson's carefully structured screenplay crosses the expressionist *Doppelgänger* motif – Olivia de Havilland plays identical twin sisters, Ruth and Terry whose dispositions are antithetical – with an explicitly Freudian analysis of the pair's behaviour, orchestrated by psychiatrist Scott Henderson (Lew Ayres). Henderson, investigating the murderous *femme fatale* Terry, falls in love with the decent homebuilder, Ruth. Scott's preference for Ruth makes Terry pathologically jealous and she seeks to destroy her rival by making her doubt her sanity, a clever inversion of the familiar Gothic motif in which the *homme fatal* is the twisted persecutor. The rather prosaic scenes between psychiatrist and patient are offset by the intensity of the scenes between the two sisters, photographed in progressively darkening light by Milton Krasner, which have a strange erotic charge composed of fear, envy and possessiveness. In the climactic scene Terry, believing Ruth has died from an overdose, tries to assume her sister's identity. When Ruth reappears, Terry attacks her own reflection in the macabre, twisted logic that she can destroy the image of herself and become whole.

Before working on *The Dark Mirror*, Siodmak was loaned out to direct *The Spiral Staircase* (1946), a co-production between RKO and David O. Selznick's Vanguard Films. Although the story is a standard Gothic noir set in turn-of-the-century New England, *The Spiral Staircase* is the most beautifully crafted of Siodmak's films, superbly paced with the suspense steadily accumulating in intensity aided by the expressive cinematography of Nicholas Musuraca. Its mute heroine Helen (Dorothy McGuire) is a maid in the Warren house-hold, presided over by the bedridden matriarch (Ethel Barrymore). Helen's life is threatened by a mysterious psychopath whose targets are women with physical impairments. The occupants move around the maze-like Gothic mansion in a *danse macabre* in which characters and actions reduplicate. First Blanche (Rhonda Fleming) descends the spiral staircase candle in hand to her doom in the cellar, before Helen descends in exactly the same way. Musuraca's chiaroscuro lighting creates huge shadows that dominate the frame creating a suggestive, dream-like space.

Siodmak commented that he collaborated with screenwriter Mel Dinelli 'to create a sort of surrealist film which put the audience into a trance, a state of hypnosis, so that they would accept the unfolding of events without asking themselves questions. Helen's thoughts were expressed through gestures . . . and Dorothy McGuire conceived her silent role as a sort of ballet. Her choreographic expression enables us to regain some of the elements of the best silent cinema.'[5] In the opening scene, a deftly executed crane shot takes us from the silent film (*The Kiss*) that the heroine is watching, up to the balcony room in which an unidentified man spies on a lame girl dressing whose form is distorted through a fish-eye lens. Siodmak cut to a close-up of the man's eyeball, the camera boring in on the retina as if to reach the diseased brain, before the figure moves forward to strangle her. Eventually this figure is revealed to be, not the obvious suspect the feckless Steve Warren (Gordon Oliver), but his elder brother, the urbane scholar Albert Warren (George Brent), another corrupt son of a long-established family in decay. *The Spiral Staircase*'s subtle craftsmanship, high production values and powerful cast made it the most successful of Siodmak's American films (Alpi, 1998, p.144).

Siodmak's next two films for Universal, *The Killers* (1946) and *Criss Cross* (1949), show the influence of another independent producer, Mark Hellinger, who was an ex-journalist attracted not to lush Gothic thrillers, but to hard-boiled fiction set in realistic locations. While both films bear Hellinger's stamp, they also clearly demonstrate Siodmak's take on the criminal thriller: a pronounced fascination with romantic love and pathological relationships.

The Killers' complex narration has already been discussed, and its real interest is not in criminal activities – the famous robbery scene, shot in one continuous three-minute take, seems expressly designed to get that action over swiftly – but in the intensity of the Swede's fatal passion for Kitty Collins, the incarnation of exotic eroticism, which results in his masochistic desire for oblivion.

Hellinger initiated *Criss Cross*, choosing Don Tracy's 1936 pulp novel for adaptation, but he died before its production was underway, which allowed Siodmak to assume far greater creative control (Walker, 1992b, p.139). Siodmak, who collaborated on the screenplay with Daniel Fuchs, starts, as in *The Killers, in medias res* with an aerial shot of night-time Los Angeles that ends with a medium shot of two lovers in a car park staring at some off-screen threat, to establish a tense atmosphere in which nothing is certain. The events leading up to this point are narrated in a series of flashbacks by Steve Thompson (Burt Lancaster), returning to his home neighbourhood of Bunker Hill. Hellinger wanted a panorama of Los Angeles life similar to *Naked City's* New York, but Siodmak concentrates almost the entire action in Bunker Hill, presenting it as a vibrant working-class neighbourhood infiltrated by gangsterism (Davis, 2001, pp.38–40).

As the story's narrator, Steve, unlike the Swede, can explore his own emotions, the irresistible attraction of the Rondo Club where he knows he will meet his ex-wife Anna (Yvonne de Carlo) and thereby initiate a train of events that he is powerless to control: 'It was in the cards. No way of stopping it . . . It was fate.' Anna's exotic attractiveness is less remote than that of Kitty Collins; Anna is a neighbourhood girl for whom the tacky, claustrophobic Rondo Club represents sophistication and liberation. Steve watches in mounting jealousy and voyeuristic excitement as she dances a hot Latin rumba with the local gigolo.[6] In a drink together the pair recall their feisty, up-and-down marriage in a moment of ingenuous affection. It is his sense that he and Anna can return to their old life together that obsesses Steve, even after Anna marries the small-time gangster Slim Dundee (Dan Duryea). In a desperate bid to win her back, Steve proposes a payroll heist to Dundee and thus initiates the act in which he is the chief victim.

This mixture of credulity and cunning characterizes Steve's actions through to the end when, pursued by Dundee whom he has betrayed, he tries to escape with Anna, bribing one of Dundee's men to take him instead to their rendezvous at a beach house, that typically liminal noir location. Appalled by Steve's naivety, Anna hastily packs to save herself and the money from Dundee, her betrayal taking Steve to the heart of loss: 'I am different. I never wanted the money. I just wanted you. After we split up I used to walk around the streets in strange cities at night thinking about you. I just wanted to hold you in my arms, to take care of you. It could've been wonderful. But it didn't work out. What a pity it didn't work out.' Steve's plangent utterance, made in a softly lit bare room, is made more poignant with Slim's arrival, the two lovers trapped, as in the first scene, but this time awaiting death. The pair die like romantic lovers, in each other's arms, murmuring each other's names; the final shot is of their bodies united in death, behind them a moonlit ocean beyond their grasp as Miklos Rozsa's lush score swells to its climax and creates a tragic *tableau* (Walker, 1992b, p.145). Such an ending would have been inconceivable had Hellinger remained in charge of the film and indicates Siodmak's fundamental romanticism.

The creative tensions between the neo-realist and romantic elements in *Criss Cross* are also evident in *Cry of the City* (1948), which Siodmak directed on loan for Twentieth Century-Fox, produced by the semi-documentarist Louis de Rochemont. The film constructs a complex portrait of New York's Little Italy through its paradigmatic male *Doppelgänger* story of the struggle between the charismatic gangster Martin Rome (Richard Conte) and the puritanical police lieutenant Vittorio Candella (Victor Mature) who both come from this intimate neighbourhood. The casting of two Italian-American actors reinforces the authenticity established by the location shooting. Siodmak reverses the familiar iconography: Candella is always dressed in black, Rome in white; Candella is a saturnine, obsessive loner, the outsider, who envies the quick-witted, attractive Rome's strong family ties and who visits the Rome household, drinking some of Mrs Rome's 'wonderful' mines-trone as if he wanted to be her son. For all that the law divides them, both men are equally ruthless, torn between sentiment and cruelty, and utterly intent on winning. Candella seems to live only for the sublimated pleasure of hunting Rome down. He confides to his indifferent assistant Collins, 'He's out there somewhere, in an alley, on a roof, looking for a way out. He's not asleep.' In a subway shoot-out, Candella is wounded by a bullet meant for Rome. This provides a further bond between the two men as Rome was wounded in a gunfight before the film opened.

Candella's ultimate objective is not just the destruction of Rome and with that his hold over his innocent girlfriend Teena Riconti (Debra Paget), but the redemption of Rome's teenage brother Tony. After Candella persuades Teena to leave Rome in a church, appropriate for a film that reverberates with Christian symbolism, the two men have their final confrontation out on the mean streets. Candella shoots Rome in the back, having asked him to stop 'in the name of the Law'. In the rear of the police car, Tony places his head on Candella's shoulder, a gesture that signifies that Candella has finally taken Rome's place. On one level this shows the victory of the Law, which would have satisfied the censors; on another it is the final move in the film's power-fully homosocial study of the deep and symbiotic relationship of gangster and policeman.

Siodmak's final film noir was *The File on Thelma Jordon* (1949), made for Paramount, which though not his most powerful work, was his most subtle and intricate study of duality and obsession. Cleve (Wendell Corey) is another of noir's ground-down husbands, a district attorney's assistant trapped in a routine and castrated by his overachieving father-in-law, a judge, who dominates his life. His encounter with the independent, attractive and determined Thelma (Barbara Stanwyck) is not merely destructive, but also liberating and enriching. Although Cleve and Thelma plot like Walter and Phyllis in *Double Indemnity* – Cleve has to collude in Thelma's murder of her aunt by bungling the prosecution case – both are less corrupt and more sympathetic. Stanwyck's Thelma is a complex creation, intelligent and sophisticated, frustrated and scheming, but also capable of tenderness and love. As she drives away with her other lover, the vicious and venal Tony (Richard Rober), she uses her cigarette lighter to blind him, causing their car to crash. Thelma, who lives long enough to absolve Cleve from any responsibility in her aunt's death, ruminates that she has always been two people, 'All my life struggling, the good and the bad'. Both she and Cleve are ambivalent, divided figures, sympathetically weak; and for Cleve there remains the muted possibility of a reunion with his wife.

In contrast to Mann, Siodmak's style is smooth, with a preference for long takes and classical *découpage*, creating more subtle effects that mark him as a European director. Colin McArthur's summary – 'Darkness, cruelty, obsession, betrayal and death are the hallmarks of Siodmak's work' (McArthur, 1972, p.112) – could almost be a description of noir itself, indicating his centrality to the main concerns of the cycle. This centrality derives from his ability to combine existentialist fatalism tempered by an equally powerful romanticism, creating a body of work that used both noir's hard-boiled and its Gothic lineage. The outstanding quality of his films is their depth and complexity of characterization. Siodmak's men and women are divided and ambivalent figures, gripped by sexual obsession. The males are weak, self-absorbed and usually destroyed by their desires; the women are often stronger, more resilient, but also more duplicitous.

FRITZ LANG

Fritz Lang was one of the most important of the Weimar directors whose influence on the development of the urban thriller, notably through *M* (1931), has already been discussed. Like Siodmak and many others, Lang fled from Nazi oppression in 1933, making one film in France before moving to Hollywood in 1936. Moving from studio to studio, Lang tried in vain to recreate the working conditions he had enjoyed in Germany where, as a celebrated *autoren* he had control over choice of subject matter, casting, scripting, shooting and editing. However, Lang worked closely with his scriptwriters, designers, cinematographers and actors and all those who worked with him, even the ones who disliked his methods, admired his mastery of every aspect of the film-making process.[7] As one of the best known émigrés, Lang's career was also blighted by xenophobia; HUAC placed him on the 'grey list' as a potential subversive (McGilligan, 1997, pp.365–96).

These difficulties meant that Lang was not invited to direct the most prestigious Hollywood films but intermediates, the occasional Western, but mainly crime thrillers, which were profoundly important to the development of the noir cycle. Lang's concern with the dark underside of modern life, the fundamental tension between individual desires and society, found a congenial vehicle in film noir. Lang's early noirs retain strong European elements, notably *Scarlet Street* (1945), but his later noirs, including another Renoir adaptation, *Human Desire* (1954), are thoroughly Americanized and more representative of noir's final phase of development than aberrant masterpieces such as *Touch of Evil* (1958). As one commentator sums up: 'If Orson Welles is the baroque master of *film noir*, then Fritz Lang is its classicist, an economical and precise craftsman whose carefully controlled effects are all the more powerful for the compression of their means' (Appel, 1974, p.16).

Lang anticipates the style and themes of film noir in his two influential prewar thrillers, *Fury* (1936) and *You Only Live Once* (1937). In *Fury* Joe Wheeler (Spencer Tracey), the archetypal 'John Doe', is imprisoned for a crime he did not commit. In the frightening central scenes, the townsfolk, who have become a lynch mob, storm the jail and Joe is apparently killed. When he returns, a dark shape in the doorway of his brothers' room, Joe is a damaged man, physically and mentally scarred from his ordeal and determined on revenge. Lang's combination of the social delineation of the primitive vindictiveness of small-town America, and the psychological study of a man who is both victim and scourge, whose desire for 'justice' overwhelms his humanity, made *Fury* a distinctive film, but one which MGM executives disliked. Lang deplored the sentimental reunion of Joe with his girlfriend (Sylvia Sydney) that the studio imposed on the film (Jensen, 1969, p.114).

Lang's second film, *You Only Live Once*, was made for Walter Wanger working at United Artists. Eddie Taylor (Henry Fonda) is another ordinary Joe whose turn to crime is the result of poverty and lack of opportunity. Attempting to go straight, Eddie is sentenced to death for a crime he did not commit. When his pardon is announced, Eddie suspects a hoax and shoots the prison chaplain whilst breaking out of the penitentiary. Eddie and his pregnant wife Jo (Sylvia Sydney) become the archetypal fugitive couple, dying together in a hail of police bullets.

These two films have the fatalism that pervades Lang's German films, but their concerns are, characteristically, more social than existential; both are powerful studies of the conflicts and tensions of Depression America. Their flawed but sympathetic outsider heroes, enmeshed in powerful forces beyond their control, prefigure many of noir's central concerns. Lang's use of low-key lighting and unusual angles in key scenes – for instance the scene showing Eddie on death row, shot in 'Caligari' chiaroscuro – create a sense of instability. Not only does Lang play on the ambiguity of guilt and innocence, but he ties this in with the ever present and ambivalent role of the modern media, hungry for sensational events and indifferent to individual lives: the excitable news cameraman in *Fury* or the compositor in *You Only Live Once*, who placidly makes up three different headlines for the outcome of Eddie's trial.

Lang's wartime espionage thrillers – *Man Hunt* (1941), *Hangmen also Die* (1943) and *Ministry of Fear* (1944) – with their psychotic Nazis, pervasive atmosphere of fear and persecuted heroes on the run, were also influential in the early development of the noir cycle.[8] *Ministry of Fear*, set in London and adapted from a Graham Greene novel, is perhaps the most powerful through its play on the deceitfulness of appearances and the instability of identity. Stephen Neale (Ray Milland) is a reluctant hero, pitched into a struggle with Nazi fifth columnists through a mistake. Even though Seton Miller's adaptation removed much of Greene's depiction of the hero's disturbed and damaged psyche, photographer Henry Sharp's use of low-key lighting and stark compositions enable Lang to evoke a paranoid atmosphere in which the extent of the Nazi organization is gradually revealed. Lang's early noirs make sparing use of unusual angles or complex montage sequences. Lang strove for a 'rational camera', knowing that 'every scene has only one *exact* way it should be shot' (Bogdanovich, 1967, p.96). Hence the classical economy of Lang's films, their strict attention to the central drama of the scene and the overall balance of the film.

Lang's further noirs may be roughly divided into two groups: the first four – *The Woman in the Window* (1944), *Scarlet Street* (1945), *Secret Beyond the Door* (1948) and *House by the River* (1949) – use Freudian themes and concentrate on individual desire; the second quartet – *The Blue Gardenia* (1952), *The Big Heat* (1953), *While the City Sleeps* (1955) and *Beyond a Reasonable Doubt* (1956) – focus on the interaction between self and society. However, there are many shared elements between the groupings, especially the problem of guilt and with it the instability of identity. Lang's other two films noirs, *Clash by Night* (1951) and *Human Desire* (1954), stand somewhat apart as they are primarily social realist melodramas. Although Lang's films are often described as dominated by an implacable fate, this applies more to his earlier films. Writing in 1948, Lang strenuously rejected this notion, arguing that audiences had become more mature following the Second World War and therefore ready to accept more complex films that dramatize the struggles of protagonists who have a certain measure of choice (Lang, 1948, pp.22–9). It is no longer chance that dominates but desire.

Both *The Woman in the Window* and *Scarlet Street* are reminiscent of the Weimar Street films with their middle-aged male protagonists infatuated by

The middle-aged victim: Professor Warnley (Edward G. Robinson) in *The Woman in the Window* (Fritz Lang, 1944)

younger women. *The Woman in the Window*, with its sophisticated and literate script by Nunnally Johnson, adopts the Weimar device of the frame tale. Professor Warnley (Edward G. Robinson) has said farewell to his wife and two children and returned to what seems to be his natural habitat, the all-male club with its atmosphere of self-satisfied professionalism and suspicious fear of women, revealed in the teasing Warnley receives when he admits to admiring the portrait of a beautiful woman in a nearby gallery. As he later passes the same painting the woman herself, Alice (Joan Bennett), suddenly appears next to him reflected in the glass. Alice is dressed like the archetypal vamp with her dark hair, hat that frames her face in dark feathers and her black, sheath-like dress. After buying her a drink and going to her apartment, Warnley stabs Alice's lover Mazard with scissors, a desperate act that plunges him into the noir world of murder, blackmail and deceit.

If his stabbing of Mazard was self-defence, Warnley uses all his professional skills to cover up the crime, until he is convinced that the situation is hopeless and he takes a fatal overdose. In a clever slow track back from his slumped body, the camera reveals that these events happened in fantasy, that Warnley has harmlessly fallen asleep in the armchair at his club. Lang's device, which borders perilously on cliché, allows him to avoid the moralizing of his source novel, *Once Off Guard* by J.H. Wallis, without risking the wrath of the Hays Office: Warnley has committed no crime and can be allowed to go free. That Warnley's erotic and violent fantasy was all a dream is hardly reassuring as this potential clearly exists within him (Gunning, 2000, p.293).

The Woman in the Window is driven by a Freudian logic – we first see Warnley lecturing to students about psychoanalytical concepts – that represents the acting out of his repressed desires. These are, partly, at least, an attempt to prove his manhood. He asks Alice if his contemplation of her painting was appropriately heterosexual: 'Did I react properly, ah, normally?' His male opponents – the explosively violent Mazard and the slimy, wheedling Heidt (Dan Duryea) – represent dual aspects of his dark self and the whole episode is a nightmare that embodies the extreme opposite of his everyday or conscious self. Some of the best scenes are those in which he seems to court discovery by his prosecutor friend Lalor (Raymond Massey) – who, like Mazard and Heidt wears a straw boater – as if wanting to feel the rigour of the law, his superego demanding that he be punished.

For *Scarlet Street*, his first film as an independent for Diana Productions, Lang was allowed the luxury of working for three months on the script with Dudley Nichols, and reusing cinematographer Milton Krasner and the principal cast from *The Woman in the Window*. In *Scarlet Street* Alex Golitzen recreated Renoir's Montmartre as New York's Greenwich Village, a sleazy Bohemia where Christopher Cross (Edward G. Robinson) another lonely, middle-aged 'little man' in a loveless marriage, becomes entangled with a *femme fatale* Kitty (Joan Bennett) and exploited by her weaselly lover Johnny (Dan Duryea). Kitty, as Eisner suggests, is an embourgeoised version of Renoir's prostitute; but she remains, in her see-through plastic raincoat, the 'lost girl' of French Poetic Realism (Eisner, 1976, p.258). Kitty, goaded on by Johnny, uses her sex appeal in a thoroughly calculating manner, not only causing Chris to embezzle company funds (he is the firm's cashier) in order to set her up in a swank apartment, but thoroughly humiliating him. In a bitterly cruel episode Kitty taunts Chris's artistic aspirations – he paints at home on Sundays, his one pleasure and emotional release – by holding out her toenails: 'Paint me Chris', she cries, a note of triumph in her voice. 'They'll be masterpieces'. In a further irony it is through Chris's paintings, passed off as hers, that Kitty gains fame and acceptance into polite society.

Chris's final humiliation comes when he observes the strength of her infatuation for Johnny. Her withering denunciation of him as old, ugly and unmanly provokes a murderous rage in which he stabs her repeatedly with an ice pick, his violent thrusts grotesquely mimicking the erotic pleasure he has been denied and underlining the film's equation of sex and death. In another bitter irony, Johnny is executed for Kitty's murder. In a cut scene, Chris was to have witnessed the execution of his rival (ibid., p.264). Instead, dismissed for peculation, he becomes a shambling tramp. In a grim, starkly expressionist scene, Chris writhes on his bed in a shabby room, the glaring light from a neon sign intermittently stabbing through the pitch darkness, haunted by the voices of Kitty and Johnny declaring their mutual passion and Kitty's refrain, 'You killed me, Chris. You're old and ugly and you killed me', intermingled with the strains of 'Melancholy Baby'. His suicide is forestalled only for a final cruel twist: he witnesses his own painting of Kitty, which he had entitled 'Self-Portrait', being bought for a handsome sum. In a dissolve, the street is emptied of people and Chris becomes the archetypal night-time urban wanderer of Poe and Maupassant, alienated modern man, still with Kitty's 'jeepers Johnny, I love you' reverberating in his head (Gunning, 2000, p.339).

Through these two films, as Tom Gunning argues, Lang laid claim to be one of the founding influences on the modern urban thriller where everyday events reveal themselves in an instant as sinister and deadly, where the characters move in a landscape of fear and paranoia which seems to arise out of the alienated urban landscape itself, and where identity is unstable and in constant threat of disintegration and collapse (ibid., pp.296–7). As key texts within the noir canon, they have the distinctiveness of centring on middle-aged eroticism, which adds an element of pathos and absurdity to the plight of the male protagonist.

Lang's concerns with desire, violence and unstable identity, are also readily apparent in *Secret Beyond the Door* and the neglected *House by the River*, which both use Gothic conventions. Lang acknowledged his debt to Hitchcock's

Rebecca, while *Secret's* male protagonist also has echoes of *Spell-bound* (ibid., pp.344–8). Lang also employed *Spellbound's* composer, Miklos Rozsa, whose experimental score adds much to the film's disturbing atmosphere. Lang collaborated closely with Rozsa, suggesting that he write the music backward and record it on tape; when the tape played forwards the sound would be normal, but strangely different (Ott, 1979, p.223).

Like *Rebecca*, *Secret Beyond the Door* has a female narrator, Celia (Joan Bennett), but unusually for the 'paranoid woman' film and to accommodate Bennett who was then in her forties, Celia is neither young nor inexperienced, though she admits to being in 'love for the first time' with the brooding, passionate Mark Lamphere (Michael Redgrave), the *homme fatal*. The film begins with their wedding and Celia's voice-over passes comment on Mark's cryptic behaviour. In flashback, we see that their first meeting is unsettlingly bound up with sex, death and the exotic as both witness a knife fight in a Mexican square. Celia's longings for erotic violence are revealed in her remarks on the pride the woman must feel to be fought over by two men. Once they return to the Lamphere mansion, Celia finds herself shut out from her husband's disturbed world. Mark is an architect *manqué* who has a passion for recreating rooms that reveal the disordered passions of their occupants, but, like Bluebeard, he keeps the seventh locked. *Secret* is replete with dream images, symbolism and mysterious journeys through labyrinthine passages as Celia probes her husband's secret: his fear of being controlled and dominated by women which derives from a traumatic event at the age of ten when his mother locked him in to go out dancing with a suitor.

Although *Secret* contains many powerful moments – including the surreal dream sequence where Mark imagines he is on trial for Celia's murder – Lang lacks Hitchcock's sure-footedness with this material and the film's dénouement is confusing. *Secret's* disastrous failure at the box-office helped dissolve Diana Productions and Lang was forced to seek work with lesser studios: *House by the River* was a 'superior' 'B' production made for Republic, anxious to upgrade its production under the direction of its new head of production, Herbert Yates. Despite the set limitations, the home of Stephen Byrne (Louis Hayward) becomes another mysterious and unnerving Gothic residence, set on the river with its sinister shimmering light and its endless movement that returns any object to its original starting point. Stephen is another artist *manqué*, a frustrated writer and shabby womanizer. In the opening scene he consoles himself after another rejection letter by fantasizing about the maid Emily (Dorothy Patrick), bathing upstairs in his wife's absence. As he crouches in the shadows and watches her bare legs as they descend the stairs his sexual arousal increases until he blocks her path and, distracted by a looming shadow at the door, inadvertently strangles her in an attempt to quieten her screams. With the low cunning of the Hollywood aesthete,

Stephen persuades his brother John (Lee Bowman) to help him dispose of the body in the river and sucks John into the web of lies and evasions that he embroiders to cover his tracks, using John's love for Stephen's wife Marjorie (Jane Wyatt) as the bait. Stephen's criminal energies fuel the creativity of a basically unstable identity continually in need of some form of stimulation, while the notoriety of his maid's mysterious 'disappearance' helps to sell his novel. Emily's body, like all things on the river, returns to haunt Stephen. Having tried to strangle his wife who has learned the truth from his latest novel, he sees Emily's ghostly image on a curtain, which, as he flees in horror, wraps around his neck and strangles him as he struggles to pull free begging her to let him go. Lang handles this macabre melodrama with great finesse through his deft choice of camera angles coupled with cinematographer Edward Cronjager's delicate lighting.

When Lang returned to film noir with *The Blue Gardenia* (1952), his shift from individual pathology to social themes was, as has been shown, typical of the change in the cycle as a whole. For Lang, the alteration was also a return to his prewar films, especially in the renewed concern for the complex relationships and exchanges between police and criminal, pursuer and pursued, villain and victim. His 1950s noirs often blur the 'distinctions between guilt and innocence, good and evil, criminality and legality' (McArthur, 1972, pp.74–6). Lang commented: 'I wanted to show that the average citizen is not very much better than a criminal' (quoted in Ott, 1979, p.214). Within this unstable modern landscape, the media, as in the prewar American films, play a powerful but ambiguous role. These films were tightly budgeted intermediates; even the most successful, *The Big Heat*, was a modest offering by a second-tier studio, Columbia (McArthur, 1992, pp.22–30).

The Blue Gardenia, made for the independent producer Alex Gottlieb, was based on a short story by Vera Caspary, who wrote the novel from which *Laura* was adapted. It is one the rare noirs that featured a working-class woman as its heroine. Nora Larkin (Anne Baxter) is a telephonist sharing an apartment with her two girlfriends, who comes to believe herself responsible for the murder of Harry Prebble (Raymond Burr), the womanizer she impulsively had dinner with after reading a rejection letter from her fiancé in Korea. In the one expressionist scene, she strikes him with a poker as he forces his attentions on her, his agonized face reflected in a mirror. In her distracted, guilt-ridden state, she places her trust in Casey Mayo (Richard Conte), an ambitious reporter whose interest in her springs from his ruse to increase circulation through his appeal, in 'Letter to an Unknown Murderess', for the woman to come forward and confess. Like Prebble, Mayo is a disaffected middle-class professional who has adopted a cynically misogynist attitude towards women and who only gradually recognizes the ways in which he is exploiting Nora. Although Mayo redeems himself when he helps the police find the real culprit, Nora's exoneration comes at the price of the punishment of another ambiguously 'guilty' woman, Prebble's pregnant girlfriend.

The film's brisk pace and yet intense claustrophobia were the result of Lang's collaboration with cinematographer Nicholas Musuraca who developed a uniquely mobile crab dolly, allowing much more fluid camerawork, where the camera could 'wander through a space like a curious person who seeks to see for himself what is happening . . . The camera in motion, therefore, becomes an important and "living" participant in the film' (Lang, quoted in ibid., pp.242–3).

In *The Big Heat*, this moral ambiguity extends to the gangster's moll Debby (Gloria Grahame), whose role has already been analysed, but centres in the honest cop Sergeant Dave Bannion (Glenn Ford), turned into a savage revenger after his wife Katie (Jocelyn Brando) is blown up by a car bomb meant for him. On one level Bannion has the fearless courage to take on a corrupt police force and expose the operations of crime boss Langana (Alexander Scourby) and his sadistic henchman Vince Stone (Lee Marvin) who control the frightened city. On another he has become a dehumanized figure, as violent and brutal as the gangsters he opposes and whose actions cause the death of four women. Bannion has become the expressionist Golem, beyond rational control or appeal and yet acting with an implacable logic. Typically, Lang does not dwell on the psychology of the split self, but on its public consequences. Only with Debby's death can Bannion regain touch with his tender emotions and his wife's memory. Lang refuses his audience any easy consolation from Bannion's victory. He remains an isolated figure, an outsider, even if he is reinstated in the police force at the end, and a morally ambivalent one. Lang described Bannion as 'the eternal man trying to find justice' turned vigilante when the law fails and through whom 'right prevails'. He added: 'Could it be that people see in him a symbol of hope in these days of taxes, insecurity and the H-bomb?' (quoted in ibid., p.246).

Lang's final American noirs, *While the City Sleeps* and *Beyond a Reasonable Doubt*, were a modestly budgeted package deal with Bert Friedlob, a producer working for RKO, a studio now in its death throes, and therefore a reminder of Lang's limited status at this point. Neither was warmly received at the time, but both can now be seen as further examinations of the ambiguous morality of American middle-class life and an increasingly powerful media.

While the City Sleeps has a serial killer – the 'lipstick murderer' – as its ostensible focus, but Lang is less interested in explaining the compulsions of Robert Manners (John Barrymore Jr) than in the motivations of the newspaper staff which seek to use the case to further their own ends. Even the most sympathetic, Edward Mobley (Dana Andrews), shares his male colleagues' contemptuous and predatory attitude towards women. Mobley is Manners's respectable *Doppelgänger*, graphically demonstrated when Mobley uses exactly the same technique to gain entry to his girlfriend's flat. Mobley is quite prepared to put her life as risk as bait to catch the killer and boost circulation. As a television journalist, he uses the new medium to directly address his other self: Manners is shown gazing at Mobley's smooth talking, confident image on the television set in his bedroom. In the dénouement one chases the other through the subway tunnels that exist beneath the city streets, both underground men.

This disturbing motif is taken up in Lang's *Beyond a Reasonable Doubt*, where Dana Andrews again plays an ostensibly virtuous figure, writer Tom Garrett, who agrees to pose as a murderer at the request of Austin Spencer (Sidney Blackmer), a wealthy publisher, in order to be brought to trial and sentenced. In proving Garrett's innocence through incontrovertible photographic evidence, Spencer will expose the law's fallibility and capital punishment as iniquitous. The plan backfires when Spencer dies before he can clear Garrett. In a desperate race against time, Spencer's daughter (Joan Fontaine), Garrett's fiancée, finds the photographs. About to be released, Garrett lets slip that he was indeed the murderer who had seen her father's scheme as a way of ridding himself of a wife who stood in the way of a prosperous marriage. Susan has to choose between her loyalty to the man she loves and the demands of justice. She chooses the latter, coaxed by the policeman who has fallen in love with her and who now sees Garrett as the impediment to his own successful marriage. The multiple ironies of these reversals are typically Langian, where innocence and guilt are impossible to untangle. At the film's centre, Garrett is a man of multiple identities: writer, prospective son-in-law, pretend murderer, wrongly accused victim, reprieved criminal and finally real murderer, who remains Susan's lover. Andrews, as has been discussed, plays the ultimate *tabula rasa*, the man without qualities or psychological depth who can, with equal plausibility be any and all of these roles.

In these 1950s noirs, working with tight budgets and short shooting schedules, Lang developed a ruthlessly pared-down style, which, whilst 'realistic' and apparently merely conventional, is marvellously economical in its suggestiveness. Lang's analytical camerawork dissects a scene piece by piece while his neat parallel editing creates juxtapositions that comment on what is being shown rather than simply depict it, generating multiple ironies that undermine appearances, where the viewer often has to infer meaning, or where information is withheld, most obviously in *Beyond a Reasonable Doubt*. It is a detached style and therefore at odds with the warmer, more sentimental approach that dominates in conventional Hollywood cinema and runs counter to the graphic melodrama of 1940s noirs. 'Lang's style in the 50s began to resemble camouflage: the films strive to resemble the very environments they critique. Lang's classicism cloaks a distance and irony which penetrated to the cold rage for order that underlies the emotional expressiveness of 50s culture' (Gunning, 2000, p.409). Lang's powerful analysis of the increasingly impersonal, corporate nature of American life marks him as a seminal modernist film-maker.

This chapter has emphasized that Mann, Siodmak and Lang had to struggle for creative control within an hierarchical producer-led studio system wedded to commercial success. However, all three found film noir a congenial form, using its repertoire of visual and thematic motifs to conduct a stimulating, occasionally profound, exploration of the darker side of American society and character. Analysis of their films shows the complex interaction between generic conventions and the agency of the individual artist, an interaction that throws light on the nature of the creative process within a commercial system.

NOTES

1. For an illuminating discussion see Naremore (1999, pp.263–78).
2. Silver and Ward note that Mann's Westerns, from *Devil's Doorway* (1950) through to *Man of the West* (1958), carry over elements of noir including existentialist doubt, an 'aura of uncertainty', bitterness and unheroic male protagonists (Silver and Ward, 1980, p.327).
3. See Deborah Alpi, *Robert Siodmak* (1998, pp.46–53). Alpi's study is a comprehensive analysis of Siodmak's career and films. An earlier book-length study, Hervé Dumont, *Robert Siodmak: Le maître du film noir* (Lausanne: Editions l'Age d'Homme, 1981), has not been translated into English.
4. Siodmak co-authored an original story, 'The Pentacle', that was made into *Conflict* (1945), directed for Warner Bros. by Curtis Bernhardt for whom Siodmak had been an assistant in Berlin in 1928.
5. Siodmak, quoted in Dumont (1981, p.181); translation, Walker (1992b, p.124).
6. Her dancing partner is played by the (then) unknown Tony Curtis.
7. Composer Miklos Rozsa thought Lang, 'a true creator, always conscious of the dramatic totality at which he worked, knowing technique to the depth without being its slave' (quoted in Ott, 1979, p.223).
8. Lang directed a fourth spy thriller, *Cloak and Dagger*, in 1946.

CHAPTER SEVEN

Neo-Noir 1

Modernist Film Noir

DEFINITIONS OF NEO-NOIR

As discussed in the opening chapter, the label 'neo-noir' has established itself as the preferred term for films noirs made after the 'classical' period (1940–59). Todd Erickson defines neo-noir as 'a new type of noir film, one which effectively incorporates and projects the narrative and stylistic conventions of its progenitor onto a contemporary canvas. *Neo*-noir is quite simply a contemporary rendering of the *film noir* sensibility' (Erickson, 1996, p.321). Although it is possible to identify the release of Lawrence Kasdan's *Body Heat* in 1981 as the moment when this contemporary sense of film noir was first acknowledged and which inaugurated the current revival, there was a distinct earlier period – 1967 to 1976 – when film noir was resurrected as part of the 'Hollywood Renaissance', a decade of radical energy at an aesthetic and thematic level which transformed several major genres. The two chapters on neo-noir are therefore divided between this earlier 'modernist' phase, and the later 'postmodern' one from 1981 onwards. As the two chapters will discuss in detail, films noirs from each period are separated by crucial differences in style, sensibility and audience orientation which reflect many of the key changes in Hollywood's production practices and its relationship to wider cultural changes over this thirty-year period. The chapter division retains this book's focus on film noir as an evolving phenomenon, best approached through historical contextualization.

THE ANTECEDENTS OF MODERNIST NEO-NOIR

If film noir was in decline after 1959, it never disappeared entirely, migrating to television most notably in *The Fugitive* (1963–67), which drew heavily on the existentialist sensibility of David Goodis. David Janssen played Dr Richard Kimble, a typically masochistic Goodis antihero, trammelled by guilt and forever haunted by his past (Ursini, 1996, pp.275–87). As David Cochran has recently demonstrated, there was an 'underground' culture that retained film noir as a critical cultural form. This underground tradition included *roman noir* authors Jim Thompson, Charles Willeford, Chester Himes and Patricia Highsmith, and 'B' film-maker Samuel Fuller with *Underworld U.S.A.* (1961), *Shock Corridor* (1963) and *The Naked Kiss* (1964), who all attacked the beneficence of American capitalism and the sanctity of the suburban family, keeping alive a habit of irony, scepticism, absurdity and dark existentialism. However, during this period noir authors were isolated figures not part of any movement, lacking a cultural climate that could make their work influential (Cochran, 2000).

The most significant developments of the noir tradition occurred in France where that climate was more congenial.[1] Not only were noir thrillers the most popular American genre in France for both *cinéfiles* and ordinary cinemagoers, but French film-makers were attracted to the mode and a transplanted tradition developed, beginning with Henri-Georges Clouzot's *Quai des Orfèvres* (aka *Jenny Lamour*, 1947) a tale of deception and betrayal, and André Hunebelle's *Mission à Tangier* (1949). Some of the most accomplished and influential films noirs were made in France, including Jacques Becker's *Touchez pas au grisbi* (*Grisbi/Honour Among Thieves*, 1954), a tale of criminal greed and betrayal set in the Parisian underworld with Jean Gabin as an ageing gangster; Clouzot's *Les Diaboliques* (*The Fiends*, 1954) with its pair of would-be female murderers; and Jules Dassin's heist film *Du Rififi chez les hommes* (*Rififi*, 1955). The most prolific director was Jean-Pierre Melville, who had changed his name as an *hommage* to one of the greatest American novelists. Melville uses noir conventions in a highly stylized way. The casting, dress and performance style of the actors is carefully regulated so that it complements the meticulously controlled mise-en-scène. The opening scene in *Le Doulos* (*The Finger Man*, 1962) depicts an unidentified figure (Serge Reggiani) in a soft hat and a belted raincoat who moves silently through a drab, menacing, urban landscape lit by single street lamps, towards a fateful rendezvous. In *Le Samourai* (1967), the existentialist hit man, Jeff Costello (Alain Delon), is the consummate lone professional, but a doomed, even tragic figure. Delon, like Alan Ladd, had a sculpted, hard, impenetrable beauty, cold and still, which matched the muted visual style where the colours of even ordinary objects, like banknotes or labels, were deliberately bleached out.

Melville's austere stylization influenced several American directors, notably Walter Hill's *The Driver* (1978), but in general terms they were more indebted to the young group of directors who formed the nouvelle vague (New Wave), especially François Truffaut and Jean-Luc Godard. Truffaut described *Tirez sur*

New Wave noir: Charles Aznavour in *Tirez sur le pianiste* (François Truffaut, 1960)

le pianiste (*Shoot the Piano Player*, 1960), adapted from the David Goodis novel *Down There* (1956), as 'a respectful pastiche of the Hollywood B-films from which I learned so much' (quoted in Insdorf, 1994, p.26). Charles Aznavour played the archetypal doomed noir hero, Edouard/Charlie, an ex-concert pianist who, unable to forgive himself for causing his wife's suicide, has changed his name and plunged into the Parisian *demi-monde* where he plays abstractedly, staring into off-screen space like Bogart. *Tirez*'s complex flashback structure, its multiple ironies and the enigmatic central figure, owed much to *Citizen Kane* which Truffaut deeply admired (ibid., p.34). But *Tirez*'s innovation, typical of the nouvelle vague, was its combination of deep seriousness and an ironic playfulness in an allusive, multilayered construction that deliberately mixed genres. Truffaut combined 'comedy, drama, melodrama, the psychological film, the thriller, the love film etc.' in order to create an unstable, oscillating tone designed to 'explode' the detective genre.[2] Truffaut used the 'edited zoom', 'a series of three or four quick shots of a detail in which each shot successively magnifies the image. This device is jarring, explicit and introspective, and it fits Charlie's fractured story well' (Monaco, 1980, p.46).

Godard's first feature, *À bout de souffle* (*Breathless*, 1959), part scripted by Truffaut, was also an affectionately critical response to film noir and the American 'B' film, dedicated to Monogram. Its male protagonist, Michel Poiccard (Jean-Paul Belmondo), is clearly modelled on the hard-boiled detective; at one point he gazes at a poster of Bogart's last film, *The Harder They Fall* (1956) and murmurs reverentially 'Bogie' as he poses in front of the image, modelling his expression on Bogart's (Vincendeau, 2000, p.164). Michel is a directionless petty criminal, infatuated with an American woman, Patricia Franchini (Jean Seberg), a modern *femme fatale* who ultimately betrays him. Godard's style is also audaciously experimental using direct address to the camera, jump cuts and sequences of oddly juxtaposed shots to create a kaleidoscopic effect. When Michel shoots a motorcycle traffic patrolman during his drive from Marseilles to Paris in a stolen car, a close-up looking down the barrel of the gun about to fire is followed by a medium shot as the cop falls melodramatically behind a tree, then by an abrupt cut to Michel sprinting through an open field in long shot. Michel's death scene is also disconcertingly tragi-comic, his protracted stagger a parody of the fabled deaths of 1930s Hollywood gangsters. In place of Truffaut's expressionist chiaroscuro, *À bout de souffle* is shot in the daytime Parisian streets often using a hand-held camera, or in Patricia's bright, modern flat where jump cuts render the interior space and the characters' relationship in a new and exciting way.[3]

AMERICAN NEO-MODERNISM (1967–76)

John Orr has given the label 'neo-modernism' to the developments in cinema that emerged at the end the 1950s in the European 'New Wave' cinemas of France and Italy, and which gradually disseminated outwards during the 1960s and 1970s. This diffuse, decentred 'movement' looked back to the great period of experimentation with film form in the 1920s, but was much more prepared to engage with popular culture and demonstrated a 'cooler', more detached and ironic attitude towards the possibilities of radical change. Neo-modernism's most pervasive concerns were with the problems of identity and memory, depicting unmotivated characters adrift in ambiguous situations beyond their comprehension which they are incapable of resolving. Neo-modern cinemas are formally self-reflexive, committed to an investigation of the relationship between representation and reality and to a Brechtian *Verfreumdungseffect*, the 'making strange' or defamiliarization of experience, which asks audiences to take a critical attitude to what is being shown rather than consume it passively (Orr, 1993). Robert Kolker, in his seminal *The Cinema of Loneliness*, argues that these European developments encouraged American film-makers to break with the coherent, character-driven causality of classical Hollywood cinema and develop a modernist American cinema marked by 'self-consciousness, the questioning of the form and content of established film genres, [and] the realignment of the relationship between audience and film' (Kolker, 1988, p.17). These films display what Frederic Jameson has described as the 'great modernist thematics of alienation, anomie, solitude, social fragmentation and isolation' (Jameson, 1991, p.11).

Such a neo-modern cinema was able to emerge in America at this point because of the continued decline of film production, cinemagoing and profitability, which the majors seemed unable to remedy. The expense of making films escalated as the market shrank so that, by the mid-1960s, production costs exceeded revenues by 2:1 (Izod, 1988, p.173). The action adventure films and musicals that dominated production schedules reflected an entrenched attempt to continue making films for a general family audience that took no account of the shift in audience composition and the migration of the family audience to television. In the 1950s and 1960s, the American cinemagoing public became younger, more affluent, more middle-class, better educated and more discriminating in their choice of films. An industry-wide crisis was precipitated when several of the big-budget musicals – *Dr Dolittle* (1967), *Star!* (1968) and *Hello Dolly* (1969) – all did poorly at the box-office and contributed to record losses of $500 million in the 1969–72 period (Belton, 1994, p.290, 302). John Boorman observed that: 'There was a complete loss of nerve by the American studios at this point. They were so confused and so uncertain as to what to do, they were quite willing to cede power to the directors' (quoted in Biskind, 1998, p.22). The huge success of Mike Nichols' *The Graduate* and Arthur Penn's *Bonnie and Clyde*, both released in 1967, persuaded the studios to be more open to writers and directors who might reach this new audience. In particular, the success of the low-budget *Easy Rider* (1969), directed by Dennis Hopper, was the 'primary catalyst' for a switch from big-budget productions to a willingness to employ new talents and produce more experimental, much lower-budget films (Lev, 2000, p.6). At the same time the Ratings system, introduced in 1968, allowed films to be released under the 'X' certificate that were adult in content; graphic displays of near-nudity, sex and violence could be much more overt.

Not only did the majors turn to émigré talent, the English Boorman and the Polish Roman Polanski, and to directors who had come through theatre and television like Penn, but also to a younger generation of film-makers like Hopper and the film school educated 'movie brats', which included Francis Ford Coppola, Martin Scorsese and Paul Schrader. These younger writer-directors were the product of the explosion in film studies courses within American higher education, and their tastes and anti-establishment attitudes reflected those of educated filmgoers who had started to stay away from insipid musicals. All these film-makers were steeped in film history and their films reflect a critical consciousness of both European and American film traditions. The increasingly influential notion of the *auteur*-director as the key creative force in film-making gave them the confidence to experiment and to see their films as vehicles for their own artistic self-expression.

Bonnie and Clyde was instrumental in gaining widespread acceptance for an irreverent, playful mixed-mode film-making in the style of the New Wave. As will be shown, neo-modern films display many formal innovations including disjunctive editing (often jump cuts), hand-held camerawork, very long takes, deliberately grainy cinematography, and a consistent preference for long shots (close-ups and reaction shots are rare or absent altogether). They used wide-screen compositions critically to show characters dwarfed by their environments, or decentred towards the edge of the frame. These techniques were all designed to prevent identification with the characters and to draw attention to the process of film-making. In particular, neo-modernists showed a keen awareness of the potential of the zoom lens which creates a very different sense of space from the tracking shot that was one of the cornerstones of the classical style. A forward or reverse zoom abstracts space by flattening or elongating it and, because it does not reproduce human perception, is overtly cinematic. John Belton summarizes: 'Spatially distorting and inherently self-conscious, the zoom reflects the disintegration of cinematic codes developed before the Second World War' (Belton, 1980–1, p.27). The gradual introduction of faster film stock allowed an increasing sophistication in the use of colour, with cinematographers able to shoot in colour at very low lighting levels. Neo-noir's deep blacks, punctuated by objects picked out using coloured gels, created striking contrasts that resembled classical noir's chiaroscuro.

These neo-modern cultural practices mediated the wider social and political history of this period. Michael Ryan and Douglas Kellner identify the key political trends as the struggle for black civil rights, the protests against the Vietnam War, the feminist movement and the New Left student movement. The assassinations of Robert Kennedy and Martin Luther King in 1968, and the 1972 Watergate scandal created disillusionment with American society, a pervasive alienation from 'Establishment' values which generated a counter-cultural creation of 'alternative' lifestyles. Overall the period was characterized by 'a high level of disaffection on the part of white middle-class youth from the values and ideals of fifties' America, the world of suburban houses, corporate jobs, "straight" dress and behaviour, sexual repression, and social conformity' (Ryan and Kellner, 1988, p.18). The generations were polarized as never before, hence the success of films about malcontents struggling against 'the system', young outsiders and outlaw couples.

AMERICAN NEO-MODERNISM AND
GENERIC TRANSFORMATION

Whereas European directors tended to abandon genre altogether for a more intellectualized art cinema, American modernists worked, for the most part, within a popular generic tradition which continued to engage with both *cinéastes* and a broader filmgoing public (Schatz, 1983, pp.217–87). In a seminal essay, John Cawelti argued that modernist American film-makers engaged in a thoroughgoing generic revisionism and transformation where the cultural myths at the heart of popular genres were subjected to a powerful critique which exposed them as defunct, inadequate or even destructive (Cawelti, 1995 [1979], pp.227–45). These transformations produced the characteristically drifting, dysfunctional male protagonist, lost and alienated.

This revisionism occurred across a range of genres, but the anti-traditionalism of film noir lent itself particularly well to a critique of American values. As noted in Chapter 1, Paul Schrader's seminal 'Notes on *Film Noir*' celebrated film noir as an exciting and iconoclastic element of Hollywood cinema that was ripe for revaluation and reappropriation. In their resurrection of film noir, modernist American film-makers attempted a radical development of the form in ways that recalled the distinguished late noirs: *Kiss Me Deadly*, *Touch of Evil* and *Vertigo*. Larry Gross identifies in these modernist neo-noirs a self-reflexive investigation of narrative construction, which emphasizes the conventions in order to demonstrate their inevitable dissolution, leading to an ambivalence about narrative itself as a meaningful activity. The misplaced erotic instincts, alienation and fragmented identity that characterized the classical noir hero, are incorporated into a more extreme epistemological confusion, expressed through violence which is shown as both pointless and absurd (Gross, 1976, pp.44–9).

The neo-noir revival began with John Boorman's *Point Blank* (1967), which Jack Shadoian identifies as 'a serious attempt to bring the genre perceptually and aesthetically up-to-date', and Foster Hirsch as 'the first truly post-noir noir' (Shadoian, 1977, p.308; Hirsch, 1999, p.17). Its modernity consists in its extreme version of the oneirism that characterizes film noir. It is never clear whether the revenge carried out by the central protagonist Walker (Lee Marvin) – we never learn his first name – is real, or his hallucination just before his death after he is shot repeatedly at point blank range by his close friend Mal Reese (John Vernon) in a cell on Alcatraz where they were engaged in hijacking the syndicate's money. The film's concern with the ambiguities of desire, memory, perception and identity, is profoundly influenced by Alain Resnais, in particular *L'Année dernière à Marienbad* (*The Last Year at Marienbad*, 1961). Walker's flashback recollections of the events that led to the shooting and his initial actions are presented in a highly elliptical narrative that deliberately mingles dream and reality. When he enters the flat of his faithless wife Lynne (Sharon Acker) and fires repeatedly into the empty bed, he seems to be trying to kill her and Reese *in flagrante*, as he had glimpsed them together on Alcatraz. When he suddenly sits down, spent, in a corner of a flat that is now strangely empty, it is as if he were back in the cell in Alcatraz. Boorman wanted to create a 'feeling of repetition, of *déjà vu*', as in Walker's passionless affair with Lynne's sister Chris (Angie Dickinson) which replays his doomed relationship with his wife, the two actresses chosen because of their strong physical resemblance (Ciment, 1986, p.78). Boorman replaces character psychology with a blank mask, using Marvin's taut, angular frame and expressionless face to suggest an animated cadaver, profoundly alienated from the bright modernity of Los Angeles with its vertiginous buildings and vast impersonal offices of plate glass and polished surfaces that house impersonal corporations: 'I wanted my setting to be hard, cold and in a sense futuristic. I wanted an empty, sterile world, for which Los Angeles was absolutely right' (ibid., p.73). Boorman employs a highly stylized colour scheme, moving from cold greys and silvers through blue and green to warmer reds. However, this 'thawing' of colour only serves to counterpoint ironically the profound futility of Walker's quest. As he retires into the shadows and the film dissolves into its final long shot of dawn breaking over Alcatraz island, we recognize the redundancy of Walker's circular story, revealed as an empty spectacle, the delusion of a man already dead.[4]

THE IMPOTENT PRIVATE EYE

Point Blank's stylistic experimentation, framed within a strong generic structure that could appeal to both *cinéastes* through its intellectual complexities whilst providing enough action and excitement for ordinary filmgoers, was highly characteristic of American neo-modernism (Palmer, 1994, pp.177–8). American neo-noir directors, like their predecessors in the 1940s, assimilated developments of European cinema without abandoning altogether the pulp fiction origins of the crime genre. Apart from *The Outfit* (1973), another story of an avenging hit man, this was nowhere more clearly demonstrated than in a group of films which reworked the image of the private eye: *Klute* (1971), *Hickey and Boggs* (1972), *Chandler* (1972), *Shamus* (1973), *The Long Goodbye* (1973), *Chinatown* (1974), *The Yakuza* (1975), *The Drowning Pool* (1976), *The Late Show* (1977) and *The Big Fix* (1978). All these films depict a bemused, vulnerable and inept investigator, lost and alienated in a world he no longer understands and is therefore powerless to master (Cook, 1999, pp.188–209). In *Hickey and Boggs*, one of the pair laments: 'I gotta get a bigger gun. I can't hit anything.' They are adrift in a society that no longer has a place for them and only survive because they are too unimportant to matter (Ward, 1996, pp.237–41).

Robert Altman's *The Long Goodbye* (1973) struck at the heart of this tradition in its radical reworking of Chandler's novel and the 'Bogart myth'. Whereas the casting of Robert Mitchum as Philip Marlowe in *Farewell My Lovely* (1975) or *The Big Sleep* (1978) was a nostalgic invocation of a vanished tradition, Altman casts against type: Elliott Gould is a shambling, scruffy, passive and above all puzzled Marlowe, whose tag-line – 'It's okay with me' – betrays his bewilderment and his attempt to disengage himself from what is going on. His laid-back attitude seems contemporary, but his ill-fitting suits and addiction to wearing a tie appear hopelessly old-fashioned. He drifts about, his actions banal or apparently inconsequential, as in the marvellous first scene where he goes to great lengths to placate his fastidious cat which will only eat a certain type of pet food.

Altman's constantly moving cinematography, where almost every shot is either a slow, never completed, zoom, or an almost imperceptible arc or track round the characters, creates a drifting, uncertain perspective, neither conventionally objective nor subjective. There is a profusion of shots through glass or reflective surfaces, which both obstructs or distorts a clear perception and draws attention to the artifice of film-making. In nearly every scene the central focus shifts in what appears to be a random way, leaving the viewer unsure what the real object of interest is (Luhr, 1991, p.169). This self-conscious, obtrusive style is of a piece with the episodic, rambling narrative that refuses orthodox emotional melodramatic climaxes (Shadoian, 1977, p.341). In a key scene, Marlowe, who has been engaged by Eileen Wade (Nina Van Pallandt) to protect her writer-husband Roger (Sterling Hayden) from the clutches of a corrupt psychiatrist, appears to be becoming romantically involved with his hostess in her candlelit dining room. But as the camera zooms slowly towards the couple, in the centre of the frame the figure of Roger appears, stumbling madly out into the night-time surf. The roar of the surf on the soundtrack becomes increasingly loud and the slow zoom only stops to linger on the rhythms of the relentlessly breaking waves of the Pacific Ocean. Eventually the pair notice Roger's predicament, but it is too late. The moment of his suicide thus arises unpredictably, jolting the viewer into an uneasy sense of the contingency of events, rather than their usual careful shaping by generic conventions. Marlowe's one moment of decisive action occurs right at the end of the film when he shoots his friend Terry Lennox, whom he has been shielding, after Lennox reveals casually how he used and betrayed Marlowe. This apparent vindication of his professional honour and integrity is undermined by the strident playing of 'Hurrah for Hollywood' on the soundtrack, returning the viewer to the film's opening, and stimulating a Brechtian, reflexive sense of the artifice of American myths in a film which is rife with allusions to other Hollywood films. It also refuses the consolation of the conventional male 'buddy' movie (Keyssar, 1991, pp.90–110). Altman commented: 'I see Marlowe the way Chandler saw him, a loser. But a *real* loser, not the false winner that Chandler made out of him. A loser all the way' (quoted in Brackett, 1974, p.28, original emphasis).

Roman Polanski's *Chinatown* (1974) critiques the 'Bogart myth' in a different way, through a deliberately deceptive period recreation of the 1930s. Polanski commented, 'I saw *Chinatown* not as a "retro" piece or conscious imitation of classic movies shot in black and white, but as a film about the thirties seen through the camera eye of the seventies' (quoted in Eaton, 1997, p.49). Screenwriter Robert Towne recreated not Spade or Marlowe with their rough integrity and drab offices, but J.J. Gittes (Jack Nicholson), a new archetype, cool, insolent, glamorous and successful. Gittes's plush chambers and the immaculate dandified elegance of his suits mask an essential vulgarity, betrayed in the pleasure he gets from the racist joke about Chinese lovemaking, which rebounds on him. John Alonzo's widescreen compositions often displace Gittes to the margins of the frame, a small figure in the dry landscape (Wexman, 1985, pp.96–7). Their surface beauty, where almost every scene is bathed in warm Californian sunlight, only serves to emphasize the rottenness that lies beneath. At its heart lies Noah Cross (John Huston) quite prepared to destroy a city and copulate with his own daughter in order to preserve his power and dynastic aspirations. As he tells Gittes, or 'Mr Gits' as he calls him, 'In certain circumstances, a man is capable of anything.'

Chinatown's sterile kingdom, dying king and drowned man (Horace Mulwray the city's chief engineer) evoke the Bible and T.S. Eliot's modernist anti-epic poem, *The Waste Land*, giving the story a mythical dimension, which is far beyond the comprehension of this slick 'bedroom dick'. In the dénouement in Chinatown, Gittes is powerless to prevent the death of the woman he loves, Cross's daughter Evelyn Mulwray (Faye Dunaway), shot by a police officer as she tries to drive away with her daughter in a last attempt to get clear of her father. Although Dunaway may evoke Lauren Bacall as Nicholson evokes Bogart, their relationship is thus brutally curtailed. Cross remains unpunished and keeps possession of his daughter/granddaughter while Gittes is led away by one of his colleagues who tells him, 'Forget it Jake, this is Chinatown', which echo the words he used to hear from his superiors in the LAPD when they wanted his investigations to cease. Gittes is another noir protagonist who is condemned to repeat the past. Robert Towne saw Chinatown as a metaphor for Gittes's 'fucked up state of mind' and a synecdoche for the city of Los Angeles where no one knows what is going on (quoted in Eaton, 1997, p.13). Towne wanted a redemptive ending in which Evelyn killed her father, but Polanski, the arch modernist, insisted on one in which the limits of human intervention are starkly revealed. As Cawelti summaries,

'The result is not heroic confrontation and the triumph of justice, but tragic catastrophe and the destruction of the innocent' (Cawelti, 1995 [1979], p.232).

Arthur Penn, like Altman, spent this period exposing the self-deluding myths of popular genres. *Mickey One* (1964), with its paranoid and trapped protagonist (Warren Beatty) and a jagged, fragmented visual style, was his first neo-noir, highly influenced by Godard and Truffaut, but the film was small-scale and went largely unnoticed (Charyn, 1996, pp.193–5). When Penn returned to noir a decade later with *Night Moves* (1975), it was as the successful director of *Bonnie and Clyde* who could command high production values and a top star, Gene Hackman, as private investigator Harry Moseby. Penn described *Night Moves* as a 'dark picture' caused by his sense of depression and loss after the Kennedy assassinations and characterized the film as a 'counter-cultural genre film, a private-eye film about a detective who finds the solution is not solvable' (quoted in Cook, 1999, pp.189–90).

Moseby is another disillusioned professional, insecure, drifting and also curiously detached from his world, even from his wife's infidelity. He confronts his cuckolder Marty who goads him: 'C'mon, take a swing at me, Harry, the way Sam Spade would', but he is unable to take decisive action. A psychological explanation for Harry's malaise is invoked, the deep trauma of his father's running away when he was a child. But characteristically, when Harry tracked his father down on a park bench in Baltimore, he turned and went away, and is now unable to explain why. Harry's lack of a true purpose or a moral centre, his nameless fears, hopelessness and impotent anger are mirrored in the film's oblique style where scenes often seem to lose their energy and drift onwards to no real purpose, only to be abruptly truncated by a disorientating cut. Even the central investigation into the disappearance and subsequent death of the promiscuous Delly (Melanie Griffith) becomes mired in Harry's doubts and lack of resolution. He warms to the friendship of Paula (Jennifer Warren), only to find that her apparently artless and heartfelt revelations about her confused feelings as they make love, are faked, designed to delay him and keep secret the smuggling activities that have claimed Delly's life. In a catastrophic dénouement, Harry lies wounded aboard the smugglers' yacht, ironically named the *Point of View*. Penn's slow reverse zoom shows the craft circling endlessly, a metaphor for a stagnant, directionless contemporary world.

THE LONE INVESTIGATOR AND POLITICAL PARANOIA

Hackman also starred in Coppola's neo-noir *The Conversation* (1974) as Harry Caul, another type of investigator, a professional electronic surveillance expert. Harry is an ordinary, even unattractive protagonist: balding, poorly dressed, greying, sallow and bespectacled. He is a loner, a guilt-ridden Catholic, obsessed by his work and paranoid about invasions of his own privacy. Harry is so wary and secretive about his own feelings that his bubbly, affectionate girlfriend asks him to stop seeing her. His suspicions about his assistants and his rival surveillance experts prevent him taking solace in male comradeship. He has a one-night stand that leads to betrayal and further loss of faith in human society. Ironically it is Harry's romantic belief in the innocence of the young couple whose conversation he has been hired by an anonymous organization to record, that leads to catastrophe and the destruction of his own home. Convinced he is now the object of surveillance, he frenziedly rips everything apart, all his carefully guarded and cherished possessions, until he finally smashes the plaster Virgin Mary, revealing nothing. In the final shot, the camera slowly pans back and forth across the wreckage of his apartment before zooming out from Harry himself, in the midst of the ruins, playing the saxophone, his one release.

Coppola creates a noir world of paranoia and confusion. It is never finally clear what the conversation means nor who is really guilty as Harry's investigation merges with his subjective fears and uncertainties. It is a narrative in which sound – distorted, magnified, endlessly replayed – dominates. The film's editor, Walter Murch commented that, 'All the content of the film is being carried by the sound . . . with a construction based on repetition rather than exposition, like a piece of music' (quoted in Pye and Myles, 1979, pp.99–100). *The Conversation*'s deconstruction of the apparent objectivity of recording devices provided a sonic equivalent to Michelangelo Antonioni's *Blow-up* (1967) where a photographer becomes convinced that his innocent shots of a tranquil London park hide a murder plot.

The Conversation forms a bridge between the private eye films and a group of political conspiracy thrillers, where noir conventions are deployed in order to create a paranoid world that displayed a deep mistrust of American institutions stemming from the Watergate revelations (Ryan and Kellner, 1988, pp.95–105). This group included *Executive Action* (1973), *Three Days of the Condor* (1975), *The Domino Principle* (1976), Aldrich's *Twilight's Last Gleaming* (1977); and Alan J. Pakula's *The Parallax View* (1974) and *All the President's Men* (1976), which both extend the fears about surveillance initiated by *Klute*, the three films coming to be known as his 'paranoia trilogy'.

The Parallax View opens with a spectacular scene atop Seattle's Space Needle where a senator is shot in a virtual re-enactment of the assassination of Bobby Kennedy. However, the event is shown through a thick plate-glass window, a typically modernist distancing device. The protagonist, journalist Joe Frady (Warren Beatty), is gradually awakened from his flippant moral torpor as he begins to understand the reach of the conspiracy controlled by the mysterious

Parallax Corporation. Like Gittes or Moseby, Frady is plunged into a world that is beyond his capacity to understand or to combat. Ironically, his murder allows the Corporation to have him blamed for the death of another senator. The circular narrative ends as it began, with an anonymous group of judges shrouded in gloom who ascribe the assassination to the work of a lone psychopath. These book-ended scenes have the dark oneirism of a noir nightmare now overtly politicised. Throughout the film, Pakula uses low-key lighting and off-centre framing, or agoraphobic widescreen compositions, to suggest a corrupt and unbalanced world in which abrupt cutting creates jarring shifts in vision and rapid reversals that unsettle the viewer and where events are presented before their cause is explained.

All the President's Men was more thoroughly chiaroscuro with its shadowy assignations in anonymous car parks, streets with silhouetted figures pushed to the edge of the frame, the dark, cramped interiors of the two journalists' apartments, the long corridors of government buildings and the night-time Washington streets shot through blue or bilious green filters. Many of the shots have one solitary source of light and cinematographer Gordon Willis, who also photographed *Klute*, was nicknamed the Prince of Darkness for his daring use of colours at very low lighting levels (Naremore, 1998, p.191). Pakula also uses the horizontal expanses of Panavision to open out space and to isolate his protagonists. For all its paranoia about the extent of government corruption, the two journalists (Dustin Hoffman and Robert Redford) are conventionally heroic – courageous, honourable and ultimately successful. Pakula commented: 'The Parallax View represents my fear about what's going on, and *All the President's Men* my hope' (Jacobs, 1977, p.16).

ROGUE COPS

In 1950s' film noirs the rogue cop was the aberration, in 1970s' neo-noirs he is the norm. Although the figure was appropriated by both left- and right-wing film-makers, both perspectives share a sense that American society is ramshackle, corrupt and venal, its legal system in disrepair, inadequate to combat the changing nature of crime and hopelessly bureaucratic. There is no longer a belief in the power of legitimate authority to dispense justice. The rogue cop shares with other modernist figures a moral confusion and his actions are ambivalent if not worryingly psychotic. He is another loner, outside the bonds of family, male comradeship, all social ties. This group of films is less formally experimental, preferring a straightforward uncluttered style, with linear narratives reminiscent of the 1940s' semi-documentaries.

The most influential example was Don Siegel's *Dirty Harry* (1971). Clint Eastwood, who had made his reputation as the Man with No Name in Sergio

Leone's 'Dollars' trilogy (1964–7) starred as the eponymous 'Dirty' Harry Callahan: a tough, laconic, unstable loner who is barely able to contain and control the often sadistic violence that wells up within him. In one of the film's most famous moments he points the huge barrel of his .44 Magnum at a trapped and wounded black criminal musing whether 'in the heat of the action' he fired six shots or only five: 'Do you feel lucky, punk?' he snarls as he pulls the trigger. It was this black humour – Eastwood delivers his mordant one-liners with the wit and savvy that the distracted private eyes have lost – that distanced the sadism as it did in the James Bond films. But in a darker moment as the killer Scorpio lies at his feet under the floodlights in the Kezar Stadium, Harry repeatedly kicks his injured leg, stamping and grinding on the wound. Siegel's camera zooms outwards as if repulsed by the scene.

Harry believes that his methods are justified by the sickness of a society capable of producing a sadistic and psychopathic killer like Scorpio (Andy Robinson) whose long hair and peace symbol belt buckle symbolize his counter-cultural affiliations. But the film repeatedly links the two figures, separated by a thin divide: at one point a shot of Harry's badge dissolves into the sniper's muzzle and, as the camera zooms outwards from the scene in the stadium, they are left together, lost in the dark and damaged world both inhabit. Harry has no home life after the death of his wife, killed in a traffic accident by a drunk, and, perpetually mired in the sleaze and corruption that constitute city life, is now confused about his ultimate motivations. He advises his wounded partner Chico to quit and when asked by Chico's wife why he continues, replies wearily, 'I don't know. I really don't.' In the final scene, having killed Scorpio on derelict ground some way from San Francisco, Harry throws away his badge as the camera again zooms back to an extreme long shot of a figure lost in a huge landscape, whose gesture lacks the moral resonance of its equivalent in *High Noon* (1952).

In several quarters the film was attacked for its uncritical endorsement of a right-wing law and order agenda (Frayling, 1992, pp.89–91). But, as the analysis above indicates, the film attempts to maintain a critical distance from the character, recognizing the dangerous seductiveness of Harry's licensed vigilantism. Siegel described Harry as 'a racist, a reactionary . . . some policemen are like Harry, genuine heroes whose attitudes I abhor' (quoted in ibid., p.93). A similar ambivalence underscores another ostensibly right-wing neo-noir, *The French Connection* (1971), directed by William Friedkin who was influenced by the European documentary thrillers, Gillo Pontecorvo's *The Battle of Algiers* (1966) and Costa-Gavras' *Z* (1969) (Biskind, 1998, p.205). Gene Hackman plays 'Popeye' Doyle, hard-boiled scourge of Harlem drug dealers, who pursues 'the Frog', Alain Charnier (Fernando Rey), the criminal mastermind behind a huge heroin shipment from Marseilles. Doyle's obsession with Charnier is a disturbing mixture of envy, hatred, fear and desire as he munches his way through a half-cooked hamburger on a freezing New York street while his adversary dines at his leisure in a top restaurant. Doyle is an unstable loner, whose violence alienates his partner Russo (Roy Scheider), horrified that in the final shoot-out Doyle appears unconcerned that he has killed a federal agent. Friedkin uses an unsettling editing style, with abrupt, jarring transitions which often suspend the viewer in mid-action without establishing shots. Friedkin deliberately eliminated bridging material to sustain a tense mixture of headlong action and 'edgy confusion' (Rubin, 1999, pp.247–50). In the 1975 sequel, *French Connection II*, Doyle is even more the alienated loner, adrift in a foreign city (Marseilles), his clothes, language and attitude all utterly out of place and seemingly ridiculous. He wins some sympathy through his utter abjection during his 'cold turkey' as he struggles to recover from being shot full of drugs after Charnier's gang kidnapped him. In an extraordinary performance, both frightening and deeply affecting, Hackman captures the terror of the powerless tough guy as he desperately clings on to the shards of his identity, his vestigial American-ness symbolized by his craving for Hershey bars. In what seems like a some-what sentimental gesture, he finally gets his man after a superhuman chase along the dockside. But the viewer is left wondering just what is left for Doyle now that he has destroyed his quarry; what meaning, if any, his life might still possess.

The critical perspective on the right-wing tough guy that these films main-tain was discarded in Michael Winner's *Death Wish* (1971) and its successors, and in Phil Karlson's *Walking Tall* (1973) and its two sequels, where the resonantly named hero, Buford Pusser, a Tennessee sheriff, uses any method to achieve 'justice'. However, the critique of legitimated authority was con-tinued in Robert Aldrich's *Hustle* (1975), which was as sceptical about the man of action as *Kiss Me Deadly*. The central protagonist of *Hustle* is Lieutenant Phil Gaines (Burt Reynolds), confused about his life, especially his relation-ship with the high-class prostitute Nicole Britton (Catherine Deneuve), and dissatisfied with the pervasive venality of Los Angeles where everyone is on the hustle. Where the response of Harry Callahan was vigilantism, Gaines is introspective, quizzical and nostalgic with his taste for 1930s' music and films, now seen as a lost age of innocence. Gaines harbours a dream of Europe – specifically Rome which he once visited on a narcotics case – as an idealized haven of civilization that he and Nicole will escape to. But the case he investigates, the death of a young woman that could be murder or suicide, plunges him back into a corrupt, ambivalent world where money speaks loudest. The girl's father, Marty Hollinger (Ben Johnson) is an un-stable Korean veteran blundering around in a world he neither knows nor understands, but who expresses the naked outrage Gaines suppresses. When Hollinger kills the unprincipled attorney Leo Sellars (Eddie Albert), one of

Nicole's clients, who may or may not have been responsible for his daughter's death, Gaines covers up for him, convincing himself that a form of justice has prevailed. En route to meet Nicole at the airport for their flight out, Gaines tries to prevent a liquor store burglary and is shot. Both Reynolds and Aldrich, co-producers, held out for this bleak ending against the advice of the studio; it ruined the film's box-office chances but retained its integrity as the expression of Gaines' instinct that he must intervene to maintain a system he knows is hopelessly corrupt (Arnold and Miller, 1986, p.193). In that futile but honourable gesture he becomes another of the modernist losers, a 'loser all the way' like Altman's Marlowe.

An isolated but prescient film was Burt Kennedy's *The Killer Inside Me* (1976), adapted from Jim Thompson's 1952 novel, a pioneering effort to adapt this most disturbing of the new generation of hard-boiled writers. Stacy Keach plays the affable small-town sheriff, Lou Ford, on the outside liberal, gentle and caring, everyone's friend, but whose murderous dark self can be easily triggered. *The Killer Inside Me* uses chiaroscuro lighting, flashbacks and voice-overs, mirror reflections, sounds and images from the past which seem to float by in distorted, repetitive fragments to convey Lou's psychological tumult (Hirsch, 1999, p.127). Lou recognizes his condition – 'I've got my feet planted both sides of the fence, going to split down the middle' – but cannot control it, his memories circling back to the traumatic primal scene when he discovered his mother in bed with her lover and was beaten by both parents for his meddling.

NEO-MODERN APOCALYPSE: *TAXI DRIVER*

The film that has become *the* representative neo-modernist noir is *Taxi Driver* (1976), which, like other major noirs, is the locus for the varied social and cultural forces that make up this historical moment. Kolker judged *Taxi Driver* to be the film that most comprehensively works through the problem of the dislocated subject (Kolker, 1988, p.181). Travis Bickle (Robert De Niro) is a richly complex figure: maladjusted Vietnam veteran, angry and inarticulate – 'I got some bad ideas going on in my head' – the lonely, paranoid, psychotic, insomniac adrift in the anomie of the night-time city, and right-wing vigilante, committed to purging the city's sleaze and corruption. Bickle's rage and alienation drew a strong response of recognition from contemporary audiences: *Taxi Driver* was the twelfth most successful film of its release year.

Taxi Driver fused director Martin Scorsese's Italian-American Catholicism with its penchant for baroque spectacle, with the puritanical Dutch-American Calvinism of screenwriter Paul Schrader who acknowledged the key influence of Robert Bresson's *Pickpocket* (1959), with its austere delineation of the existential crisis of a petty criminal. Scorsese drew inspiration from the fevered imagination of Dostoevsky's alienated protagonist in *Notes from the Underground* (Taubin, 2000, p.9). Both men, through their film-school education, could draw upon a wide knowledge of European and American cinema. Scorsese cites the importance of John Ford's *The Searchers* with John Wayne's Ethan Edwards as a prototype for Travis, another man who has 'just fought in a war he believed in and lost' (quoted in Thompson and Christie (eds), 1989, p.66). Both men had a deep interest in film noir evident in Travis's voice-over narration. Scorsese remembered the formative influence of *Murder by Contract* (1958) which offered 'an inside look into the mind of a man who kills for a living' (ibid.). Travis conforms to Schrader's conception of the late noir protagonist who has lost his integrity and stable identity, the prey to 'psychotic action and suicidal impulse'.

Both Scorsese and Schrader wanted the story to have a topical element and Travis' diary was based on the one kept by Arthur Bremer which was serialized in newspapers and published as *An Assassin's Diary* in 1974. Travis's plans to kill a presidential candidate align *Taxi Diver* with the paranoid conspiracy films, but his aborted assassination attempt is illogical – why should he want to kill the politician who promised to clean up the city? – an index of his loosening hold on reality. He becomes possessed by morbid fantasies of the masochistic disciplining of the flesh that will create the true warrior, emerging onto the New York streets in a bizarre combination of US Army combat gear and Mohican hair-cut. In one of the most famous scenes Travis stares at his mirror reflection as if it were his ultimate antagonist: 'You talkin' to me? You talkin' to *me*? Who the fuck do you think you're talkin' to?' It is a memorable image of the schizophrenic solipsist, waging war on himself. As in Scorsese's earlier *Mean Streets* (1973), De Niro's method acting, at once intense, meticulously planned, and apparently improvised and unpredictable, captures the unstable identity of contemporary urban man where Travis's masculinity has become a succession of performances.

Like Dirty Harry, Travis is revolted by what he sees, but compulsively fascinated by it: 'It's that idea of being fascinated, of this avenging angel floating through the streets of the city, that represents all cities for me' (Scorsese, in ibid., p.54). In order to capture this 'fascination', Scorsese had to create a style that would create an ambiguous world that hovers between dream and reality, what Scorsese referred to as 'that sense of being almost awake' (ibid.). It is a style that merges a subjective and objective perspective: 'Sometimes the character himself is on a dolly, so that we look over his shoulder as he moves towards another character, and for a split second the audience would wonder what was happening. The overall idea was to make it like a cross between a Gothic horror and the New York *Daily News*' (ibid.). The jump cuts and edited zooms, the frenetic hand-held camerawork, apparent randomness of the drifting narrative and the jagged editing, are all inspired by the New Wave directors.[5] But *Taxi Driver* also shows a profound debt to Expressionism (by way of classical noir) in its mise-en-scène. In the memorable opening sequence Michael Chapman's wide-angle lens captures Travis' distorted view of the glare and tawdry glamour of the neon signs in their saturated primary colours, or the strange eruptions of steam through the manhole covers in the timeless drift of the cab through the dark night-time streets. Chapman recalled that Godard's influence allowed many audacious cuts that give the film its free-flowing improvisatory feeling (Biskind, 1998, p.299). Chapman also customized the tracking dolly with golf cart tyres, thereby enabling the crew to track just about anywhere.

Travis's schizophrenia comes through most strongly in his relationships with women, polarized between the sculpted beauty of Betsy (Cybill Shepherd) the virginal madonna dressed in white, and the gamine Iris (Jodie Foster), the twelve-year-old prostitute he tries to protect, in her hot pants. He is incapable of relating to Betsy, taking her to a blue movie on their first date, but can relax with Iris even though he is unsure what he wants from her. In the penultimate scene he 'rescues' her from the pimp (Harvey Keitel) in what becomes an escalating bloody massacre of the occupants of the bordello, a demonic parody of the avenging hero, the selfless martyrdom of his namesake who commanded the Alamo garrison, and the purgation of all the post-Nam violence and rage that festers inside him. In an ironic ending, this psychotic slaughter is rendered heroic: the camera pans slowly over newspaper cuttings of 'Taxi Driver Hero To Recover' as we listen to the voice-over of Iris' grateful father congratulating Travis on returning their daughter to them. In the final scene Travis is once again in his cab, looking as he did in the opening scene, but driving Betsy who shows a far greater interest in this media celebrity. Travis's smile is enigmatic as he drops Betsy off and drives endlessly on to the sound of Bernard Herrmann's moody jazz score. It is another circular narrative whose dénouement is ambiguous. Scorsese commented that, 'although at the end of the film he seems to be in control again, we give the impression that any second the time bomb might go off again' (quoted in Thompson and Christie (eds), 1989, p.62). The film functions as a modern apocalypse, a profound, pervasive alienation that cannot be cured and whose pessimism grows out of the failure of American myths to provide satisfying answers to society's ills (Sharrett, 1993, pp.220–35).

The neo-modernist phase of film noir is characterized more by quality than quantity. There were relatively few films noirs released, but those that were constituted a significant revision of the paradigms that had been established in the classical period. The use of colour, zoom lenses, highly mobile cameras and widescreen compositions redefined noir's visual style, while the noir protagonist was also reconstructed, his alienation and paranoia became more extreme as his existential crisis deepened. In many ways Gene Hackman emerged as the representative star: middle-aged, shabby and uncertain of purpose. The narrative paradigm also shifted. Modernist neo-noirs abandoned the crisp fast-paced trajectory of their predecessors in favour of meandering, episodic and inconclusive stories, circling back on themselves. Above all modernist noir was self-reflexive, drawing an audience's attention to its own processes and self-consciously referring not only to earlier films noirs, but also to the myths that underpinned their generic conventions. Neo-modernist noirs demanded a great deal from their audiences, who were challenged rather than consoled. The key limitation of modernist film noir was its inability or refusal to take up two of the major socio-cultural movements that were transforming American society: black civil rights and women's emancipation. Only *Klute* seemed to be interested in the contemporary independent woman in a period in which the *femme fatale* became a marginal figure.[6] Many of these features of neo-noir were to change profoundly in the 1980s and 1980s as noir entered its postmodern phase.

NOTES

1. For overview discussions see Vincendeau (1992a, pp.50–80); Forbes (1992, pp.85–97); Buss (1994).
2. Truffaut in 'Questions à l'auteur', *Cinema* 61 (January 1961), quoted and translated in Monaco (1980, p.41).
3. Claude Chabrol also made a series of films noirs, deeply indebted to Hitchcock, over an extended period, but he was less influential in America; see Austin (1999, pp.92–4, 135–66).
4. See Boorman's comments in Ciment (1986, p.78).
5. For a detailed contextual study see Leighton Grist, *The Films of Martin Scorsese 1963–77* (2000).
6. *Klute* is analysed in detail by Gledhill (1998, pp.20–34, 99–114); and Martin (1997, pp.67–8).

CHAPTER EIGHT

Neo-Noir 2

Postmodern Film Noir

Postmodern film noir may be dated from 1981, the year of *Body Heat* and the remake of *The Postman Always Rings Twice*, which inaugurated a new phase of prolific development. Neo-noir has established itself as an important contemporary genre within a restabilized, expanding Hollywood cinema. Films noirs are now a staple of cinema exhibition, terrestrial and cable television programming and video rental. Their production is no longer characterized, as it was in the modernist period, by a sporadic but intense revisionism spurred by a political critique of American myths, but by a more commodified reworking of classical noir whose seductive, instantly recognizable look – known in the trade as 'noir lite' – forms part of a knowing, highly allusive postmodern culture. Film Noir has generated its own 'mediascape': in a resurgent hard-boiled fiction, television series, interactive video games, magazines, cover art, websites, comic books and graphic novels, even tourist industry simulations (Naremore, 1998, pp.254–77). Although this commodification means that film noir is no longer clearly an oppositional form of film-making, postmodern neo-noir retains the capacity, handled intelligently, to engage with important issues. The darkness of postmodern noirs is not simply a borrowed style but a continuing exploration of the underside of the American Dream.

This chapter attempts a broad overview of postmodern film noir using the categories established in the earlier chapters: its conditions of production and reception, style, themes and narrative strategies, construction of gender and auteur directors, with additional sections on two key developments, the use of film noir by women and black directors. It begins by considering the fundamental characteristics of postmodernism and how these were represented in the two paradigmatic postmodern noirs, Lawrence Kasdan's *Body Heat* (1981) and Ridley Scott's *Blade Runner* (1982).

THE EVOLUTION OF POSTMODERN NOIR

Postmodernism, like modernism, is a complex term that connotes both an aesthetic style and a more general 'historical condition', which Jean-François Lyotard characterizes as defined by a scepticism about 'metanarratives' (over-arching, explanatory systems of thought) and a concomitant belief in a non-hierarchical diversity and difference (Lyotard, 1984, p.xxiv). As an aesthetic style that derives from this radical relativism, postmodern cultural practices characteristically employ *la mode retro*, which appropriates past forms through direct revival, allusion and hybridity, where different styles are used together in a new mixture. This borrowing and recycling of images from earlier forms is a condition of creativity itself, but the scale and intensity of these intertextual references are what differentiates postmodern practice from earlier periods. Such practices signal 'a fundamental shift in the conception of artistic pro-duction in which creativity is no longer conceived in terms of pure invention but rather as the re-articulation of preexisting codes' (Collins, 1995, p.92). Not only has a romantic conception of originality been abandoned, but also the modernist project of evolving a new style that can express changed social and cultural experiences. Where modernism posits a dream of authenticity, a meaning and truth that is elusive but nevertheless theoretically possible, postmodernism understands 'truth' as another discourse that has no neces-sary legitimacy. Jean Baudrillard has postulated that we are no longer part of the drama of alienation, rather we live in the 'ecstasy of communication' (1983, pp.126–34). However, this reappropriation of past forms can be highly creative and meaningful, not necessarily the empty, nostalgic pastiche that Frederic Jameson discerned (Jameson, 1991, pp.19–21).[1]

Two basic tendencies are at work in postmodern noir, revivalism, which attempts to retain the mood and atmosphere (*stimmung*) of classical noir, and hybridization where elements of noir are reconfigured in a complex generic mix.[2] The revivalist mode was inaugurated by *Body Heat* which recreated the ambience of classical noir that Kasdan found intellectually and emotionally stimulating, 'a world that I found very sensual and exciting . . . For me, that dark side speaks to my own hidden obsessions . . . What's great about *noir* is the blending of the life we present to other people and our secret life. It's all about desire' (quoted in Chute, 1981, p.53). Citing *Body Heat* as 'a child of *The Maltese Falcon* and *Double Indemnity* and *Out of the Past*, but used for my own purposes', Kasdan attempted to understand the loss of innocence – 'the expectation that the world would be wonderful and it wasn't' – that his 'baby boom' generation felt and which he saw as analogous to the feel-ings experienced by those returning from the Second World War (ibid.). *Body Heat* therefore combines these two periods, portraying in Ned Racine (William Hurt), 'someone of my generation who just happens to find himself

The birth of postmodern noir: off-angle composition in *Body Heat* (1981), Lawrence Kasdan's remake of *Double Indemnity*, with William Hurt as Ned Racine (Lawrence Kasdan, 1981)

in the *film noir* world' (quoted in Fuller, 1994, p.125). Hence the film's retro-modern small town Florida, contemporary but without air conditioners, caught in limbo, like Ned himself, a small-time rather unsuccessful lawyer who lacks the resolve to better himself or move away. Like Walter Neff, he sees in Matty (Kathleen Turner) the promise of something more, a fantasy of sex and success that will restore his self-esteem even if, or because, it involves murdering her husband.

The film's style attempts to create Ned's drowsy, oneiric confusion: 'I wanted *Body Heat* to have the same kind of languid, sensual feel that envelopes Ned . . . That's why I wanted to move the camera a lot – to have that kind of grace' (quoted in Chute, 1981, p.54). Hence the slow, gliding tracking shots and lap dissolves, and the low-lit, mutedly chiaroscuro interiors of Matty's house where they make love. The colour scheme is carefully controlled: the warmth of the yellows, browns and reds gradually gives way to cool blues and greys as Ned realizes he is the victim of Matty's wiles. If Ned's victim-loser was classical, Matty was a modernized, unpunished *femme fatale*, relaxing on the exotic beach she had dreamed about since college days, even if her enigmatic expression hints that she is unfulfilled. Much more than the lacklustre remake of *The Postman Always Rings Twice* that slightly preceded it,

Body Heat rekindled the possibilities of film noir for a new generation of film-makers and their audiences. Reviewers saw in *Body Heat* the recreation of a mood and sensibility they thought had been abandoned, whose eroticism was now more graphic and explicit (ibid., p.50).

Released six months later, Ridley Scott's *Blade Runner* (1982) melded noir and sci-fi to create a hybrid 'future noir' that depicted a nightmare Los Angeles of 2019 as an entropic dystopia characterized by debris, decay and abandonment. From the air, Los Angeles has become a vast industrial sprawl belching out huge fireballs of gaseous waste, while at street level a crowded, polyglot community jostles for space in perpetual darkness beneath the unending acid rain. *Blade Runner* has been cited as the 'quintessential city film: it presents urbanism as lived heterogeneity, an ambiguous environment of fluid spaces and identities' (Bukatman, 1997, p.12). It is a city of recycled objects, assorted styles – Graeco-Roman columns mingle with Oriental motifs and the neo-Mayan pyramid of the Tyrell Corporation – and discontinuous spaces, unlike the homogeneous monumentality of Lang's *Metropolis* (1926) which was an important influence. Scott used actual locations, including the run-down Bradley Building whose design was famously futuristic when it was built in 1893, but integrates these into the huge studio space that was 'retrofitted' (putting new add-ons to existing buildings) over the 1929 New York Street set that Warner Bros. used for its gangster movies. *Blade Runner's* densely textured style is evident in almost every frame, but particularly in such set pieces as the 'retiring' of the replicant Zhora which takes place amidst a bewildering cacophony of sounds, objects and twitching neon signs, picked out in saturated colour gels, that penetrate the gloom created by the use of low-key lighting and blue filters which has become the standard contemporary chiaroscuro or 'noir lite'. Using the 'steadicam', where the operator's movements are not transmitted to the camera, Scott can trace the replicant's sinuous movements through the clutter before 'her' slow motion demise through the splintering plate glass window, where each successive image is shown in pin-sharp detail, allowing the viewer to savour every instant.

In addition to its dark, layered visual style, *Blade Runner* also references classical noir through its central protagonist, Deckard (Harrison Ford), both modern law enforcer, a blade runner, and archetypal 1940s private eye in his battered trench coat, whose voice-over narration (in the studio version of the film), recaptures the cynical world-weariness of the hard-boiled 'dick'. Scott thought Ford 'possesses some of the laconic dourness of Bogey, but he's more ambivalent, more human. He's almost an antihero' (quoted in Sammon, 1996, p.89). His ambivalence comes from his increasing sense that the replicants are not rogue automata but more human than their creators, a confusion compounded by his love for Rachel (Sean Young) – whose bobbed, swept-back hair recalls Joan Crawford – a further stage in genetic evolution whose 'life-span' is undefined. Deckard's dilemma is not whether he can trust her or not – she has proved her loyalty by shooting another replicant – but what kind of entity she is and what their life together might be. Scott's director's cut, released in 1992, leaves their future uncertain, huddled in a lift shaft hoping for escape.[3]

THE PRODUCTION AND RECEPTION
OF POSTMODERN FILM NOIR

Modernist noirs were part of a waning film industry that was unsure of its direction. Postmodern noirs are made within a vigorous contemporary Hollywood stabilized by the 'blockbuster' where production levels are higher than ever (Schatz, 1993, p.10). The old studios have evolved into 'consolidated' media conglomerates such as Time-Warner/AOL (Gomery, 1998, pp.47–57). These global media conglomerates control the diverse markets within which films are now sold, including part financing the massive multiplex building programme that has more than doubled the number of cinemas in America between 1975 and the present (Schatz, 1993, p.20). Whereas roughly three quarters of a film's revenue used to come from its cinema release, now only one quarter to a third comes from that source, the rest coming from 'ancillary' markets: video cassettes bought and rented, screenings on cable, satellite and finally terrestrial television, and from associated product merchandizing (Balio, 1998, pp.58–73).

The other key element to contemporary Hollywood is the rapid and sustained growth of 'independent' or 'Indie' cinema: film-making that takes place outside the direct control of the majors, often with unconventional financing. This sector of the industry is associated with the creativity, formal innovation and challenging subject matter that characterized European art cinema, or the modernist American *auteurs* in the 1970s. Indie cinema is very diverse, both in subject matter and style, and lacks any overriding cohesive ideology, but it offers a cultural space for experimentation and artistic self-expression. Indie cinema now has a high public profile in both America and Europe (Levy, 1999).

Within this dynamic if volatile film industry, production levels of film noir are now comparable to the heights of the classical period (Silver and Ward, 1993, p.442). R. Barton Palmer argues that the 'erotic thriller' – a 'direct descendent of film noir' – is the most popular genre of the 1990s (Palmer, 1994, p.168). Films noirs are rarely blockbusters, those that are tend to be hybrids, such as *Face/Off* (1997), where director John Woo combined a dark *Doppelgänger* story with the high-speed action sequences through which he made his name in Hong Kong cinema. *Face/Off* is replete with the breathtaking special effects that are the *sine qua non* of high-budget productions. As before, most noirs are medium-budget intermediates, for instance the remake of *Night and the City* (1992) starring Robert De Niro and Jessica Lange. But there is now a modern equivalent to the erstwhile 'B' feature, the low-budget straight-to-video/cable films budgeted at under one million dollars, which rely on the basic appeal of sex and violence (Silver, 1996, pp.331–8). The videocassette cover of one representative example, *Body Chemistry* (1990), invites viewers to take 'an erotic journey into the sexual danger zone'. As in the 1940s, the noir style can serve to disguise impoverished production values, small casts and limited sets or locations, which make it a popular option. Over half the films made by Showtime, a company specializing in the made-for-cable market, were films noirs (Lyons, 2000, p.163).

Films noirs are also popular with Indie film-makers. The success of Joel and Ethan Coen's *Blood Simple* (1984), costing only $1.5 million, demonstrated the potential of film noir for Indie film-makers who could make visually sophisticated films with a subversive content on small budgets. The Coen brothers commented: 'We've liked that type of story for a long while . . . It's a genre that really gives us pleasure. And we also chose it for very practical reasons. We knew we weren't going to have much money. Financing wouldn't permit other things. We could depend on that type of genre, on that kind of basic force' (quoted in Woods, 2000a, p.65). Indie directors have produced many of the most thoughtful and innovative postmodern noirs (Levy, 1999, pp.218–48).

As in the classical period, there are few hard and fast divisions between these production strands, which should be understood as overlapping practices in a state of dynamic tension. The horror-noir *The Silence of the Lambs* (1991) was a 'sleeper', i.e. an intermediate 'A' feature which becomes a surprise success over a relatively lengthy period largely by word of mouth. Its popularity as the third highest grossing film of 1991 allowed the long-awaited sequel, *Hannibal* (2001), to be marketed as a blockbuster. John Dahl's *Red Rock West* (1992) and *The Last Seduction* (1994) originated as made-for-cable productions, but were given a cinema release because they were judged, correctly, as having the potential to be successful with cinemagoers. Some Indie films can 'cross-over' into mainstream distribution. After the film's success at Cannes, Quentin Tarantino's *Pulp Fiction* (1994) was aggressively marketed by its producers Miramax who coupled its critical status with an emphasis on its generic qualities as a sexy noir thriller, thereby broadening the film's audience while securing widespread distribution. *Pulp Fiction* went on to attain cult status, readily available on video and regularly screened on television. In the 1990s the boundary between Indies and the majors became increasingly blurred, with 'independent' companies that specialized in financing Indies, such as New Line Cinema, now part of media conglomerates. This permeability of production boundaries reflects a wider process that characterizes postmodernism: an accelerating cultural relativity that erodes cultural distinctions. Many films noirs straddle what is becoming a diminishing divide between art house films and mainstream cinema.

This blurring of boundaries between mainstream and independent cinema is dependent upon more knowledgeable audiences. Modern media-saturated viewers are likely to be more cineliterate than their predecessors, able to respond to the numerous references that postmodern films, including noirs, mobilize. Contemporary audiences have been characterized as simultaneously both naive and ironic, innocent and knowing, able to grasp and enjoy the multiple allusions without necessarily struggling to fit these into a coherent cultural matrix (Ray, 1985, p.244). Postmodern viewers – 'hyperspectators' – retain an essentially innocent delight in film – appreciating effects, enjoying the fantasy, accumulating knowledge – no longer the estranged, detached, rational viewer that neo-modernist filmmakers solicited (Cohen, 2001, pp.152–63). The massive home consumption of films on video and now DVD has been an integral part of this process, leading to the growth of the 'popular archivist', the collector who amasses a home library of films (Klinger, 2001, pp.132–51). The collector's cineliteracy does not presume the academic or systematic acquisition of knowledge, but rather the enthusiasm of the autodidact which may well include classical film noir as these films have been assiduously marketed by video companies as worthy of the film 'connoisseur'. Hence the growth of cult films as opposed to 'great films'; cult films, which include many noirs, are ones that 'become the property of any audience's private space' and which can be enjoyed in a variety of ways (Corrigan, 1992, pp.80–5). This said, some clear divisions within contemporary taste remain. The straight-to-cable noirs are aimed at 18–30 year old males who are looking for 'good-quality B movies – B for beer, biriani and bonking'.[4] Indie noirs appeal to older and better educated audiences, looking for thought-provoking pictures in the absence of the widespread distribution of European films (Hillier, 1993, p.31).

NOIR STYLE: EXCESS AND HYBRIDITY

The two paradigm films delineated the leading tendencies of postmodern noir, either a careful attention to an overall mood in which the style strives for a generic purity where all the elements work in unison, as in *Body Heat*; or the hybridized 'excess' that characterized *Blade Runner* (Collins, 1993, pp.242–63). The former style was dominant in the 1980s and included John Dahl's accomplished first noir *Kill Me Again* (1989) where Jacques Steyn's smooth, languorous tracking shots carefully establish time and place including the entry of the *femme fatale* Fay (Joanne Whalley Kilmer) into Reno where the night-time neon signs glide sinuously over the car windscreen, or the blue-filtered night exteriors are wreathed in mist as the private eye Jack (Val Kilmer) dumps the car to fake Fay's death.

The latter style dominates the 1990s by which time *Blade Runner* had become a cult film and gained a theatrical re-release. In these films the tight economy of the classical period is completely abandoned. Instead, every aspect of the viewing experience is intensified: a spectacular mise-en-scène, insistent multichannel soundtracks and running times that are often over two hours (Dixon, 2000, pp.4–5). Editing and camerawork tend to be taken to extremes using a hypermobile camera, rapid zooms, shock cuts and ultrafast montage sequences. As Thomas Elsaesser argues, disruptive spectacle is now preferred to coherent diegesis or causality. Instead of being solicited as the ideal observer of the unfolding action, the postmodern spectator is now 'engulfed' in an often overwhelming sensory experience, a virtual spectacle that viewers inhabit rather than watch (Elsaesser, 1998, pp.242–63). Contemporary films are often 'modular', consisting of loosely connected set pieces, bursts of energy and excitement, that cause them to resemble music videos or advertisements (Wyatt, 1994, pp.17–23). In Dahl's *Unforgettable* (1995), his first high-budget noir made for MGM/UA, the camera movements are more extravagant, the use of blue-grey filters for the interiors more pronounced and the saturated colour gels that pick out Seattle's neon signs in the night-time city, more strident. *Unforgettable*'s organization is modular, concentrating on the intense moments when Dr David Krane (Ray Liotta), a police pathologist, relives the experiences of the victims of a serial killer, including his wife, by injecting himself with a serum based on their spinal fluids, a variation on the Jekyll and Hyde archetype. These moments are conveyed through spectacular, disorientating montages that burst onto the screen; the images rush over the viewer, some in slow motion, but all in a whirl of angles that approximate the confusions of memory. They are anchored by shots of Krane himself physically experiencing the events. Such is the power of these moments that they tend to overshadow the intervening narrative, which often slides into melodramatic cliché.

One of the most influential recent noirs has been David Fincher's *Seven* (1995) where these two tendencies are combined. *Seven*'s cinemtographer, Darius Khondji, an admirer of German Expressionism as well as Greg Toland, demonstrated the eloquent subtlety that is now possible with modern high-speed negatives that provide exceptional sharpness at very low lighting levels. Khondji used a sombre, oligochromatic colour register, 'composed of a very limited, closely related range of colours: white, cream, grey, slate, ochre, beige, brown, black and dirty, acidic greens' (Dyer, 1999, p.62). In postproduction, silver, normally eliminated to save money, was put back in order to give the blacks greater richness and desaturating other colours. The processing was graduated so that in some scenes the blacks were less dense according to the overall mood (Darke, 1996, pp.18–20). In this way each interior is a shadowy and confusing labyrinth in which the horror of the serial killer's 'artistic' crimes are gradually revealed, but also partly obscured, allowing an audience's imagination to work. Fincher withholds establishing shots, and the partially glimpsed unidentified city (inspired by *Blade Runner*), which is insistently noisy and soaked in perpetual rain, is the perfect breeding ground for such a killer. The final scene, the only one shot in sunlight amidst an open country landscape, is the most horrific.

THEMES AND NARRATIVE PATTERNS

Postmodern noir's 'excess' is also evident in its themes and narrative patterns. The paranoia, alienation, existential fatalism and Freudian psychopathology that were the core themes of classical noir have been retained but intensified. In Steven Soderbergh's *The Underneath* (1995), a remake of Siodmak's *Criss Cross*, the motives of its protagonist Michael Chambers (Peter Gallagher) are more ambiguous and enigmatic than those of his predecessor (Burt Lancaster). Michael's compulsive gambling appears both destructive, alienating his loving girlfriend Rachel (Alison Elliott), and unfathomable, part of Michael's alienation, the self-negating contradictions of a man without qualities (Andrew, 1998, pp.272–3). The Freudian elements are played up as it is Michael's stepfather who is killed in the armoured van robbery and the suspicious police investigator is his own brother David (Adam Trese), who seems to harbour homoerotic desires towards his younger brother as well as desiring Rachel. In Soderbergh's fatalistic universe there is no romantic finale, only deceit and betrayal. As Rachel drives off with the money, she is followed by the corrupt boss of the security firm (Joe Don Baker).

Many postmodern noirs retain classic noir's conception of the corrupt city including future noirs such as Kathryn Bigelow's apocalyptic *Strange Days* (1995) set in end-of-the-millennium Los Angeles, or Curtis Hanson's enthralling *L.A. Confidential* (1997) set in the 1950s, adapted from the third instalment of James Ellroy's four-part 'secret history' of Los Angeles which exposes an endemic corruption and deceit. But the new development was 'country noir' set amidst the wide-open spaces of redneck America (Orr, 1998, pp.210–21). Country noir is anti-pastoral, the countryside is no longer the innocent, wholesome idyllic retreat from the depraved city that it was in *Out of the Past* or *The Asphalt Jungle*, but claustrophobic and corrupt, its small towns – 'two bit shitholes in the middle of nowhere' as the villain in *Breakdown* (1997) puts it – riven by incest and murderous hatreds. The panoramic establishing shots, often arresting in their beauty, serve only as an ironic contrast to the sordid dramas that unfold. The paradigm film was *Blood Simple* (1984). It opens with a montage of shots that evoke the bleak, barren Texan landscape, with its sleazy motels, sinister incinerators and a dead buzzard on one of the ramrod-straight highways that seem to go nowhere. The narrator – 'what I know about is Texas, and down here, you're on your own' – is the reptilian private detective Visser (M. Emmet Walsh) in his canary yellow suit and stetson hat, prepared to do anything if the price is right. Inspired by Dashiell Hammett's *Red Harvest* – which contains the observation that after a murder a man 'goes soft in the head, blood-simple' – and James M. Cain, *Blood Simple* is a highly complex tale of adultery, betrayal, but above all the false suspicions and confusion that characterize this ingrown community. The lugubrious Marty (Dan Hedaya), owner of the Neon Boots bar with its tawdry flamboyance, employs Visser first to spy on and then kill his wife Abby (Frances McDormand) and his employee Ray (John Getz), only to be double-crossed and shot by Visser. Ray, finding Marty in his office and believing Abby shot him, tries to dispose of the body in a deserted field. In a blackly comic scene he has to club the partially recovered Marty with a spade before burying him alive. Visser, wrongly assuming the couple know about his deception, kills Ray but is finally killed by Abby in another grotesquely violent and protracted scene where she imagines it is Marty who is attacking her.

Blood Simple is a rich hybrid of noir, Greek tragedy, southern Gothic, Grand Guignol and the low-budget horrors Ethan Coen had previously worked on, shot in an intricate style that recalled Bertolucci as well as Hitchcock, Lang and Welles, providing sophisticated entertainment for a cineliterate audience (Hinson, 1986, p.14). Its influence is clearly visible in John Dahl's *Kill Me Again* (1989) and *Red Rock West* (1992), slow-paced, intricately plotted tales of double and triple cross set in the yawning mountain and desert landscapes of Nevada and Wyoming respectively, Oliver Stone's *U Turn* (1997) located in the depths of Arizona, or the Coens' own *Fargo* (1996), a 'white noir', set in the wintry snow-filled landscapes of their home state of Minnesota with its resonantly named town Brainerd.

NARRATIVE PATTERNS

Postmodern noir's excess is also evident in its highly complex narratives where the convoluted plots often circle back on themselves, and by a pervasive uncertainty about the reliability of what is being shown or told. A flashback structure is common, but, as John Orr notes, postmodern flashbacks are more visceral, oblique and ambiguous than their classical predecessors

(Orr, 2000, p.158). In Indie noirs, such as Peter Medak's *Romeo Is Bleeding* (1994) and Bryan Singer's *The Usual Suspects* (1995), this unreliability is pushed towards a radical indeterminacy. In *Romeo Is Bleeding* the confessional flashback narrative of corrupt New York cop Jack Grimaldi (Gary Oldman), told to an imaginary interlocutor, is self-serving and deceitful (Martin, 1997, pp.131–7). He becomes increasingly emotionally entangled in the events he is relating, rearranging their sequence and distorting others' motives. Grimaldi's recollections are frequently interrupted by dream sequences, making it unclear whether the whole story is real or a self-lacerating fantasy created out of a profound fear and mistrust of women. The final scene, in which his wife Natalie appears and then fades away, calls into question her existence, Grimaldi's story of secreted money, and his whole narrative. In *The Usual Suspects*, the events that led up to the opening explosion are narrated by Verbal Kint (Kevin Spacey) under interrogation. Kint's story zigzags back towards this starting point in a series of flashbacks that unfold events in meticulous detail, but explain nothing. It may all be embroidered from the names he sees on the police noticeboard in the interrogation room. Kint may or may not be the monstrous Keyser Soze whom he identifies as the evil genius behind the robbery. Nothing definite is resolved as the film allows us no access to an objective viewpoint. *The Usual Suspects'* popularity shows that contemporary audiences can cope with ambiguity and uncertainty.

Christopher Nolan's *Memento* (2000), set in present-day Los Angeles, is an extreme version of the noir tradition of amnesiac narratives. Insurance investigator Leonard Shelby (Guy Pearce) has lost his short-term memory through a head injury and the trauma of his wife's rape and murder. Not only does he blunder around in a confused state, taking Polaroid photographs to provide him with memories or consulting messages written on post-it notes or tattooed or drawn on his body, but the action happens in reverse, often literally, working backwards from Shelby's shooting of a man called Teddy, convinced he is his wife's murderer from the 'evidence' of a Polaroid photograph with its caption 'Don't believe his lies. He is the one. Kill him.' But in the course of the narrative, in which he trusts a woman, Natalie (Carrie-Anne Moss) who appears to betray him, it becomes clear that Shelby's own motives are suspect and that he may have accidentally killed his wife through a lethal dose of insulin and constructed a fabricated narrative to hide this appalling possibility. At one point he asks himself 'Do I lie to make myself happy?' only to reject this notion and continue his pursuit of the 'killer', becoming both victim and murderer (Darke, 2000, pp.42–3). This basic confusion of roles is part of *Memento's* thoroughgoing jumble of subjective and objective states where it is impossible to separate 'facts' and knowledge from lies or self-protecting fantasies, pushing generic fiction close to the radical ambiguity associated with European art house cinema.

CHARACTERIZATION AND GENDER

Male Protagonists: Drifters and Victims

Body Heat's reworking of the Cain paradigm retained noir's central male protagonist: the victim, duped by the lure of sex and success. All the 'country noirs' have their male victims, outmanoeuvred and outsmarted by women. In Dennis Hopper's *The Hot Spot* (1990), Harry Maddox (Don Johnson), an archetypal drifter, finally accepts a fallen world: 'I've found my level. Now I'm living it', muses Harry as he lolls back in the front seat of the car beside a woman he knows will betray him without a second thought. In that memorable phrase Harry defines the morality of the new postmodern victim.

To the conventional cast of itinerant or lower-middle-class victims, postmodern noir has added the upper middle-class dupe in a subcycle of 'yuppie horror' films that included *Bad Influence* (1990), *Shattered* (1991), *Poison Ivy* (1992) and *The Temp* (1993) (Grant, 1998, pp.280–93). These films express a yuppie paranoia that even the most well fortified bourgeois home can be breached or that the plush office is no longer safe from destructive rivals. Michael Douglas appeared in several noirs, including *Fatal Attraction* (1989) discussed below, where 'normal' (white middle-class) masculinity was in 'crisis'. In *Disclosure* (1994), he played Tom Sanders, a computer executive, seduced and supplanted by his new boss Meredith Johnson (Demi Moore), whose advances are the screen for a corporate take-over engineered by the managing director Bob Garvin (Donald Sutherland), thereby combining the corrupt patriarch with the yuppie *femme fatale*. The overweening lawyer was the favourite victim: Harrison Ford in *Presumed Innocent* (1990) or Kenneth Branagh in Altman's *The Gingerbread Man* (1997), which returns to one of noir's roots in southern Gothic.

The Rogue Cop

In postmodern noir it seems that only Afro-American actors are allowed to play decent cops: Morgan Freeman's cultivated black Sherlock Holmes in *Seven* (1995), *Kiss the Girls* (1997) and *Along Came a Spider* (2001), or Denzel Washington in *The Bone Collector* (1999). The white policeman is psychotic, another characteristic of conventional masculinity in crisis, but extending noir's established tradition of rogue cops. Many films use the *Doppelgänger* motif. In *Tightrope* (1984) detective Wes Block (Clint Eastwood) shares many disturbing characteristics with the serial killer he pursues relentlessly through the New Orleans *demi-monde*. Mike Figgis's *Internal Affairs* (1990) explores the duel between the corrupt Dennis Peck (Richard Gere) and the arrow straight Raymond Avila (Andy Garcia) investigating his activities for the bureau of internal affairs. In ways that recalled *Touch of Evil* because of Avila's insecurity as an Hispanic outsider in a white community, a complex psychic and emotional exchange takes place between the outgoing, sensual, but ruthless Peck and the repressed, impotent and puritanical Avila, around the figure of Avila's successful yuppie wife. In *Unlawful Entry* (1992) Ray Liotta played an outwardly charming and attractive cop who has become perilously violent and psychotic through his dealing with 'scum'. In a different spin on the 'yuppie horror' motif, he is the dark self of the young executive (Kurt Russell), married to the woman they both desire. *Copland* depicted the establishment of an entire rogue community.

Damaged Men, Psychopaths and Serial Killers

These rogue cops were part of wider contemporary fascination for damaged, psychopathic male protagonists. The revival of interest in the fiction of Jim Thompson with five recent adaptations – *The Kill-Off* (1989), *After Dark, My Sweet* (1990), *The Grifters* (1990), *The Getaway* (1994) and *This World, Then the Fireworks* (1997) – demonstrated this trend, as Thompson's fiction deals with difficult psychological terrain, even for film noir. The protagonist of *After Dark, My Sweet*, played by Jason Patric in James Foley's adaptation, is a brain-damaged ex-boxer, haunted by memories of the fight in which he killed his opponent, struggling to make sense of his apparently aimless existence and the deeper meaning of the kidnapping that he has been sucked into with the neurotic, alcoholic widow (Rachel Ward) and the venal 'Uncle Bud' Stoker (Bruce Dern). It is unclear whether his apparent idiocy is an act or gives him the sublime wisdom of the holy fool and whether the final sacrifice of his life will redeem Rachel. Is it nobly heroic, misguided or infantile?

Michael Oblowitz's *This World, Then the Fireworks* uses a surrealistic-Gothic style to render the strange, distorted world of Marty Lakewood (Billy Zane) locked into a destructive, incestuous relationship with his sister Carol (Gina Gershon). The pair's corruption stems from a childhood trauma when they witnessed their father kill his neighbour after being caught making love to the man's wife. As Marty comments in laconic voice-over 'The man on the floor didn't have any head, hardly any head at all. And that was funny, wasn't it . . . Dad and the woman. Dad who went to the electric chair, and the woman who committed suicide. Standing there naked.' Forged in this moment, neither Marty nor Carol recognize any moral boundaries to their actions, which include poisoning their mother when she turns on them. Like all Thompson's protagonists, they have moved beyond good and evil.

This interest in amoral, disturbed personalities has been most fully developed in a distinct subgenre of noir-horrors that depict the serial killer, the ultimate transgressor, a mythical figure composed of Gothic elements (the 'fatal man' and the vampire) together with the deviant criminal and noir psychopath (Simpson, 2000, p.15). This mixture shows the deep parallels between the Gothic and the postmodern including eclectic appropriations, indeterminacy of meaning, fluidity of gender, and a fascination with terror, evil, the repulsive, sex and death (Smith, 1996, pp.6–19). All of these facets are condensed in serial killer narratives which are themselves hybrids of Gothic romance, police procedural, murder mystery, horror story and noir thriller.

One type of serial killer is the neo-primitive white trailer trash. The narrative of *Kalifornia* (1993) takes the form of an inverted westwards journey in which the middle-class researcher Brian (David Duchovny) the bookish liberal, discovers America's Third World and its elemental amoral killers like Early Grayce (Brad Pitt) with his strange visions. Oliver Stone's *Natural Born Killers* (1994) argued that its outlaw couple Mickey (Woody Harrelson) and Mallory (Juliette Lewis), two conscienceless killers, were produced by a contemporary American society and media that was in love with crime and violence, turning killers into celebrities. The other type of serial killer was the criminal mastermind, most famously embodied by Hannibal 'the Cannibal' Lecter in three films based on Thomas Harris's novels: *Manhunter* (1986), *Silence of the Lambs* (1991) and *Hannibal* (2001). *Seven* (1995), whose style has already been discussed, is the darkest of these 'mastermind' films. Its hyperintelligent murderer 'John Doe' (Kevin Spacey) parodies the expected behaviour of the 'classic' serial killer.

Hommes fatals

In postmodern noir the *homme fatal* is no longer confined to period Gothic, but fully contemporary (Cohen, 1992–3, p.114). The new figure emerged in *Jagged Edge* (1985) where Jeff Bridges played a highly desirable and attractive widower, immaculately groomed, rich, affable and apparently innocent of his wife's murder. His lawyer Teddy (Glenn Close) falls in love with him, clinging to her emotional belief in goodness until she finally shoots him when, masked and knife-wielding, he attacks her in the same way as he murdered his wife in the film's opening scene, an attack that resembles a violent rape by an unknown assailant. The lawyer-client relationship was repeated in Sidney Lumet's *Guilty as Sin* (1993) with Don Johnson and Rebecca de Mornay. *Masquerade* (1988), *Betrayed* (1988) and *A Kiss Before Dying* (1991) were more conventional uses of the type, but *Deceived* (1991) was consistently inventive in the unexpected depths of the *homme fatal's* deceit. Jack Saunders (John Heard) has constructed a series of surrogate identities for himself as he overcompensates for his deprived background.

Femmes fatales

The most striking character type in postmodern film noir is the *femme fatale*, so conspicuously absent in modernist noir. Several commentators identify the paradigm film as the hugely successful *Fatal Attraction* (1989) where Glenn Close plays a glamorous, successful and sexually insatiable single professional woman whose propensity for psychotic violence threatens the bemused, frightened yuppie (Michael Douglas) and his family. Unlike her 1940s forebears, the new *femme fatale* competes with her male victim in the job market as well as seducing him, but her transgressions continue to be expunged by death. In *Fatal Attraction* the wronged wife, homebuilder and good mother, who has the strength that the infatuated male victim lacks, kills her rival. The film's traditional sexual politics were often read as a backlash against feminism; but it is noticeable that it is women's resourcefulness not male prowess that the film celebrates (Pidduck, 1995, pp.65–72). The *femme fatale* is the staple of the erotic thriller that dominates the marketplace including the straight-to-cable *Body Chemistry* (1990) and *Sexual Malice* (1994), but also high-budget versions including *Body of Evidence* (1992), which reduced the trangressive performativity of Madonna to a conventional, if characteristically excessive, sexual spectacle. In demonic form the figure recurs as the vampiric psycho-femme in 'slasher-noirs', such as *The Hand That Rocks the Cradle* (1991) with its crazed nanny (Rebecca de Mornay), and *Single White Female* (1992), which hybridize melodrama and horror with noir in which the victims are primarily women. *Single White Female* mingles lesbian desire with murderous intentions as Hedy (Jennifer Jason Leigh), traumatized by guilt about causing the death of her twin sister in childhood, attempts to steal the identity of her flat-mate Allie (Bridget Fonda) by first resembling, then destroying her rival.

Paul Verhoeven's *Basic Instinct* (1991), which made a star of Sharon Stone as the seductress Catherine Trammell, was one of the most successful and widely discussed examples. Catherine is an amalgam of male fantasies – blonde, beautiful, wealthy (an heiress), successful (a best-selling authoress) and erotically uninhibited – and fears: bisexual (does she prefer women?), insatiable, highly intelligent and probably homicidal, suspected of the violent murder of a retired rock star with which the film begins. Like Phyllis Dietrichson in *Double Indemnity*, Catherine is witty and provocative, and, in the permissive 1990s, allowed to talk directly about sex in front of her police interrogators – 'Are you sorry he's dead?' 'Yes. I liked fucking him'. She is overpoweringly desirable to Nick (Michael Douglas) another unstable cop with a hair-trigger, known as 'The Shooter'. 'All accidents?' Catherine goads as she tells Nick that he is the subject of her new novel. As their relationship develops, it is Catherine who always appears in control, verbally and physically. In the final scene, the killer apparently apprehended, Nick rolls over comfortably in bed beside her musing about their future together, only for the camera to close in on the ice pick, the killer's preferred weapon, under their bed. Verhoeven's misogynist gloss on the ambiguous ending is that

Catherine will simply wait another few months before murdering Nick and that 'her behaviour only makes sense when you really assume she's the devil' (quoted in Cohan, 1998, p.267). Indeed, *Basic Instinct* marks all its women – Catherine, Beth, Roxy and Hazel – as bisexual killers, creating a generalized fear about the homicidal sexual violence of the castrating female psychotic or *femme castratic* (Creed, 1993, p.123).

Basic Instinct was a controversial film. Verhoeven's graphic and explicit style – the frequent sex scenes are shot like a soft-porn film, which then explodes into frenzied, horrific violence – deliberately pushed at what was permissible in mainstream cinema. It generated protests from gay and lesbian groups who objected to the association of bisexuality with psychotic violence. But although Stone is clearly offered as an erotic object, she is also more than that. Even the notorious interrogation scene, where Catherine flashes her crotch at the assembled officers, is a critique of male voyeurism rather than a simple endorsement. *Basic Instinct*'s male victim is not sympathetic – Nick is complacent, crudely carnal and unstable – the attractive figure is Catherine who offers potential pleasures for women viewers as a strong character with wit and style, enjoying sex and money but not punished for her appetites.

The figure of the successful, unrepentant *femme fatale* reached its apotheosis in John Dahl's *The Last Seduction* (1994) where Bridget Gregory (Linda Fiorentino) lays waste all the men who cross her path. Bridget is another

The ultimate *femme fatale*? Linda Fiorentino in *The Last Seduction* (John Dahl, 1994)

successful professional, first shown bossing her male workers in the office to increase sales, who moonlights in drug deals with her vain husband Clay (Bill Pullman) whom she double crosses. Bridget embodies the yuppie ethos of upward mobility, ambition and greed, city qualities that she takes with her in her flight upstate from New York into 'cow country', where she seduces the hick Mike (Peter Berg) who has failed in his attempt to break away from his small town. Mike is fascinated and appalled by Bridget's belligerent sexuality which is detached from any romantic feelings, where her demonstrations of soft, vulnerable femininity are simply a performance – 'Maybe I could love you . . . Will that do?' – a self that she can display and discard at will. The hapless Mike is drawn into her scheme to kill Clay, where, in a final double cross that inverts the woman-as-victim scenario, she goads Mike into raping her as she dials the emergency number, ensuring that he is caught by the police and blamed for Clay's murder. In the final shots Bridget climbs into a gleaming limousine, betraying none of the discontent that seems to haunt Matty at the end of *Body Heat*.

The Last Seduction has a postmodern playfulness and irony that allows Bridget to 'have it all': power, sexuality, femininity and wealth. As Stella Bruzzi notes, *The Last Seduction* recontextualizes the erotic attractiveness of the *femme fatale* 'within a narrative constructed around a female subject' whose hard-edged image is under her own control, not simply a trap for men even if it can be used in that way (Bruzzi, 1997, p.128). Like Catherine Trammell, Bridget offers a post-feminist image of a strong and attractive woman who is both feminine and feminist, uniting what were previously incompatible qualities in a way that is particularly appealing to young women.[5]

The Independent Woman

'Successful' *femmes fatales* who go unpunished are part of contemporary Hollywood's wider investment in the figure of the independent woman which is often more robust than the fragile and circumscribed image that was developed during the classic period. Several postmodern noirs have used women investigators: Kathleen Turner played Sara Paretsky's serial private eye in *V. I. Warshawski* (1991); Jodie Foster was an FBI agent in *Silence of the Lambs* (1991); *Betrayed* (1988) and *Impulse* (1990) have Debra Winger and Theresa Russell respectively as undercover investigators; Linda Fiorentino plays a homicide detective in *Bodily Harm* (1995). All these women experience the attraction of criminal figures or lifestyles, both thrilling and forbidden, which foregrounds questions of desire and sexuality in situations which are both threatening and exciting and which are specific to the investigator's gender (Tasker, 1993, pp.91–113). This was developed in a different ways by *Black Widow* (1987) where Russell and Winger were paired. Russell played the glamorous *femme fatale*, Winger the drab FBI investigator who becomes sexually obsessed by her quarry who acts as her dark self, prepared to murder to attain the lifestyle that both crave.

Several films constructed a strong version of the 'wronged woman', one who displays miracles of tenacity and courage to undertake her revenge. *Eye for an Eye* (1995) and *Double Jeopardy* (1999) have typically middle-class female professionals, but *Mortal Thoughts* (1991) was one of the very few recent noirs to depict working-class women. *Mortal Thoughts* is told almost entirely through the flashbacks of an unreliable narrator, Cynthia (Demi Moore). As her story disintegrates under questioning, it nevertheless reveals the profound bond of loyalty between Cynthia and her best friend Joyce (Glenn Headly), forged in childhood, but cemented through the brutal or venal actions of their despicable husbands. The film consistently shows Joyce being abused by her husband Jimmie (Bruce Willis), 'but only Cynthia ever tries to intervene. Everyone else regards violence as an integral part of working-class marriage' (Holmlund, 1993, p.142). Both men resent their wives' friendship, seeing it as a threat and an accusation that their emotional and psychological needs cannot be satisfied by men, and both react by violence, either physical or legal. Cynthia kills Jimmie in self-defence when he tries to rape her; later Joyce kills Cynthia's husband who was threatening to take her children away from her.

Overall, as Sharon Willis argues, films about *femmes fatales* and independent women mobilize a pervasive anxiety about gender boundaries and the new dynamics of sexual relationships, dramatizing a central confusion about what men want from these women and what the women themselves ultimately desire (Willis, 1997, pp.60–97). Where classical and modernist noir almost always adopted a male perspective, postmodern noirs have been much more prepared to offer a female one, particularly in the films of women directors.

WOMEN DIRECTORS AND FILM NOIR

Under the notoriously patriarchal studio system women were rarely in positions of power in the creative process. A woman director, such as Ida Lupino who made several noirs including *The Hitch-Hiker* (1953), was an exceptional figure. Though far from genuinely hospitable, contemporary Hollywood is more accommodating and several women directors have left independent cinema for mainstream film-making, where their work has helped to deconstruct the gender politics of popular genres including film noir. Mary Lamb's *Siesta* (1987) invested a female protagonist (Ellen Barkin) with the disturbed paranoia of the noir male in an oneiric, ambiguous art-thriller. Tamra Davis's *Guncrazy* (1993), which struggled to find wide distribution but gradually became known through word of mouth, reworked the outlaw couple motif and in particular Joseph H. Lewis's 1950 film of the same name, by privileging the subjectivity and experiences of the woman partner, Anita (Drew Barrymore). Lizzie Borden's *Love Crimes* (1991) was a 'woman's psychothriller' which, like *Sleeping with the Enemy* (1991), *Copycat* (1995) and *Double Jeopardy*, depicts the ways in which women try to overcome their own victimization by men. *Love Crimes* reworked this subgenre because it was prepared to explore how women might collude in their own erotic exploitation, though Miramax cut four scenes that dealt explicitly with sexual perversity (Lane, 2000, pp.138–9). The film's heroine Dana (Sean Young) is a repressed, masculinized professional woman, an assistant district attorney, whose pursues a sensual but sadistic photographer David Hanover (Patrick Bergin), who specializes in luring women into performing their sexual fant-asies while he photographs them. This encounter releases her own childhood trauma of being locked in the closet while her father slept with various women and witnessing his murder of her mother when she found out. In a complex psychic exchange between the two, David begins to understand his vulnerability and Dana her own masochistic tendencies, her desire to be both aroused and dominated. Borden's challenging film refuses to offer any easy resolution to these issues.

Equally complex was Kathryn Bigelow's *Blue Steel* (1990), a noir police procedural thriller with a female protagonist. Contemporary Hollywood affords many examples of action heroines in what were previously male-only genres, but, like Linda Hamilton in the 'Terminator' films, they are often presented as replicas of their male counterparts. In contrast, *Blue Steel*'s heroine, Megan Turner (Jamie Lee Curtis), is a woman caught in a web of contradictions. Her graduation as a police officer gives her confidence, self-belief, upward mobility, what she sees as a clear identity and is a statement that she will never be subjected to domestic abuse like her mother. But her role and her phallic weaponry make her the prey of the psychotic serial killer Eugene (Ron Silver), who becomes obsessed with Megan after seeing her shoot a supermarket robber on her first night's duty. Because Eugene secretly removed the thief's gun from the crime scene, Megan is suspended, forced to operate outside the law as both Eugene's target and his pursuer who wants revenge for the death of her best friend. In the process, Megan's dark side is revealed; she is both fascinated and appalled by her own capacity for violence and the consequences of her strangely enhanced sexuality. Eugene recognizes their kinship – 'We're two halves of the same person' – an association she must repudiate in her increasingly frenzied pursuit which leads to psycho-logical disturbance expressed through her tormented flashbacks. In the final confrontation she is in a trancelike state. Bigelow's slow-motion photography, odd juxtapositions of place and time and oneiric imagery create an ambiguity about the scene's ontological status, dream or fantasy? After Eugene's death Megan sits immobile, as if she had killed part of herself (Margolis, 1993, p.72). Like Borden, Bigelow refuses to simplify the complexities of sexual politics whose disturbing ambiguities contribute significantly to the instabilities of gender roles that characterize postmodern noir.

BLACK NOIR

In separate but analogous ways, black directors have also tried to widen the parameters of neo-noir. Classic noir, reflecting the racist limitations of Hollywood cinema as a whole, very rarely attempted to deal with Afro-American experience (Lott, 1997, pp.81–101). Black characters were marginal figures, jazz musicians in hothouse dives or menials. The rare exceptions included *No Way Out* (1950) starring Sidney Poitier as a black middle-class doctor, the first of many roles in which Poitier was cast as an ebony saint (Bogle, 1994, pp.175–82), and *Odds Against Tomorrow* (1959), where the black criminal played by Harry Belafonte is eventually united in death with his racist white partner (Robert Ryan).[6]

A form of black cinema emerged in the 'blaxploitation' films of the early 1970s, notably *Shaft* (1971) in which Richard Roundtree's eponymous hero was the 'superspade', a bold, resourceful and intelligent private eye performing like a black James Bond (Leab, 1975, pp.248–63). Pam Grier starred as the resourceful action heroine in *Coffy* (1973), *Foxy Brown* (1974) and *Sheba Baby* (1975) – 'The baddest One-Chick Hit-Squad that ever hit town!' – who defeats white drugs gangs after being drugged, tortured and raped. For the first time the work of the black hard-boiled author Chester Himes reached the screen in *If He Hollers Let Him Go* (1968) and *Cotton Comes to Harlem* (1970), but these films were unrelated to other modernist noirs.[7]

After this cycle petered out, Afro-American film-making became the preserve of independent cinema, but was revived commercially through the merging of Indie and mainstream cinemas which affords innovative black directors such as Spike Lee the opportunity to have their films widely distributed. Mario Van Peebles's sensationalist *New Jack City* (1991) and John Singleton's *Boyz 'N the Hood* (1992), a coming of age story set in south central Los Angeles which gained critical acclaim and an Oscar nomination, convinced the majors of the commercial potential of black cinema (Lott, 1999, pp.211–28). Black noirs formed part of a wider project to reveal the complexity and heterogeneity of black experience, exploring what Manthia Diawara has labelled 'black rage': 'a set of violent and uncontrollable relations in black communities, induced by a sense of frustration, confinement and white racism' (Diawara, 1993, pp.261–78). *Dead Presidents* (1995), produced and directed by Allen and Albert Hughes, attempts to use the noir matrix to explore the story of a black Vietnam vet who cannot readjust to civilian life. Charles Burnett's *The Glass Shield* (1995) reversed the police procedural by centring on an idealistic young black cop who is assigned to a corrupt division. Bill Duke's *A Rage in Harlem* (1991), adapted from a Himes novel set in the 1950s, explored black rage, but also reconciliation, between violent and non-violent blacks: 'the tolerance the brothers arrive at for each other is an important message for the black community' (Duke, quoted in Hillier, 1993, p.158). Duke went on to direct *Deep Cover* (1992) where Larry Fishburne gave a compelling performance as a divided noir protagonist whose opening voice-over and flashback reveals that his decision to become a policeman derives from the time when as a ten-year-old he witnessed his junkie father killed when robbing a liquor store. His unwanted assignment to infiltrate and expose a drugs cartel by posing as a dealer, brings out all the contradictions of his situation including the suppressed rage and violence he feels. Eventually he vindicates himself by exposing the political machinations that lie behind the police operation.

The most widely discussed black noirs are the pair directed by Carl Franklin, *One False Move* (1992) and *Devil in a Blue Dress* (1995). The first was a noir road movie that subtly explored the complexities of interracial relationships through the figure of Fantasia (Cynda Williams) on the run in the company of two drug-dealing killers, her boyfriend Ray (Billy Bob Thornton) and his black partner Pluto (Michael Beach). Fantasia is heading home, returning to her roots in Star City, Arkansas, where she has a son. Captured by local police chief Dale 'Hurricane' Dixon (Bill Paxton) determined to make the major arrest that will fulfil his naive dreams of being a somebody, Fantasia or Lila as he knows her, reveals that the boy is Dale's son. After a bloody shoot-out in which Lila, Ray and Pluto die and Dale is badly injured, father and son meet for the first time, symbolic of the hope for a better future. Franklin never allows plot to dominate characterization or to obscure the tragic destiny of Lila/Fantasia who left Star City to become an actress and whose violent death provides the possible catalyst for change.

Devil in a Blue Dress (1995) was Franklin's high budget adaptation of Walter Mosley's best-selling novel set in 1948 Los Angeles. Easy Rawlins (Denzel Washington) is the archetypal veteran down on his luck and out of work, who accepts a job that requires his descent into the underworld. Tak Fujimoto's beautiful widescreen photography recalls *Chinatown*, but the presence of a black protagonist forces an audience to understand familiar scenes from a new perspective, to observe how his colour creates barriers and threats at every turn. In the course of the action – his search for a black woman who is passing as white, itself a comment on segregation – the social and cultural spaces of the city are rewritten with the white world shown as the site of terror, brutality and alienation (Naremore, 1998, pp.249–53). Unlike *Chinatown*, the black suburb where Easy owns a bungalow is an uncontaminated haven of peace and security to which he finally returns. As a group, black noirs have not only mapped out a new terrain for the genre, but can be invested with hopes for redemption and reconciliation that 'white' noir conspicuously lacks.

THE POSTMODERN NOIR *AUTEUR*

The development of Indie cinema has created a space for the avant-garde *auteur* within American cinema, allowing the creative control and the development of a personal vision that is difficult to achieve in studio-based production. But, as Indie increasingly merges with mainstream practice, there is pressure to create more marketable genre films where the director's 'signature' is less evident. The role of the *auteur* has itself become more commodified, increasingly seen as a commercial strategy that is a highly marketable tool for selling films. Modern directors are encouraged to develop distinctive public personalities and their magazine interviews, appearances on chat shows and trailers are 'a commercial performance of *the business of being an auteur*' (Corrigan, 1992, p.104; original emphasis). These performances exist alongside their films as another way of capturing audience interest and creating a cult following. Although a case can be made for three postmodern noir *auteurs* – David Lynch, the Coen brothers and Quentin Tarantino – I have chosen to analyse Tarantino as he is the postmodern commodified artist *par excellence*.[8]

QUENTIN TARANTINO

Quentin Tarantino was *the* 1990s celebrity director whose films, published screenplays and personal appearances were all media events (Dawson, 1995, p.13). Tarantino has cultivated his persona as a 'film geek', someone who is passionately devoted to films, possessing enormous erudition and enthusiasm about trash culture. There are endless magazine articles and websites devoted to the minutiae of his work and six book-length studies that are journalistic rather than scholarly (Polan, 2000, pp.7–18, 64). His films have inspired numerous imitators – 'Tarantinees' – including Roger Avery's *Killing Zoe* (1993) for which Tarantino was executive producer (Levy, 1999, pp.144–51). Although the debate continues as to whether he is a clever but superficial and empty stylist, or a genuine *auteur*, there is no doubt that *Pulp Fiction* (1994) has become a contemporary classic, quintessentially postmodern, the most extreme of neo-noir hybrids.

The most obvious element of Tarantino's films is their obsessive allusions, verbally and visually, to an eclectic range of popular culture. Tarantino, whose idiom is as distinctive as Raymond Chandler's, populates his films with compulsive talkers, preoccupied with the telling distinctions that mark them as pulp connoisseurs, whether it be song lyrics, television programmes, varieties of fast food or movies. Their conversations show that the central experience of modern Americans is their engagement with the forms and images of popular culture, which shape memories, emotions, attitudes, a whole sense of being and identity. Visually, the films' narrative structures and mise-en-scène make reference not only to Hollywood genres, but to Hong Kong action cinema, spaghetti westerns (their choreographed violence and extreme close-ups recall Sergio Leone), Italian pulp horror (notably Mario Bava), as well as the French New Wave. Tarantino named his production company A Band Apart in *hommage* to the fresh, improvisatory playfulness of Godard's early films, which also characterizes his own film-making. These citations and borrowings summon up particular times, not only the 1970s culture in which Tarantino grew up, but also the 1940s and 1950s which, as a member of the video generation, he could experience almost as if they were part of the same, continuous cultural fabric. Images and songs circulate and recirculate in and through his films as if in an eternal present where all items can have a place, either cool or eccentric. Spotting these allusions is a central part of his films' appeal and their profusion – carried to deliberate excess in some scenes, notably when Vincent (John Travolta) and Mia (Uma Thurman) go to the 1950s retro restaurant Jack Rabbit Slim's in *Pulp Fiction* – encourages the repeated viewings or frame-by-frame inspection beloved of the fan. His main actors – Pam Grier, Harvey Keitel, John Travolta or Bruce Willis – are not only skilled performers, but icons whose presence summons up cycles of films.

If Tarantino's films are lavishly eclectic, their central reference point is crime fiction and film noir, but seen through the eyes of a postmodern sensibility that adapts and changes their form, which is why he insists 'I don't do neo-*noir*' (Tarantino, 1994, p.10). His style, very noticeably, eschews chiaroscuro. *Pulp Fiction* was shot by Andrej Sekula on 50 ASA film stock whose lustrous image was the closest contemporary equivalent to 1950s Technicolor (Woods, 2000b, p.71). Tarantino commented that he 'wanted to subvert the Hollywood staples, but with respect, not in a pastichey way', and to tell simple stories in a structurally complex manner (quoted in ibid., p.66). *Reservoir Dogs* (1991) updated the noir heist film – Huston's *Asphalt Jungle* or Kubrick's *The Killing* – and Lawrence Tierney's crime boss provided a link to that time, just as Harvey Keitel's Mr White was the link to the 1970s and Scorsese's modernist noirs which Tarantino admired. Its structural complexity – in which action sequences of the heist itself punctuate the prolonged aftermath in the warehouse – facilitate a depth of characterization as the various relationships between the gang members play themselves out. *Pulp Fiction*'s debt to noir was more pronounced but also less restrictive, a reinvention of the pulp thriller that 'made it challenging to myself and my audience' (quoted in ibid., p.108).

Pulp Fiction has an intricate narrative in which the time sequence is carefully rearranged so that the audience is continually trying to make sense of the events. It was partly inspired by *Le Doulos* which Tarantino described as 'my favourite screenplay of all time. You don't have any idea of what's going on until the last 20 minutes' (quoted in ibid., p.25). In *Pulp Fiction*, the characters circulate between three stories which helps build up audience interest and their temporal manipulation avoids ending either with the downbeat, banal death of hitman Vincent (John Travolta) or with the potentially excessive sentimentality of the escape of Butch (Bruce Willis), the battered pug making his bid for freedom. Instead it returns to the opening scene, the hold-up in the diner where Vincent's partner Jules (Samuel L. Jackson) spares the lives of the inexperienced 'outlaw couple' as part of his conversion to a mystical Christianity. Tarantino argued that his film was about mercy and redemption, but the scene is shot through with a characteristically postmodern irony that refuses to insist on this reading and is another circular narrative.

Dana Polan argues that *Pulp Fiction*'s narrative blends noir with sitcom, cartoons and comic strips, forms which allow for interruptions and suspensions, marked variations in the pacing of scenes or in the tone of events, and dramatic shifts from one storyline to another. This demands the constant alertness of young spectators used to 'channel-hopping', surfing the web, or playing computer games, together with a wide-eyed delight in the multiplicity of styles available in the electronic age (Polan, 2000, p.24ff.). Into this narrative flux, Tarantino inserts his carefully orchestrated set-piece scenes. When Butch makes the moral choice to rescue his erstwhile black boss Marcellus (Ving Rhames) from being sodomized by two psychotic white assailants in the basement of a general store, he reaches for a handy weapon. Butch rejects the mundane hammer he first picks up, then the baseball bat that Buford Pusser used in *Walking Tall*, then the chainsaw that alludes to Leatherface in *The Texas Chainsaw Massacre*, finally choosing the Samurai sword that was used by Tanaka Ken in *The Yakuza*. It is a typical Tarantino scene, mixing genuine emotion with horror, and black comedy that is funny even if all the references are not picked up. As in the ear-lopping scene in *Reservoir Dogs* or the earlier scene where Mia overdoses on heroin, its radical shift in tone confounds expectations and makes complex demands on the audience. Tarantino commented: 'I want to take these genre characters and put them in a real-life situation' (quoted in ibid., p.124).

Jackie Brown (1997) was Tarantino's first adaptation, based on Elmore Leonard's *Rum Punch* (1995), a modern pulp noir whose characters are ordinary people with modest dreams, which they still find difficult to realize. Tarantino takes the tone and mood, as well as much of the storyline, from Leonard, but crucially makes the heroine black not white. Tarantino's forty-something air hostess Jackie is played by Pam Grier, the blaxploitation icon. In this leisurely paced, elegiac film, Tarantino subtly delineates the hopes and fears of a middle-aged woman in a dead-end job who sees her big chance. At the centre of the film is her relationship with bail bondsman Max Cherry (Robert Forster) another middle-aged figure tired of 'nineteen years of this shit', who treats Jackie with admiration and old-fashioned chivalry. As Jackie, with $500,000 of stolen money, urges him to join her in flying to Spain, he hesitates too long and, in a poignant moment, stares into the now empty street. Jackie too is saddened, but she is a survivor and a winner, listening to 'Across 110th Street' on the car stereo, which celebrates breaking out of the ghetto.

Jackie Brown seemed an answer to Tarantino's detractors who held that he possessed the same adolescent sensibility as his core fans, adored clever talk and edgy violence (the film is less violent than Leonard's novel) and was incapable of understanding women. Jackie is, of course, not only a strong, intelligent and independent woman, but she is black which also seems a response to the somewhat racist black stereotypes in his earlier films. With its basically linear narrative and noticeably less allusive style, *Jackie Brown* shows Tarantino moving away from postmodern ironic playfulness towards a traditional concern with rounded characterization.

In the twenty years since the release of *Body Heat* in 1981, a time-span as long as the classical period, postmodern noir has established itself as a rich and complex body of films which represent an important contribution to contemporary Hollywood cinema. There is no sign that its production is slowing down; at time of writing the Coen brothers' latest neo-noir *The Man Who Wasn't There* (2001), shot in black and white, is about to receive its London première.[9] Postmodern noirs have engaged with many of the most significant issues in contemporary American culture, with alienation, racism, the role of women, male sexual fantasies, violence and paranoias and, perhaps above all, with the complexity of memory and identity, of the difficulty men and women currently have in locating themselves within a meaningful personal and social history. In these ways postmodern noir continues to explore some of the more difficult areas of contemporary experience, ones that are often suppressed or disavowed. As John Orr argues, film noir 'is the one genre which challenges the continuing power of money in the mythology of the American dream' (Orr, 1998, p.210).

Contemporary noirs are often hybrids, caught up in a web of transformations that are redefining the experience of cinema, the nature of cultural traditions and the relationships between past and present artefacts, and with that the constitution of popular genres. Jim Collins argues that genres no longer, as in the classical model, exhibit the traditional three-stage model of consolidation, variation and decline, but rather, in an era of 'hyperconscious intertextuality', we must now look for transformations across genres as part of 'the perpetual circulation and recirculation of signs that form the fabric of postmodern cultural life' (Collins, 1993, p.246). In this sense, postmodern film noir does not constitute a period in the same way as its predecessors, which is also why it shows no sign of ending.

NOTES

1. For a more positive account of postmodernism see Collins (1989).
2. There have also been numerous direct remakes. For a comprehensive study see Ronald Schwartz, *Noir, Now and Then* (2001).
3. *Blade Runner* is a 'cyberpunk' story, before the term was coined by William Gibson in his novel *Neuromancer* (1984). 'The link between noir and cyberpunk was neither superficial nor coincidental, but was connected to those "intolerable spaces", once *urban*, now *cyber*. The task of narrating urban alienation and separation now fell to the hybrid of crime fiction and science fiction that was cyberpunk' (Bukatman, 1997, p.51).
4. Dave Lewis of Medusa films (quoted in Williams, 1993, p.13).
5. For stimulating overviews see Jones (1991, pp.297–320); Stables (1998, pp.164–82); Read (2000).
6. Abraham Polonsky scripted *Odds Against Tomorrow*, often seen as the last of the 'classic' films noirs, but was uncredited because of blacklisting; see Buhle and Wagner (2001, pp.179–86).
7. Himes had been fired from Warner Bros. in 1942 when Jack Warner decreed that 'I don't want no niggers on this lot' (quoted in Millikins, 1976, p.56).
8. Lynch's influential *Blue Velvet* (1986) has been lucidly analysed by Atkinson (1997). The cryptic narrative of Lynch's other neo-noir, *Lost Highway* (1997), is explored in Warner (1997, pp.6–10). For studies of the Coens see Bergan (2000) and Mottram (2000).
9. *The Man Who Wasn't There*'s themes, characterization and visual style are discussed in 'Dead Man Walking' (2001) *Sight and Sound* 11 (10) pp.12–15.

CHAPTER NINE

British Film Noir

Film noir is not solely an indigenous American form. Other European cinemas have also created their own film noirs, notably France, Germany and Spain, where a *cine negro* which emerged in the 1950s continues to form a significant component within contemporary popular Spanish film-making (Jordan and Morgan-Tamosunas, 1998, pp.86–96, 101–5). However, it is arguably British cinema that has produced the second most important corpus of films noirs outside Hollywood. British film noir was part of the same broad cultural interaction that gave rise to its American counterpart, the meeting of blood melodrama with European modernism, and shares many of its characteristics, occupying a similar but somewhat longer period, 1938–64. Though influenced by American noir, British film noir has its own energies and distinctiveness, providing a vehicle for the exploration of the social and sexual discontents that bubbled under the surface of British life. For a long period British noir was forgotten, undefined or ignored, part of the 'lost continent' of British film-making: vulgar, unruly and critically despised (Petley, 1986, pp.110–11). However, accounts by William Everson, Robert Murphy, Laurence Miller and Tony Williams have begun the process of mapping out the terrain, which this chapter tries to build on and extend.[1]

THE PRODUCTION AND RECEPTION OF BRITISH FILM NOIR

There is as yet no definitive filmography of British film noir. Everson's 'rough and non-definitive check list' contains 135 British noirs for the 1938–63 period while Miller estimates that there are 331 examples between 1940 and 1959, 16.3 per cent of all feature film production, though he does not list the titles (Everson, 1987, pp.341–7, Miller, 1994, p.160). As in America, the early British noirs were a mixture of 'B' features and intermediates, both Gothic romances and crime thrillers, with the occasional more prestigious feature such as *Odd Man Out* (1947), directed by Carol Reed. The status of British noirs declined in the 1950s when they became more exclusively crime films, most of which were second features sold at a flat rental. These noirs were supplied by small production companies including Anglo-Amalgamated, Butchers, Danzigers (American brothers who started producing British films in 1955), Independent Artists, Tempean, and Hammer Films, reformed in 1947 as the production arm of the distribution agency Exclusive to supply low-budget British support features for the ABC cinema circuit (McFarlane, 1997, pp.48–70). All were capable of producing interesting and imaginative noirs – Anglo-Amalgamated's *Street of Shadows* (1953) or *Face of a Stranger* (1964); Butcher's *There Is Another Sun* (US title: *Wall of Death*, 1950); Independent Artists' *The Man in the Back Seat* (1961); Tempean's *Impulse* (1955) co-written and directed by Cy Endfield; Hammer's *Thirty-Six Hours* (US title: *Terror Street*, 1954) and *The Stranger Came Home* (US title: *The Unholy Four*, 1954) directed by Terence Fisher – which stood out amidst the more formulaic noirs. This mode of film production reached its peak between 1959 and 1963 and although three-quarters of these were 'B' features, there were a number of important films.

Following the disappearance, around 1964, of the double bill and therefore the second feature, film noir lost its production base and indigenous crime films were replaced by Cold War spy thrillers and caper films funded by Hollywood Majors (Murphy, 1992, pp.215–18). Only the John le Carré adaptations – *The Spy Who Came in from the Cold* (1965), *The Deadly Affair* (1966) and *The Looking Glass War* (1969) – with their webs of deceit, betrayal and paranoia, had noir elements. Hammer produced a series of sub-*Diaboliques* thrillers beginning with *Taste of Fear* (1961), written and produced to a rigid formula by Jimmy Sangster, where a beautiful, innocent young woman is preyed on by an older *femme fatale* and her scheming lover, a mini-cycle that petered out by the late 1960s. After that point, only the occasional film noir surfaced, notably *Performance* (1970) and *Get Carter* (1971), both financed by Hollywood studios (MGM and Warner Bros. respectively) just before the withdrawal of American finance which blighted the British film industry in the 1970s (Walker, 1986, pp.441–65). They were isolated examples, which could not generate a cycle of films. The history of British neo-noir is characterized by short bursts of activity, quiescence and the occasional important film, not a sustained development, as British film production limped along behind a culturally ascendant television industry. The situation altered to some extent in the 1990s as cinema became more buoyant. A populist, post-modern British cinema emerged that included made-for-cable noirs such as *Killing Time* (1998), and an important cycle of gangster films whose main market was video rental.

British film noirs were often heavily censored. Although the British Board of Film Censors (BBFC) had no written code, its officials applied a harsh and rigid moral standard where murderers and other criminals must always be punished, while the police, the clergy, the monarchy and the armed forces were to be shown as free from any corruption. Several potential films noirs were halted at the scenario stage by the ferocity of censors' attacks. The Board's chief censor observed of *They Made Me a Fugitive* (US title: *I Became a Criminal*, 1947): 'This type of film is not to be encouraged as in my opinion it is far too sordid but I cannot see on what grounds we can turn it down' (Spicer, 2000, pp.121–4).

Reviewers were equally severe in their admonitions, which often revealed a deep-seated hostility towards what they perceived as a pernicious American influence on British cinema. *Sight and Sound*'s reviewer, Arthur Vesselo condemned *They Made Me a Fugitive* and several other 'morbid burrowings', because of their 'parade of frustration and violence, an inversion and disordering of moral values, a grasping into the grimier recesses of the mind' (Vesselo, 1947, p.120). He and several other critics saw these films as symptomatic of a pervasive 'morbidity' that had disturbing parallels to Weimar Germany after the end of the First World War. In the House of Commons, the Board of Trade Secretary Harold Wilson denounced the spate of films depicting 'diseased minds, schizophrenia, amnesia' which he thought aberrant and unpatriotic (quoted in Barr, 1986, p.14). These attacks died down in the 1950s largely because crime films were thought beneath notice. By the end of that decade a more liberal censorship regime under John Trevelyan was slightly more accommodating to noirs and reviewers were less morally censorious.

Despite this hostile climate, many British noirs were successful. *Odd Man Out* (1947), *They Made Me a Fugitive* (1947), *The Upturned Glass* (1947), *The October Man* (1948) and *Silent Dust* (1949) were all listed in the trade press as 'box-office winners', while *The Third Man* was the highest grossing British film of its release year, 1949, as was *The Blue Lamp* in 1950.[2] *Odd Man Out* was a prestige film, the others were all intermediates with popular stars. The success of the second features is impossible to judge, but their sheer number suggests a receptive audience, particularly young working-class males, estranged by the middle-aged, middle-class orientation of British film producers (Gans, 1959, pp.60–8). *Performance* (1970), *Get Carter* (1971) and *The Long Good Friday* (1980), though they attracted little critical approval at the time of their release and were not widely distributed, have established themselves as cult classics and enjoyed a theatrical re-release in the 1990s as part of the current 'gangster craze', while the 'Scottish noir' *Shallow Grave* was the top-grossing British film of 1995. At the time of writing, Mike Hodges' *Croupier* (1999) is enjoying considerable popularity on its re-release in Britain following its success in the States.

THE GENESIS OF BRITISH FILM NOIR

British noirs show the influence of German Expressionism, French Poetic Realism, Hollywood gangster films and the influx of émigré European talent, including set designer Alfred Junge, and cinematographers Mutz Greenbaum (Max Greene), Otto Heller, Erwin Hillier, Günther Krampf and Wolfgang Suschitzky (Gough-Yates, 1989, pp.135–66). During the McCarthyite era, various blacklisted American directors made noirs in Britain: Edward Dmytryk: *Obsession* (US title: *The Hidden Room*, 1949), Jules Dassin: *Night and the City* (1950), Robert Siodmak: *The Rough and the Smooth* (US title: *Portrait of a Sinner*, 1959) and several by Cy Endfield and Joseph Losey. Hitchcock's British crime thrillers were influential, notably the expressionist *The Lodger* (1926) and *Blackmail* (1929), and *The 39 Steps* (1935) and *Young and Innocent* (1937) with their falsely accused men-on-the-run. Fundamentally, like its American counterpart, British film noir developed from hard-boiled crime stories and Gothic fiction, but their polarity was reversed: in Britain the Gothic strand was, initially at least, the more powerful and important.

English Gothic Fiction

From its beginnings in the late eighteenth century, Gothic fiction has formed a vital and subversive element within English culture (Pirie, 1973, pp.11–21). 'Blood and thunder' Gothic melodrama became the staple of nineteenth-century British popular culture – on stage, in music-hall sketches, in the 'penny dreadfuls' and in the 'sensation novels' (James, 1976, pp.83–7; Mighall, 1999, pp.27–77). It exerted a potent influence on Dickens's novels, which had strong Gothic elements. The importance of this tradition to the development of British horror films has long been recognized, but it was also formative in the development of crime thrillers. James Chapman has drawn attention to the importance of the 'shocker', a combination of fast-paced action and the macabre, in 1930s British cinema (Chapman, 1998, pp.75–97).

The master of the shocker was Edgar Wallace whose fiction, with its gloomy Gothic dwellings, fiendish master criminals and trembling heroines, was adapted for the screen far more frequently than the better known English detective fiction; over fifty Wallace adaptations were made between 1925 and 1939. Like their Victorian forebears, 1930s shockers often critique the hypocrisies of the middle classes and the aristocracy who can be corrupt, sadistic, and frequently psychotic. Wallace's *The Frightened Lady*, filmed in 1932 and 1940, was set in a baronial mansion, Marks Priory, the seat of the Lebanons. Lady Lebanon, obsessed by continuing the dynasty, conceals the crimes of her mad son (Marius Goring) who uses a scarf to strangle his victims, an imitation of the Thuggee technique he observed during his so-journ in India.

Home-Grown Hard-Boiled

The other disreputable strand of British crime fiction was the Americanized school of hard-boiled writers that included John Creasey, James Curtis and Walter Greenwood, who alternated his social fiction with crime stories (Murphy, 1986, p.288). They appealed to male working-class readers, alien-ated by the middle-class tone and attitude of English detective fiction (Worpole, 1983, pp.29–48). James Hadley Chase (René Raymond) was the most sensational; his *No Orchids for Miss Blandish* (1939), a pastiche American gangster story, was a *cause célèbre* as novel, play and finally film, released in 1948 starring the American Jack la Rue. Peter Cheyney was highly successful with his short stories about the American private eye Lemmy Caution and a British (actually Irish) version, Slim Callaghan, which blended American laconic toughness with the refined elegance of the West End club.[3] Marcel Duhamel's translation of two novels by Cheyney and one by Chase formed the beginning of his *Série noire* from which French critics derived the noir label. Several of Arthur la Bern's novels, with their mixture of hard-boiled and Gothic elements, were adapted, notably *It Always Rains on Sunday* (1947) and *Good Time Girl* (1948). Gerald Kersh, whose novels were even more savage and macabre, wrote the 1938 thriller that formed the basis of Dassin's *Night and the City*. The market for these British pulps was stimulated by the war when servicemen could indulge their tastes free from the constraints of home and family (Chibnall, 1995, pp.131–49). This growth created a new breed of sensationalist publisher which generated a postwar paperback boom, whose covers were as lurid as their American rivals (Holland, 1993).

The writer who combined elements of both traditions was Graham Greene, whose evocative prose created its own sordid, seedy and venal world – 'Greeneland' – where paranoid, mentally disturbed and doomed anti-heroes lurk in shadows. Greene, strongly influenced by the French Poetic Realist films he wholeheartedly admired, attempted to create blood melodramas infused with the existential complexities of European modernism. His novels were able to 'dive below the polite level' of middle-class fiction and develop a 'poetic drama' of ordinary life that drew strength from Elizabethan and Jacobean revenge tragedy (Naremore, 1998, p.69). Greene's influence was felt on both sides of the Atlantic. American examples include *This Gun for Hire* (1942) based on the 1936 novel *A Gun for Sale*, and *The Ministry of Fear* (1944). Greene's 1938 novel *Brighton Rock* was filmed in Britain by the Boulting Brothers in 1948, but his most celebrated work was the original story and screenplay for *The Third Man*.

THE EXPERIMENTAL PERIOD: 1938–45

It was Greene who provided the story and adaptation for the first British noir, *The Green Cockatoo* (US title: *Four Dark Hours*), filmed in 1937. Mutz Greenbaum's chiaroscuro photography depicts London's shadowy *demi-monde*, Soho, the 'square mile of vice', with its sleazy nightclubs and vicious, marauding criminals who pursue the innocent couple (John Mills and René Ray). Only 65 minutes long, *The Green Cockatoo* was a Fox-British 'quota quickie' (produced very cheaply in order to fulfil quota requirements) that was not released in Britain until 1940 (Falk, 1990, p.14). By contrast, *They Drive by Night* (1938), adapted from a Curtis novel, was made after the passing of the 1938 Cinematograph Act that imposed a minimum cost requirement if films were to be eligible for the British quota. Warner-British lavished considerable care and attention on this production, a classic noir tale of the falsely accused man. 'Shortie' Matthews (Emlyn Williams), a petty criminal, visits an old flame on the day of his release, only to find she has been strangled. Believing that he would be the obvious suspect, Shortie takes flight, plunging into a nocturnal world of overnight hauliers and seedy roadhouse cafés. Director Arthur Woods and his cameraman Basil Emmott modulate the typically brutal Warners' realism into a noir register through atmospheric lighting, night-for-night photography, perpetual rain and even a Gothic element in the shadowy deserted mansion where Shortie takes refuge. *They Drive by Night* casts a sympathetic eye upon the tribulations of the working class – cold, wet, hungry and broke – and its murderer turns out to be a degenerate middle-class psychopath, Ernest Thesiger's camp bibliophile, seething with sexual perversions. The final scenes in his elegant flat use expressionist compositions and lighting with confidence and panache. The adaptation softens the novel's social critique (there is no police brutality) and early scenes that questioned the legitimacy of capital punishment were cut by the censors (Murphy, 1986, pp.289–90). However, *They Drive by Night* shows the passage from the macabre shocker to modern film noir, revealing a paranoid world of social and sexual corruption that exists as the dark underside to respectable British society.

Equally impressive was Joseph Somlo's *On the Night of the Fire* (US title: *The Fugitive*, 1939), adapted from F.L. Green's novel, and directed with typical sensitivity by Brian Desmond Hurst, a riveting psychological study of that favourite English victim, the disgraced petit bourgeois. Will Kobling (Ralph Richardson), an East End barber, steals the money that he sees invitingly unprotected behind an open window because he longs to escape from the 'dirty tuppences' of his customers and the 'stink of the street'. His wife Kit (Diana Wynyard) uses most of it to pay off her debt to the usurious draper Pilleger, who blackmails the couple after the police trace the money to his shop. On the night of the fire, Kobling strangles Pilleger in a macabre scene that uses expressionist lighting and deep-focus compositions alternating with choker close-ups to convey bewilderment and fear. Blundering out into the night, Kobling trudges catatonically round the rainswept streets and claustrophobic alleyways before returning to his home, now a dark, gloomy morgue. From this point he becomes the pariah, estranged from his wife and young child whom he sends away, the butt of rumours, insinuations and then violence as a hostile mob smash his windows. The London he now inhabits has a Dickensian gloom – fog-bound, blighted and menacing – where his every movement is shadowed by the police. Hearing that Kit has been killed in a car accident, he deliberately gets himself shot by the police, his face expressing relief as he falls to the ground.

On the Night of the Fire, with its sustained doom-laden atmosphere, Günther Krampf's expressive cinematography, its adroit mixture of location shooting and Gothic compositions and Richardson's wonderful performance as a lower middle-class Everyman, desperate to better himself and his family but sinking ever deeper into the abyss, clearly shows that an achieved mastery of film noir existed in British cinema before the war.

Both these films were prepared to show the social, sexual and psychological problems of a rigid, class-bound society where goods and money were scarce and unemployment and criminality ever-present. However, the development of British film noir was arrested at this point, displaced by a wartime cinema committed to consensual values and pulling together, stories of servicemen or civilians acting heroically *in extremis*, spy thrillers with vicious Nazis, or cheerful comedies designed to boost morale. Two Gothic thrillers, Thorold Dickinson's *Gaslight* (US title: *Angel Street*, 1940) and Lance Comfort's *Hatter's Castle* (1941), were exceptions, both coruscating exposés of the hypocrisy of the Victorian paterfamilias. Dickinson's mobile camerawork and atmospheric direction showed the influence of Carné and French Poetic Realism (Richards, 1986, pp.68–83). The UFA-trained Anton Walbrook conveys with great subtlety the *homme fatal*'s refined sadism, 'le vice Anglais', as he humiliates and tortures his innocent wife (Diana Wynyard).[4] In *Hatter's Castle*, the brutality of the paterfamilias (Robert Newton) assumes epic proportions, finally consumed in his own Gothic pile. There were occasional low-budget shockers, including *The Night Has Eyes* (US title: *Terror House*, 1942), which tried to give a Gothic tale topicality by explaining the misanthropy of its hero (James Mason) as the result of his traumatic experiences fighting in the Spanish Civil War. The main vehicles for Gothic 'excess' were Gainsborough's remarkable series of costume dramas beginning with *The Man in Grey* (1943). *Fanny by Gaslight* (US title: *Man of Evil*, 1944), stylishly directed by Anthony Asquith, was the only noir, based on Michael Sadleir's best-selling exposé of the nether world of vice that lay beneath respectable Victorian society, frequented by the dissipated and sadistic Lord Manderstoke (James Mason), though the adaptation was silent about his proclivity for child prostitutes (Barefoot, 2001, pp.59–64).

However, it was only towards the end of the war that British noir regained its momentum. Ealing's Gothic *Dead of Night* and RKO-British's realist *Great Day*, both released in 1945, were the first noirs to be concerned with psychological breakdown. In 'The Haunted Mirror' episode of *Dead of Night*, directed by Robert Hamer, the middle-class Everyman, Peter Courtland (Ralph Michael), is gradually possessed by his *Doppelgänger* reflection, a crippled, murderously jealous Regency aristocrat, as if to acknowledge the dark and violent desires that had been repressed by Ealing's wartime documentaries. Cavalcanti's 'The Ventriloquist's Dummy' episode, which recalls Von Stroheim's *The Great Gabbo* (1929), was even darker, using a range of expressionist devices to evoke the breakdown of Maxwell Frere (Michael Redgrave) who suffers from an uncontrollable schizophrenia. *Great Day*, directed by Lance Comfort and photographed by Erwin Hillier, was the first exploration of what was, as in America, a key noir concern, the maladjusted veteran.[5] In focusing on the plight of a First World War ex-serviceman, Captain John Ellis (Eric Portman), *Great Day* could rehearse the problems that were anticipated from the current crop of returning combatants.

In a parallel development several films appeared which foregrounded the underside of urban working-class life, depicting a society where competition and criminality has replaced co-operation and consensus. Launder and Gilliat's *Waterloo Road* (1945) introduced the figure of the spiv, the petty criminal whose appearance imitated the Hollywood gangster. British National's *Murder in Reverse* (1945) was much darker. William Hartnell played Tom Masterick, a Limehouse stevedore, wrongly accused of the murder of Fred Smith (John Slater) who is having an affair with Doris, Masterick's wife, the first British *femme fatale*, played by the silent screen siren Chili Bouchier. After fifteen years inside Masterick is released and, frustrated by the indifference of the police, tracks down Smith and brings him to the house of the trial judge expecting the law to take action. The indifference of his 'betters' incenses Masterick, who shoots Smith dead on the spot. It is a stark, brutal and unexpected moment that proclaims the manifest inequalities of the British class system.

HIGH NOIR: 1946–51

By contrast with the experimental development of film noir, which consisted of somewhat isolated films, the 'high' noir period was one of concentrated production. This outburst of dark films may be grouped into four sub-cycles:

Gothic melodramas that continued the exploration of Victorian hypocrisy; psychological thrillers that probed the mental traumas produced by the war; crime thrillers that investigated the social upheavals and discontents; and a small group of semi-documentaries which, like their American counterparts, were an unstable mixture of social realism and noir melodrama. The reformist postwar Labour Government under Clement Attlee (1945–51) has been described as the Indian Summer of Victorian liberal philanthropy (Addison, 1995, p.ix). These films noirs explored the dark underside of this altruistic paternalism and represented the unleashing of the subversive energies that had been held in check by the war.

High Noir (1): Gothic Noir

Cineguild's *Blanche Fury* (1947), Two Cities' *The Mark of Cain* (1947) and Paramount British's *So Evil My Love* (1948) – all based on novels by Joseph Shearing, lavishly adapted and using popular stars – have been called Victorian films noirs (Richards, 1997, p.121). All centred on deceptively strong-willed independent female protagonists and Byronic young men (*hommes fatals*) with whom they become involved, in a heady mixture of class-based ambition, deceit, adultery and murder. Their rebellious, morally ambivalent and obsessive young protagonists, with their dark secrets and double lives, are sympathetic figures, often driven mad in their struggle against the dead weight of sexual repression and patriarchal tyranny. The same themes coursed through Ealing's *Pink String and Sealing Wax* (1945) and *Kind Hearts and Coronets* (1949), both directed by Robert Hamer, whose sympathies were with outsiders and rebels, Two Cities' *Carnival* (1946) and also Gainsborough's *Jassy* (1947), a residue of the wartime cycle. In *So Evil My Love* and David Lean's *Madeleine* (1949), Ann Todd played the sympathetic heroine whose repressed desires are aroused by self-centred dandies who defy convention. Todd's glacial stillness and repose – the 'British Garbo' – allow her passionate outbursts to carry immense weight. *Corridor of Mirrors* (1948) produced by the UFA-trained Rudolph Cartier, and Dickinson's *The Queen of Spades* (1949) photographed by Otto Heller, were the most formally adventurous, blending high Expressionism with English Gothic, partly to disguise the poverty of the sets, but also to provide a visual equivalent to their studies in male psychological breakdown. Their tragic protagonists are men born out of time whose desires can never be satisfied.

Several adaptations of Dickens explored similar issues: Cineguild's *Great Expectations* (1946) and *Oliver Twist* (1948), both directed by David Lean; and Ealing's *Nicholas Nickleby* (1947) directed by Alberto Cavalcanti. All combine a sub-expressionist visual style with sensational Gothic melodrama to create a Victorian society that is dark, menacing and predatory. In *Great Expectations* the transformation of Pip (John Mills) into a gentleman is not based on aristocratic beneficence, as he fondly believes, but on tainted money. When the source of that money returns in the guise of the convict Magwitch, the reawakening of a dark past shatters Pip's world. However, Lean opts for the cosier of the novel's endings, allowing Everyman Pip to be reunited with Estella, the *femme fatale* who has been created to break men's hearts, and to lead her into a sunlight world, a social democratic revolt against the oppressiveness of the Victorian age.

Under the veil of history, these Gothic noirs, directed with great style and imagination by talented film-makers often with full studio resources at their disposal, could broach difficult issues with a licence that would have been impossible in contemporary melodrama. Seen in their context, they are remarkably frank and adventurous in their willingness to explore transgressive sexual desire and the wounds of class, the longing to break free from the oppressive legacy of Victorian Britain and the need for a more fluid and tolerant class structure that could accommodate social mobility. In a society that was officially committed to returning women to their traditional roles of housewives and mothers and servicemen to their former occupations, a society still strangled by an ideology of deference and respect for elders, they provided a cultural space for the rebellion of the young.

High Noir (2): Psychological Thrillers

These films noirs have a contemporary setting and concentrate on male protagonists who are all identified as sensitive and tormented men engaged in a moral struggle within their own natures which makes them more complex and ambivalent than their American counterparts (Wolfenstein and Leites, 1950, pp.23, 228). In almost every case, the protagonist returns or re-engages with his present life after a period away, only to find that he is no longer able to cope. Women are the obvious target for his frustrated impotence, either explicitly identified as faithless and duplicitous *femmes fatales*, or long-suffering, victimized home builders.

Mine Own Executioner (1947) and *The Small Back Room* (1948), both adapted from dark novels by Nigel Balchin, and *The Small Voice* (US title: *Hideout*, 1948), all explicitly identified the war as the source of psychological trauma that expresses itself in the males' fits of uncontrolled violence, a deep misogyny and anti-social withdrawal. *Mine Own Executioner* was the bleakest. Its damaged pilot, Adam Lucian (Kieron Moore), shot down in flames near Rangoon and incarcerated in a Japanese POW camp, harbours intense guilt at breaking under torture, coupled with the ecstasy of killing the camp guard and making his escape. Under analysis, he relives these defining moments, rendered as subjective point-of-view shots. Still unable to control his compulsive, psychopathic behaviour, Lucian shoots his loyal and loving wife as he imagines her metamorphosing into the camp guard. His analyst, who has failed to understand the depth of his condition, is unable to prevent his suicide.

The October Man (1947) and *Forbidden* (1949) had gentler, more intro-spective protagonists and the drama hinges on their belief that they are cap-able of murder. *The October Man*'s protagonist, Jim Ackland (John Mills), is the quintessential English Everyman, attempting to rebuild his life after hos-pitalization and attempted suicide and therefore a metaphoric veteran. The boarding house he moves into is a microcosm of traditional British society, a world of decaying middle-class gentility united by its hostility to outsiders. Director Roy Ward Baker uses chiaroscuro lighting and unbalanced, cluttered compositions to create a repressive, claustrophobic environment in which Jim comes to believe that he has indeed murdered fashion model Molly Newman (Kay Walsh), the *femme fatale*. Whereas an American noir hero would strive to prove his innocence, Jim is plunged into an existential nightmare, assailed by crippling self-doubt, confessing to his girlfriend Jenny Carden (Joan Green-wood) that there is 'something in my mind, a sort of fear, as if it's dangerous to stay alive'.

The traumatized Everyman: John Mills in *The October Man* (Roy Ward Baker, 1947)

Jim eventually pulls himself together and resists the urge to plunge in front of the oncoming express train, but his existentialist fatalism recalled the prewar French Poetic Realist thrillers. These also inspired ABPC's *Temptation Harbour* (1947), based on a Simenon novella, starring Robert Newton and photographed in sombre grey tones by Otto Heller; Two Cities' *Odd Man Out* (1947) adapted from an F.L. Green novel, with James Mason as the tortured protagonist; and Sydney Box's *Daybreak* (1946), set in a sub-*Quai des brumes* world of barges on the Gravesend reach, its doomed hero Eddie Tribe (Eric Portman), dressed and lit like Jean Gabin. In each case the male victim is driven by stronger compulsions than his own conscious will, as if courting his own destruction. In both *Temptation Harbour* and *Daybreak* he is the middle-aged victim of a *femme fatale*, though in the latter Frankie (Ann Todd), a rootless dancer, whose shiny raincoat and cap echo the garb of the 'lost woman' in the French thrillers, is a complex mixture of innocence and weakness. Reginald Wyer's unobtrusively moody photography, which avoids the jarring contrasts of expressionist chiaroscuro, keeps the focus on the complex, shifting motivations of the characters.

Whereas the Poetic Realist films had working-class protagonists, another group, more Gothic in inspiration but using the same male stars, displayed the torments of the refined middle class. In *Dear Murderer* (1947) and *Obsession* (1949), Portman and Newton respectively, play men whose minds are consumed by sexual jealousy over their faithless wives, becoming aesthetes of crime, creating a strange, macabre bond with their victims who must appreciate the logic, and the beauty, of their fate at the hands of a man of far greater sensitivity and depth of feeling. In *Obsession* the rival is an American serviceman, which makes the war's resonance clear. In *The Upturned Glass* (1947) Mason played another cultivated murderer, Michael Joyce, a brain specialist whose interest in criminal psychology becomes actualized by his desire to revenge the murder of his fiancée by her sister-in-law, another *femme fatale*. In *Wanted for Murder* (1946) Portman, the most prolific male noir actor, played an introspective, psychologically driven serial killer, his mind possessed by the legacy of his grandfather, a Victorian public hangman, whose waxworks effigy he smashes in an attempt to break free.

High Noir (3): Topical Crime Thrillers

The films in this group show the encounter of the criminalized veteran with a shadowy London underworld replete with flashy spivs and foreign mobsters. The middle-class veteran was addicted to the excitement, sense of danger and legitimated violence that the war had provided, attitudes that could not be discarded along with their service uniform. The metropolitan criminals had grown fat and greedy through profiteering and the black market, which spilled over into the postwar Austerity period when there were chronic shortages of consumer goods (Zweiniger-Bargielowska, 2000, pp.151–202). This encounter dramatized fears about the effects of wartime dislocation and a much publicized postwar 'crime wave'. A number of these films were 'B' features of uneven quality: *Dancing With Crime* (1947), *The Flamingo Affair* (1948), *Night Beat* (1948) and *Noose* (US title: *The Silk Noose*, 1948), whose creaking plot was compensated by Edmond T. Greville's expressionist direction with its sophisticated use of composition and reflecting surfaces.

The key film was Warner British's *They Made Me a Fugitive* (1947), marketed as 'fresh as today's headlines'. Clem Morgan (Trevor Howard) is the paradigmatic maladjusted veteran, the ex-RAF pilot quite prepared to embrace crime out of sheer frustrated boredom on the toss of a coin. His tempter is the dandified gangster Narcy (Griffith Jones), another product of social dislocation, 'not even a respectable crook, just cheap, rotten, after the war trash'. In Cavalcanti's expressionist direction and Heller's grim tonal range, the London underworld he inhabits is at once contemporary and thoroughly Gothic; the gang's macabre East End front – the Valhalla Funeral Parlour – recalls the prewar shockers where bodies could also be disposed of by dropping them

Coffins, contraband and crooks: gang boss Narcy (Griffith Jones) surrounded by his hoods in the Valhalla Funeral Parlour in *They Made Me a Fugitive* (Alberto Cavalcanti, 1947)

into the Thames. Clem and Narcy are *Doppelgängers*: Narcy is what Clem would be if he abandoned all restraint; Clem has the effortless breeding, the *class*, and the woman to which Narcy aspires. Unlike the psychological thrillers, Clem's response to being framed is to battle to clear his name in a dog-eat-dog world where the police use him as bait, a middle-class woman propositions him to murder her husband, and his only ally is Sally (Sally Gray), Narcy's spirited ex-girlfriend, which completes the 'exchange' between the two men. Clem, laconic and hard-bitten with a fine line in mordant ripostes like a British Bogart, finally triumphs over his rival amidst the lurid glare of the neon-lit 'Valhalla Funeral Parlour' sign, but fails to clear his name. The bleak conclusion is only softened by Sally's loyalty.

If Clem retains audience sympathy, the criminalized veterans played by Nigel Patrick in *Uneasy Terms* (1948), based on a Peter Cheyney novel, and *Silent Dust* (1949), are despicable; the latter a Gothic monstrosity who has indeed abandoned any restraints. This sense of the monstrous pervades what is the most famous, prestigious and acclaimed British noir, *The Third Man* (1949), a second collaboration, after *The Fallen Idol* (1947), between Graham Greene and Carol Reed.[6] The film's British producer Alexander Korda was able to use his currency earnings abroad and his connections to facilitate extensive preparation and a long location shoot, while his American partner, David O. Selznick, provided the international stars for the lead roles. Greene's story plays up the contrast between prewar Vienna with its 'glamour and easy charm', and the postwar divided, devastated city where the population eke out an existence from the rubble or are involved in a black market where 'amateurs can't stay the course like professionals'. Robert Krasker, also Reed's cinematographer on *Odd Man Out*, was encouraged to use extensive back-lighting and extreme wide-angle lenses that distorted the buildings, and emphasized the wet cobblestone streets, which, together with Reed's frequently tilted compositions, create a nightmare city. Intensely claustrophobic moments are often followed by agoraphobic spaces and shots of magnificent baroque buildings intercut with shots of rubble, to produce an unstable, vertiginous setting in which nothing is what it appears to be. The true citizen of this distorted world is Harry Lime (Orson Welles), the racketeer, whose home is the city's labyrinthine sewers. The cosmopolitan, European-ized Lime has his *Doppelgänger*, his boyhood friend Holly Martins (Joseph Cotten), a dull-witted innocent abroad, a stolid corn-fed American Everyman (Gomez, 1971, pp.7–12). In the extraordinary scene on the Great Wheel with its unstable, constantly shifting perspective, Holly receives his brutal education in the postwar sensibility, a world without heroes where anything is permitted to those who have the daring to break free from bourgeois restraint and embrace the aristocratic bravura of the Borgias who created the Renaissance.

Ambivalent expurgation: Harry Lime (Orson Welles) about to meet his end in
The Third Man (Carol Reed, 1949)

In Welles' charismatic performance *The Third Man* retains a rich ambivalence in its dramatization of the clash between conventional morality and existential modernism. At the end of the bravura chase sequence in the sewers when Holly kills Harry, he rids the city of corruption, but in the process extinguishes his own more imaginative and creative self, symbolized by

Harry's fingers as they poke through the grill towards freedom. Holly's hollow 'victory' is represented in the final scene where Anna (Alida Valli), who has steadfastly retained her sense of Harry's nobility, walks past Holly right out of the frame, despite the camera position predicting a stop, leaving Holly an isolated, defeated figure framed against a row of barren trees in a graveyard. This refusal to endorse conventional morality preserves the ironic scepticism that pervades the whole film. In its clash of European decadence and Anglo-American self-righteousness, its blending of an existentialist modernism with vigorous melodrama and its mapping of wartime dislocation onto Cold War tensions, *The Third Man* condenses the major themes of classic film noir and, like all seminal films, was the nexus for the varied social and cultural forces that were in play at this historical moment.

High Noir (4): Semi-Documentaries

This group of films are essentially hybrids, documenting a social problem in a restrained, sober style, often with extensive location shooting that showed the influence of a neo-realist aesthetic, but frequently making recourse to a noir register in order to give shape to the dark forces that were reshaping British society. This visual tension reproduces the thematic clash between an overt law-and-order framework and the thrilling world of depravity. Sydney Box's *Good Time Girl* (1948) and *Boys in Brown* (1949) explored the topical problem of delinquency and combined a documentary approach with sensational subject matter. Both created sympathy for the plight of the delinquent that was at odds with the homiletic framework. In *Good Time Girl*, based on an Arthur la Bern novel, Jean Kent is allowed the space to create a spirited performance as a woman whose real 'crime' is to be desired by men who all try to exploit her. Her progressive degradation has a grim irony as she finally becomes the moll for two desperate American army deserters who rob and kill the one man who had been decent to her.

Ealing Studios, always stronger on realism than Gothic, dominated the noir semi-documentary. Robert Hamer's *It Always Rains on Sunday* (1947), combined the sensational material of another la Bern novel with a conspectus of East End life, but the chief exponents of the form were the pairing of director Basil Dearden and producer Michael Relph, whose documentary-thriller *Pool of London* (1951), was promoted as 'Britain's *Naked City*' (Higson, 1997, p.163). From *Frieda* (1947) through to *A Place to Go* (1963), their films consistently combine a documentary-style exploration of a topical issue with an evocative use of a noir visual register. The thread running through their films is the effects of wartime dislocation on the lives of ordinary British people, the struggle between duty and desire, conformity and lawlessness. Their most successful and influential film was *The Blue Lamp* (1950), the clash between

the ordered community of the police whose routines are carefully documented, and the delinquent, identified as a 'class apart', the result of 'a
childhood spent in homes broken and demoralised by war'. Tom Riley (Dirk
Bogarde) is the representative 'restless and ill-adjusted youngster' and cinematographer Gordon Dines uses chiaroscuro lighting, tight framing and low-
angle shots to create the atmosphere of unstable volatility that surrounds
Riley and his girlfriend Diana (Peggy Evans), another casualty of a broken
home. In state of near-hysterical panic, Riley shoots PC Dixon (Jack Warner),
the personification of cheery paternalistic authority whose home is shot in
a neutral style to emphasize its representative ordinariness. Riley is finally
disarmed by PC Mitchell (Jimmy Hanley), the figure of the stable, decent,
boy-next-door and Dixon's surrogate son. Although critics warmed to Dixon
and condemned the delinquent, *The Blue Lamp*, like all the Dearden-Relph
films, exhibits an unconscious ambivalence embodied in the sexy charisma of
Bogarde's villain.

INTERIM: 'B' FEATURES AND STRAGGLERS, 1951–56

After the relatively high investment in films noirs in the immediate postwar
period as a number of Britain's most important film-makers attempted to
explore the dark undercurrents in a volatile society readjusting after the war,
this subsequent period, 1951–56, was characterized by more routine second
features. The energies of British production went into war films and romantic
comedies that essentially made the British feel better about what had passed
or embrace a burgeoning consumerism that promised a classless society to
come. Many British noirs were openly derivative of Hollywood models.
Hammer's *The Flanagan Boy* (US title: *Bad Blonde*, 1953) with the muscular
Tony Wright as a weak-willed boxer in thrall to a *femme fatale* (played by
Hollywood lead Barbara Payton) was clearly Americanized, as was Butchers'
Marilyn (1953, reissued as *Roadhouse Girl*), an intrepid attempt by director
Wolf Rilla at an English *The Postman Always Rings Twice*.[7] Producer Robert
Baker, one half of Tempean, was 'very keen on American *film noir*' and several
of his films, notably *Impulse* (1955), were inspired by American developments
(quoted in McFarlane, 1997, p.45).

Indeed, the noirs that best exemplify this interim period are those of writer-
director Ken Hughes who 'thought the great secret of making a picture was
to emulate Hollywood' (Eyles, 1971, p.42). Hughes's first feature, *Wide Boy*
(1952), shows how his emulation was also a form of cultural assimilation.
Although indebted to *Night and the City*, wide boy Benny Merce (Sydney
Tafler) is a thoroughly British spiv, flashy and street-wise, but trapped in a
miserable world of drab cafés and seedy bedsits that are carefully delineated.

His desperate bid to be somebody is handled with compassion, as is his fall, wrongly convinced that his girlfriend has betrayed him. *The House Across the Lake* (US title: *Heatwave*, 1954), adapted by Hughes from his own novel *High Wray*, was a sub-Cain crime melodrama narrated in Chandleresque idiom by American hack novelist Mark Kendrick (Alex Nicol). 'With some men it's liquor. With me it's always women. Women like Carol Forrest,' he muses as he becomes entrapped by the tall, blonde and ruthless *femme fatale* (Hillary Brooke). Carol is the faithless wife of financier Beverley Forrest, a lonely, terminally ill man played with conviction by Sid James, whom Mark befriends even as he betrays him. Hughes uses deep-focus compositions and chiaroscuro to evoke a world of brittle charm and sinister evasions against the backdrop of Lake Windermere. *Black 13* (1954), Anglicized from a 1948 Italian thriller, boasted a strong performance from Peter Reynolds as a sympathetic killer, but it was in *The Brain Machine* (1955) that Hughes deepened his exploration of criminal psychology. Maxwell Reed, who could convey both menace and vulnerability, played the brain-damaged gangster, Frank Smith, who hunts down the murderer of his girlfriend and then waits passively for the authorities to take him. His grim fatalism elicits a fascinated horror and sympathy from the psychiatrist who has become involved with his case. Josef Ambor's accomplished cinematography creates an evocative underworld of sleazy West End tenements, seedy Soho nightclubs and the dreary lock-up under a railway arch that Smith inhabits. By contrast with these four films made for Anglo-Amalgamated, Hughes's two gangster films for Columbia – *Confession* (US title: *The Deadliest Sin*, 1955) and *Joe Macbeth* (1955) – with their second-division Hollywood stars, were more straightforward and less interesting American pastiche, the latter with a laboured neo-Shakespearean framework.

British intermediates were rare in this period, but important noir 'stragglers' included Robert Hamer's *The Long Memory*, Carol Reed's *The Man Between* and Guy Hamilton's *The Intruder*, all released in 1953; Romulus' *The Good Die Young* (1954), Dearden-Relph's *The Ship That Died of Shame* (1955) and Rank's *Tiger in the Smoke* (1956) which all merit detailed analysis. For reasons of space, I shall concentrate on ABPC's *Yield to the Night* (US title: *Blonde Sinner*, 1956), directed by J. Lee Thompson with its innovative concern with female criminality, usually consigned to the rigid archetype of the duplicitous *femme fatale*.

Yield to the Night's story and screenplay were by Joan Henry, whose memoirs of a spell in prison had been filmed sympathetically by Lee Thompson as *The Weak and the Wicked* (1954). *Yield* was designed as a strategic intervention in the debate about the merits of capital punishment: the film's poster asked 'Would <u>You</u> Hang Mary Hilton?' Its reception became enmeshed in the furore that surrounded the execution of Ruth Ellis, the last woman to be hanged in

Britain, which Henry's novel predated (Chibnall, 2000, pp.56–103). The long scenes in the condemned cell, where the viewer's attention is maintained by Lee Thompson's nimble camerawork, underline the irony of the endless pains the authorities take to ensure that Mary (Diana Dors) is fit and well to be executed. The casting of Dors was crucial to the film's success. Not only was 'Britain's blonde bombshell' apparently cast against type so that the deglamorized scenes in the cell offer an unexpectedly intimate glimpse of a vulnerable, unsure woman, but her sexual allure in the flashbacks and in the poster help to create a woman who is sensual, intelligent and ambitious, who needs more than she can find in a conventional marriage. She is no victim, but an anti-heroine, making a confused rebellion against the repressive forces that circumscribe a working-class woman so tightly. In the film's opening sequence, a bravura piece of metonymic narrative economy with the oneiric quality central to noir sensibility, Mary seems to move distractedly, as if under compulsion, an inexorable force that will blow apart the suffocating class divisions of British society. These are focused in the intercut shots of the clothes and shoes of the two women, Mary and her upper-class rival Lucy, whom she shoots repeatedly before throwing the gun on the mews cobblestones and walking away. The clarity of *Yield*'s thematic analysis, its arresting visual style, which consciously distances the viewer in order to provoke critical thought rather than emotional empathy, was modernist and anticipated the developments which were to come in British noir. However, its impact at the time was muted by the imposition of an 'X' certificate, much to Lee Thompson's dismay (ibid., p.96).

LATE NOIR: THE NEW REALISM, 1957–64

The consensus that had underpinned 1950s British society began to break up towards the end of the decade. Writing at the time, Kenneth Allsop discerned a 'dissentient mood', which was inchoate and unfocused, but united in its rejection of the values and style of established culture (Allsop, 1958, pp.7–42). Arthur Marwick has identified this dissentience in films of the British 'New Wave' beginning with *Room at the Top* (1959) and argued that their aggressive, provincial working-class iconoclasm was the start of a 'cultural revolution' that rejected the dominant middle-class values (Marwick, 1998, pp.3–22). Steve Chibnall has argued persuasively that noir crime thrillers formed part of this cultural realignment. Like the New Wave films, crime films used location shooting and harsher, more naturalistic lighting to create a realist aesthetic that concentrated on criminals as ordinary people not a detached underworld (Chibnall, 1999, pp.94–109).[8] The macabre elements of British noir, still strongly present in *Tiger in the Smoke* (1956), were moulded into a distinct and separate genre, Gothic horror, beginning with Hammer's *The Curse of Frankenstein* (1957), which became the principal vehicle for the exploration of psychological disorder, disturbed sexuality and pathological violence. This separation of Gothic horror from the brutal realism of the crime films gave late noir its distinctive tone and themes.

This shift is first discernible in Cy Endfield's *Hell Drivers* and Ken Hughes's *The Long Haul*, both released in 1957, which concentrated on the hard brutality of haulage driving that requires toughness merely to survive amidst endemic corruption. Endfield, taking his inspiration from Warner Bros. films such as *They Drive by Night* (1940), argued that there was 'plenty of natural drama in the everyday jobs of men with physical contact with reality' (reported in *Kinematograph Weekly*, 20 March 1958, p.25). *The Long Haul*, financed by Columbia, was more Americanized, but its use of Liverpool locations was representative of late noir's turn to northern industrial cities, which carried with it, as in the New Wave films, connotations of virile working-class masculinity, imbued with tough masculine traits as opposed to the effeminacy of the south. *Violent Playground* (1958), *In the Wake of a Stranger* (1959) and *Beyond this Place* (US title: *Web of Evidence*, 1959) were all set in Liverpool, *Tread Softly Stranger* (1958) in the composite steel town of 'Rawborough', *Hell Is a City* (1960) in and around Manchester, while Anglo-Amalgamated's *Payroll* (1961) used Newcastle as its setting. *Payroll*, the story of a heist gone wrong, indebted to *The Asphalt Jungle* and *Criss Cross*, was imbued with the new brutalism, its opening hold-up of a security van as violent as anything that had been seen on British screens. At its centre is the corrupt *femme fatale* Katie (François Prevost), the glamorous wife of timid payroll clerk Dennis (William Lucas), whose discontent with their mundane existence makes him take the desperate step of becoming the gang's inside man. Katie has no compunction in abandoning Dennis in favour of the gang leader Johnny Mellors (Michael Craig), tough and cruel, often photographed in grainy close-ups that show the open pores and the sweat. Katie finally tries to double cross Johnny, but he defeats her, only to be frustrated by the actions of the obsessive revenger, Jackie Parker (Billie Whitelaw), the wife of the murdered van driver.

Stanley Baker's tough cop Inspector Martineau in *Hell Is a City* was modern British man: violent, unstable, ambitious and working-class, a product of the forces that were re-shaping British society, but Baker's key role was as Johnny Bannion in Joseph Losey's *The Criminal* (US title: *The Concrete Jungle*, 1960), which transposed the American prison film to a British setting (Spicer, 1999, pp.87–91). Bannion, based on the notorious racetrack criminal Alfred Dimes, embodied what was to become the key trope of British neo-noir, the gangster whose values are outmoded. In Losey's Brechtian analysis, Bannion is a man moving inexorably towards his doom, gripped not by fatalism but by the dialectical logic of social forces represented by Mike Carter (Sam Wanamaker), the Transatlantic 'organization man', the smooth front of the corporate businesses that were the new power in British crime (Chibnall, 1999, pp.103–4). Bannion meets his end in a nondescript bleak field, whose eloquent starkness is the culmination of Krasker's harsh, alienating visual style, the opposite of the romantic Expressionism of his work for Carol Reed.

BRITISH NEO-NOIR 1: MODERNIST NOIR, 1965–93

Losey's detached, rational and sceptical analysis of social forces were the hallmarks of neo-modernist films noirs in Britain as well as in America. There was a diverse group of unrelated noirs produced between 1968 and 1972 that included *The Strange Affair* (1968), *Villain* (1971), Hitchcock's *Frenzy* (1972), *The Offence* (1972) and *Sitting Target* (1972) and the two that were most influential and innovative: Mike Hodges' *Get Carter* (1971) and Donald Cammell's *Performance* (1970).

Get Carter, based on Ted Lewis' novel *Jack's Return Home* that launched a new wave of provincial crime fiction, links the metropolis to the north in its story of London gangster Jack Carter (Michael Caine) returning to his home town, Newcastle. Like its modernist American counterparts, *Get Carter* is highly aware of the generic conventions – Carter reads *Farewell My Lovely* as he journeys north – but transforms them in an abrasive critique of 1960s affluence and permissiveness. In Wolfgang Suschitzky's observant cinematography, Newcastle is no longer a raw and vital city, but decadent and corrupt, its main business under-age prostitution and pornography. Hodges' elliptical editing, which moves the action rapidly from one sharply observed scene to another, excises a great deal of conventional narrative baggage, focusing on Caine's compelling performance as the fastidious, chilling professional whose face is a blank mask, armoured by his laconic black humour and a strict code that gives sleazy villains their just deserts. Despite the justice of his scourging, Carter, like his Jacobean avatars, is a melancholic loner, incapable of love and more ruthless and implacable than Bannion. But, like Bannion, he is another doomed anti-hero whose moment has passed. On a desolate beach punctuated by the inexorable movement of the coal hoist, itself a symbol of a bygone age, Carter is killed by an anonymous assassin. Like Walker in *Point Blank*, Carter never understands his own ultimate irrelevance.

Performance, whose release was delayed for over two years by anxious Warner executives, was also a critique of permissiveness and of the narcissistic underworld hard man, Chas Devlin (James Fox), set amidst a squalid and corrupt London (MacCabe, 1998). Chas has also become an embarrassment, 'an ignorant boy, an out-of-date boy', exiled from the underworld because, like Carter, he mixes business with personal revenge, the killing of his boyhood friend Joey Maddocks. *Performance* is not so much interested in retribution as transformation through Chas's confrontation with a counter-cultural 'underground' and his *Doppelgänger*, rock star Turner (Mick Jagger), who has lost his 'demon' and retreated into an alternative world. Through this encounter the identity of Chas, the sadomasochistic 'performer' of sex and violence, is remodelled. The capable Pherber (Anita Pallenberg) holds a mirror so that her breast appears on his chest. But, as Chas gradually discovers his feminine self and clothes himself in hippie attire, the vampiric Turner absorbs his hard male energy and takes over the East End gang. In the final scenes their identities have become interchangeable.

Performance begins as a conventional thriller, albeit with disconcertingly rapid-fire cuts which dissect a scene rather than merely record it, but modulates through director Nicolas Roeg's increasingly rococo, allusive and self-reflexive visual style, into a radical transformation of the genre, a funda-mental re-examination of the myth of the hard man with his fabled self-possession based on violence and homoerotic narcissism. In the heady summer of 1968 when *Performance* was filmed, Roeg and writer/co-director Donald Cammell could construct a social and sexual transformation that was not ironic even if it was wrapped in an ambiguous mystical allegory that permitted numerous readings. Its modernist stress on the fluidity of identity recalled European directors such as Antonioni and Ingmar Bergman, espe-cially *Persona* (1966) (Sinyard, 1991, pp.11–24). Most unusually, *Performance* blends modernism with the Gothic – Turner's Notting Hill house is a Gothic mansion – drawing on the strength of both traditions in its critique of the legend of the notorious Kray twins and of the new media myth of baronial, drugged-out rock stars.

In the 1980s British noirs continued the focus on the gangster and through him mounted a critique of Thatcherism (Hill, 1999a, pp.160–71). The earliest and most influential was John Mackenzie's taut thriller *The Long Good Friday* (1980) scripted by the left-wing playwright Barry Keefe. Its East End gang boss Harold Shand (Bob Hoskins) embodies the contradictory ideology of Thatcherism: its Little Englandism, a parochial veneration of British tra-ditions, coupled with a belief in unfettered international enterprise. Shand is another doomed *fin-de-siècle* figure, his 'Corporation' shattered by the IRA whose members cannot be bought and whose political cause Shand cannot understand. Hoskins's memorable performance, which captures Shand's energy, charisma, his wit and rugged charm, his bursts of uncontrolled violence and also his moments of vulnerability, were reminiscent of Cagney in *White Heat*, whose fall also has a tragic grandeur. The later films – Ron Peck's *Empire State* (1987) also set in London's transforming docklands, Mike

Figgis's *Stormy Monday* (1989) set in Newcastle where the locals are preyed on by American capital, and *Tank Malling* (1990) which showed a debauched and disintegrating society, its hard-bitten journalist hero (Ray Winstone) becoming a pawn in a sinister right-wing coup – were equally critical of the changes that were reconstructing British society.

Mike Newell's *Dance with a Stranger* (1985) and Neil Jordan's *Mona Lisa* (1986) were more overtly noir in theme and style. *Dance with a Stranger* was one of a group of films that revisited a (loosely defined) 1950s, critiquing Thatcherism through exploring another time of repressive, intolerant Conservatism where it was difficult for oppositional forces to be heard. The films depicted 'a mix of criminals, deviants, and social misfits . . . who are in protest against the drabness and conformity of the society around them' (Hill, 1999b, p.125). Like Lynch's *Blue Velvet*, these British films revealed the fractures that lay beneath the surface calm. *The Krays* (1990) and *'Let Him Have It'* (1991) both locate the problems as the result of wartime dislocation, and concentrate on the damage inflicted on insecure working-class males who turn to violence as a refuge from their social and sexual inadequacies in a postwar British society depicted as hypocritical, intolerant and oppressive. *Scandal* (1988) dramatized the notorious Profumo Affair, making call-girl Christine Keeler (Joanne Whalley-Kilmer) a sympathetic protagonist.

Dance with a Stranger, based on the true story of Ruth Ellis, the last woman to be hanged in Britain, provided the most searching analysis, recalling *Yield to the Night* in its depiction of a female protagonist in revolt against the limited horizons that her life offers her. The collaborative team – producer Roger Randall-Cutler, director Mike Newell and screenwriter Shelagh Delaney, who wrote the only feminist New Wave film (*A Taste of Honey*, 1961) – were not interested in Ellis's early life, the precise facts of the case and its legal repercussions; instead they focus entirely on the doomed, destructive love affair between Ellis (Miranda Richardson) and the shallow playboy David Blakely (Rupert Everett). Its intense, episodic narrative is pared down to their key encounters where both display complex emotions: masochism, self-pity, sadism, revenge, obsession, jealousy and resentment. As they begin to destroy each other, the lovers become the vectors of the complex and incompatible social forces that each represents, but which they themselves cannot comprehend. Ellis is a capable, ambitious and calculating working-class woman whose life is wrecked by her passion for a man she knows is feckless and untrustworthy. Blakely personifies a careless and shallow upper class, but is also gripped by a passion that makes him behave compulsively and violently, causing Ellis to miscarry. In order to create the affair's fatalistic intensity, Newell deploys the full visual resources of noir: claustrophobic mise-en-scène, chiaroscuro lighting, distorted compositions and frequent mirror reflections, creating an unstable and unfathomable world. When Ellis shoots Blakely, she is, like Mary Hilton in *Yield to the Night*, possessed by forces that overwhelm her. As Randall-Cutler commented: 'We never set out to explain why she did it. We simply presented the circumstances that precipitated the action, putting in sufficient evidence to substantiate an understanding of those events . . . The film shows people in the grip of things that they are unable to deal with, but have to suffer anyway' (quoted in Park, 1990, p.183). *Dance with a Stranger* makes high demands of its audience and, unsurprisingly, was not as commercially successful as the shallower *Scandal* with its set-piece sex scenes and conventional concluding courtroom melodrama.

Mona Lisa was set in contemporary Britain, but its dark and oneiric world was equally stylized. *Mona Lisa*'s London is a world of under-age prostitution, pornography, drug-dealing and heroin addiction, where the Thatcherite gangster Mortwell (Michael Caine) supplies whatever perverted fantasy his upper-class clients want. Mortwell is a powerful but peripheral presence. At the centre of *Mona Lisa* is the figure that seemed to have been lost to British cinema, the flawed Everyman. George (Bob Hoskins), a decent, ordinary bloke who has taken to crime, is the quintessential alienated noir protagonist adrift in a world that has changed radically during his seven years in prison. *Mona Lisa* recalls *Taxi Driver* as George cruises round the distracting glare of a neon-lit nocturnal city, driving Simone (Cathy Tyson), a black prostitute in the pay of Mortwell, to her various clients. Simone is the catalyst for his re-education. Her feisty independence forces George to abandon his misogyny and racism along with his old-fashioned clothes, but at the same time she is his entrée into a darker underworld than he had ever imagined. The pair revisit the street in King's Cross where the down-and-out prostitutes gather in their search for the fifteen-year-old Cathy (Kate Hardie), a street lit to resemble a hell's mouth. Baffled, unsure, his identity dissolving, George falls in love with this 'tall, thin, black tart', only to have his romantic dreams crushed when he realizes that she will deceive and betray anyone, not for money but for Cathy whom she protects and desires. In a moving scene on Brighton pier George, in his funfair glasses, becomes the tragic clown Harlequin from the *Commedia Dell'Arte*, weeping at the indifference of his Columbine whose glasses are heart-shaped. After a grisly dénouement in which Simone shoots Mortwell, George retreats to his haven in his friend's garage, an alternative world, and is reunited with his daughter, as if the whole story had been a grotesque nightmare. But his anger and outrage – 'I sold myself for a pair of dykes' – has modulated into wistful, sentimentalized compassion: 'She was trapped . . . like a bird in a cage'. *Mona Lisa*'s radical sexual politics transform its generic framework, as Jordan was to do again in his modernist political thriller, *The Crying Game* (1992).

BRITISH NEO-NOIR 2: POSTMODERN NOIR

The modernist phase of British film noir, whose basic inspiration was European art cinema, extended for such a lengthy period because of its important engagement with Thatcherism, an ideology that persisted through to the end of John Major's government in 1997. Because of the sporadic nature of British film production, a more populist, commercially orientated postmodern cinema was slower to evolve in Britain, emerging by the mid-1990s. The inspiration for this cinema was Hollywood and many of the postmodern British noirs were unimaginative imitations of American models. The future noir *Shopping* (1994), set in a sub-*Blade Runner* near future of urban decay, was visually striking but undermined by its flimsy storyline. Noir-horror serial killer films such as *Beyond Bedlam* (1994) and *Darklands* (1996) were clumsy and derivative. Crime thrillers, including *The Young Americans* (1993), *The Innocent Sleep* (1995) and *The Criminal* (2000), with their persecuted innocents, attempted to hide second-hand plots behind an overloaded visual and aural stylization that reduced their London settings to empty pastiche. David Hayman's *The Near Room* (1995), a 'Glasgow noir' set in Britain's second city with its reputation for violent crime, was more accomplished. Its screenplay reproduces the dark, hard-boiled style of the young writers whose tales of sex and violent crime in gritty urban settings were creating a new boom in crime fiction.[9] *The Near Room* uses 'noir lite', elliptical editing, unusual angles and shadowy, distorted compositions to convey the disordered perceptions of the drifting and alienated narrator, journalist Charlie Colquhoun (Adrian Dunbar). Colquhoun is the archetypal noir anti-hero haunted by his past, whose search for his estranged daughter leads him ever deeper into a morbid world of pornography, child prostitution and civic corruption.

The most successful postmodern British noir was *Shallow Grave* (1995), a knowing modern fable of greed that drew its inspiration from American Indie cinema. Screenwriter John Hodge, director Danny Boyle and producer Andrew Macdonald admired the sophistication and witty self-consciousness of the Indies as a model for an intelligent populism; *Shallow Grave*'s black humour, inventive visual style and blending of the realistic and the macabre is indebted to *Blood Simple*. Like the Coens, Macdonald and Hodge saw that film noir offered the possibility of stylish, subversive film on a budget of around £1 million. Most of the film takes place inside a fashionable Georgian flat in Edinburgh's New Town, filmed in striking colours and with a sense of hidden, unfolding space, not claustrophobia. Boyle's camera prowls around, like Kubrick's, investigating the dark secrets of this world as the smug yuppie trio disintegrate through their decision to keep the suitcase full of money they discover in the room of their new lodger Hugo, who has died of a drug overdose. The doctor Juliet (Kerry Fox), accountant David (Christopher Eccleston) and journalist Alex (Ewan McGregor) are deliberately unlikable, shallow young professionals, whose callousness and latent violence is relentlessly exposed; at one point the film was going to be entitled *Cruel* (Bennett, 1995, p.35). Juliet degenerates into a scheming *femme fatale*; David regresses into a psychopathic paranoiac, traumatized by cutting off Hugo's limbs in the Grand Guignol scene where they bury his body; while Alex reveals the essential venality beneath his charismatic façade. In a clever dénouement each ruins the others' chances of profiting from the cash.

There were noir elements in the 1990s revival of the gangster film, which, as Steve Chibnall has shown, exploited the British public's continued fascination with a semi-mythical criminal underworld where the deaths of the Kray twins and the return of Great Train Robber Ronnie Biggs were media events. The current cycle dates from four films released in 1997: *Face, Hard Men, Mojo* and *Resurrection Man*, which, in their very different ways, engaged with the hard man/gangster myth. The success of Guy Ritchie's comic take on the myth, *Lock, Stock and Two Smoking Barrels* (1998) helped fuel the cycle, which numbered over twenty films, more than in the previous twenty years, and caused a new critical outcry at these supposedly tawdry and meretricious productions, and police protests at their glamorization of violence (Chibnall, 2001). As Claire Monk argues, the contemporary revival of the gangster film is nostalgic, a harking back to the securities of the homosocial communities that characterize these films. For a young male audience, it was part of a knowing 'laddist' culture busy appropriating past forms and styles of aggressive, hedonistic masculinity in the absence of social structures, including traditional male occupations, that might support it (Monk, 1999, pp.172–88). However, the more intelligent films in the cycle, those with a distinct genuine noir sensibility rather than the empty pastiche of *Circus* (2000) with its battery of knowing allusions, critique rather than glamorize this male culture.

Gangster No.1 (2000) was an attempt to recover the roots of the genre in its story of the rise and fall of the eponymous Gangster (Malcolm McDowell), whose hubris, his ruthless desire to be Mr Big has led only to emptiness and emotional annihilation. *Sexy Beast* (2000) revived the central British figure, the gangster whose hour has passed, but offered a fresh take on the story. Gary 'Gal' Dove (Ray Winstone) who has retired to the Costa del Sol, the nirvana of all British gangsters, is not a tragic figure but a sympathetic Everyman who survives the assault of his nemesis, psychotic hard man Don Logan (Ben Kingsley), and his return to the noir world of London gangland for a final job, to rest again by his pool with his devoted wife DeeDee (Amanda Redman). Terry Winsor's *Essex Boys* (2000), based on an actual incident, was the darkest of the group, a thoroughly noir tale of deception and betrayal. In addition to being well plotted, *Essex Boys* has a real feeling for the distinctive Essex landscape: its deserted, winding country lanes, bleak coastline, flat marsh-lands and the tawdry neon glitz of Southend, all within a stone's throw of the metropolis. The narrator, Billy (Charlie Creed-Miles) is part innocent, part gangster wannabee, who gets increasingly out of his depth as minicab driver turned chauffeur of the psychotic gangster Jason Locke (Sean Bean), his louche boss Peter Chase (Larry Lamb) the vulgar, fly entrepreneur, quintes-sential 'Essex Man', and their leering sidekick Chippy. In a series of sordid and ugly scenes, *Essex Boys* deglamorizes macho gangsterdom. Jason's drug-crazed rape that ends in the death of the hapless Nicole (Amanda Lowdell) is brutal and revolting, her body dumped at sea by the gang's middle-class, refined but ruthless partner John Dyke (Tom Wilkinson), who plays at being the county squire. Dyke lures the trio to their doom, only to be foiled by Billy who escapes across the spectral marshes and drives off with the drugs haul. In the end both Dyke and Billy are outmanoeuvred by Jason's wife Lisa (Alex Kingston), who is poised to go into partnership with their former rival. 'Essex boys? She done the lot of us,' muses Billy, half in admiration as the police arrive. Lisa is neither the conventional *femme fatale*, nor the brainless tart in white stilettos, the butt of endless media jokes about 'Essex Girl'. Her strength and ruthlessness stem from a life spent being bullied, patronized and abused by men, including Jason whom she idolized and coveted since her school days. Her triumph shows the new image of the successful entrepreneur.

The outstanding recent British noir is Mike Hodges' *Croupier* (1999) whose protagonist Jack Manfred (Clive Owen) is the archetypal existentialist anti-hero, a would-be novelist typing away in his cramped basement bedsit, searching for his subject and his fictional hero, and through them his true identity. At the behest of his reprobate father, Jack takes up a post in a casino, a noir world of tawdry glamour, shimmering surfaces and distorting reflec-tions. Trained in the art, Jack rediscovers the fascination of being a croupier, cool, professional, detached and in control.[10] He takes to dressing in his work tuxedo to travel on the underground, as if he were playing in an orchestra. This narcissism and love of appearance is the outward indication of what Jack's deadpan voice-over narration comments on: that he is gradually assuming the identity of his dark self, Jake, who has understood that the object of life is to 'fuck the world over'. Jake becomes the protagonist of Jack's novel, *I, Croupier*, which is a number 1 best-seller in a world fascinated by cynical greed.

Jack's contact with his former life is severed when his sensible girlfriend Marion (Gina McKee) is killed by a hit and run driver, which may have been a revenge killing from her time as a WPC. Marion was Jack's 'conscience' and with her death Jake takes over from Jack, his identity now crystallized into the cynical manipulator of the sad losers who gamble at his table, able to accept with equanimity his exploitation by his father who set up the raid on the casino working through the *femme fatale* Jani (Alex Kingston). He moves in with the worldly-wise Bella (Kate Hardie), an ex-prostitute and croupier who accepts Jack as Jake, not for what he could be, but what he is. Now in control of his life and insulated from the temptations of money, Jake dedicates himself to the pure pleasure of his self-created completeness, master of chance and fate.

For Hodges, Jake is a modern anti-hero, making his way in a insecure world of casualized labour where everyone is on his own and 'there's an enormous amount of gambling in all our lives' (quoted in Darke, 2001). Screenwriter Paul Mayersberg's original screenplay is a contemporary fable that asks an audience to form their own opinion as to what Jake's triumph represents. On its initial UK release *Croupier* was very poorly distributed, but after critical eulogies plus an extended and highly successful art house run in America, it had a successful re-release in Britain in summer 2001, playing at major circuit cinemas and extensively reviewed (Gilbey, 2001). Eventually *Croupier* may attain the cult of status of Hodges' earlier *Get Carter* with which it shares a similarly exact and tightly focused style where not a scene is wasted.

There is no sign that the current energies of British film noir are diminishing. It continues to provide both established and novice film-makers with a style and a sensibility that can enable a sharp critique of the myths that underpin what is still a class-ridden, racist and misogynist British society. Although frequently indebted to American models, British film noir has evolved in a distinctive way, giving a voice to attitudes and anxieties that were repressed by official discourses, providing a cultural space that has allowed the exploration of dark and hidden undercurrents. In particular it has been preoccupied with a critique of male prowess, potency, sexuality and criminality, concerns that persist from the late 1930s through to the current cycle of gangster films. It deserves to be better known and even celebrated as an important contribution to European cinema, British culture and the evolution of film noir.

NOTES

1. Everson (1987, pp.285–9, 341–7); Murphy (1989, pp.168–190); Miller (1994, pp.155–64); Williams (1999, pp.242–69); and Spicer (2001, pp.161–77). I am also indebted to various essays by Steve Chibnall, cited in the text.
2. These were films mentioned in the annual round-ups of 'box-office winners' in *Kinematograph Weekly* and the *Motion Picture Herald*.
3. See Knight (1995, pp.165–9). Raymond Chandler's fiction was even more popular in Britain than America, though not so popular as in France; see Phillips (2000, p.275).

4. *Gaslight* was admired by critics and popular, but its influence was curtailed by MGM's decision to buy the rights from British National and destroy all the prints in order to pave the way for its own 1944 version. Fortunately Dickinson preserved a print, but his film remained unseen for many years (Richards, 1986, pp.79–82).

5. For discussion of the maladjusted veteran see McFarlane (1998, pp.93–107); Williams (1999, pp.256–60, 267–8); Spicer (2001, pp.26–7, 161–77).

6. *The Third Man* was voted as the best British film of all time in the BFI Millennium Poll; it was re-released theatrically in 1999. For a thorough background study see Drazin, *In Search of the Third Man* (2000). The screenplay has been published (Faber and Faber, 1988).

7. Rilla remade *The Asphalt Jungle* as *Cairo* (1963).

8. The exceptions were the vice and prostitution films made in the wake of the Wolfenden Report (1957) such as *Passport to Shame* (1959), the British equivalent of American 'city exposé' films.

9. See Ripley and Jakubowski, 'Fresh Blood: British Neo-Noir' (1998, pp.317–22). The revival of noir extends to some television crime series, notably *Rebus* starring John Hannah.

10. *Croupier*'s roots lie deep in the noir tradition, stretching back to *The Student of Prague* and invoking *Double Indemnity* where, as discussed in Chapter 4, Walter Neff congratulates himself on his insider's knowledge of insurance which allows him to 'crook the wheel': 'I'm a croupier in that game. I know all the tricks. I lie awake at night thinking up tricks, so I'll know them when they come at me.'

FURTHER READING

Altman, R. (1999) *Film/Genre* (British Film Institute, London).

The most wide-ranging and stimulating discussion of genre theory and practice currently available, covering a huge range of films and a wide sweep of cinema history.

Cameron, I. (ed.) (1992) *The Movie Book of Film Noir* (Studio Vista, London).

A stimulating collection of essays including important accounts by Maltby, 'The Politics of the Maladjusted Text', Vincendeau on French film noir and Walker on Siodmak. Walker's 'Film Noir: Introduction' is the most useful short account of film noir yet published.

Chibnall, S. and Murphy, R. (eds) (1999) *British Crime Cinema* (Routledge, London).

The first collection to undertake a systematic and serious study of the British crime film which includes a number of essays that are pertinent to understanding British film noir. Contains an extensive filmography.

Elsaesser, T. (2000) *Weimar Cinema and After: Germany's Historical Imaginary* (Routledge, London).

A richly detailed and scholarly study of one of the most important influences upon film noir, including a chapter on noir itself.

Gunning, T. (2000) *The Films of Fritz Lang: Allegories of Vision and Modernity* (British Film Institute, London).

Not only the most rigorous and penetrating account of Lang written so far, but a model of *auteur* studies which is sensitive to context, both modernism as a cultural phenomenon and Lang's career as a film-maker.

Hirsch, F. (1999) *Detours and Lost Highways: A Map of Neo-Noir* (Limelight, New York).

The most detailed and wide-ranging study of neo-noir currently available, well illustrated and with a bibliography and filmography.

Kaplan, E. Ann (ed.) (1998) *Women in Film Noir* (British Film Institute, London).

A seminal study, first published in 1978, which contains a number of important feminist essays. The revised edition includes newly commissioned essays, which analyse women in neo-noir.

Kolker, R. (1988) *A Cinema of Loneliness* (Oxford University Press, New York and Oxford).

Now in its third edition (2000), Kolker's book remains the most important overview of modernist cinema in America, largely conducted through a study of significant *auteurs*: Penn, Kubrick, Scorsese, Spielberg and Altman. Extended discussion of film noir in this context.

Krutnik, F. (1991) *In a Lonely Street: Film Noir, Genre, Masculinity* (Routledge, London).

The most detailed analysis of the representation of masculinity in film noir, but one which concentrates almost exclusively on the 'tough' thriller.

Levy, E. (1999) *Cinema of Outsiders: The Rise of American Independent Film* (New York University Press, New York).

The most detailed treatment yet to appear about 'Indie' cinema; accessible and informative with a chapter on the 'Resurrection of Noir'.

Martin, R. (1997) *Mean Streets and Raging Bulls: The Legacy of Film Noir in Contemporary American Cinema* (Scarecrow Press, Metuchen, New Jersey).

The first book to deal systematically and in detail with neo-noir. It is organized by decade and is attentive to both text and context; includes a filmography and an extensive bibliography covering both noir and neo-noir.

May, L. (2000) *The Big Tomorrow: Hollywood and the Politics of the American Way* (University of Chicago Press, Chicago and London).

A fresh and absorbing account of the development of Hollywood cinema from the thirties through to the late fifties, situating film noir as part of the movement towards the 'counterculture' of the sixties.

Naremore, J. (1998), *More Than Night: Film Noir in its Contexts* (University of California Press, Los Angeles and London).

A scholarly, far-reaching and perceptive study of film noir, offering a broad cultural history of noir and neo-noir as a discursive practice as well as a form of film-making.

Neale, S. (2000) *Genre and Hollywood* (Routledge, London).

A comprehensive account of the theory and practice of generic film-making in America, with a very detailed chapter on the various attempts to define and elucidate film noir.

Neve, B. (1992) *Film and Politics in America: A Social Tradition* (Routledge, London).

Neve's study concentrates on a generation of radical film-makers – including Welles, Kazan, Dassin and Polonsky – whose contribution to film noir was highly significant. Contains a valuable chapter on 'film noir and society'.

Palmer, R. Barton (1994) *Hollywood's Dark Cinema: The American Film Noir* (Twayne, New York).

Less wide-ranging than Naremore, but a thoughtful account of noir and neo-noir, concentrating on detailed analyses of selected films.

Palmer, R. Barton (ed.) (1996) *Perspectives on Film Noir* (G.K. Hall, New York).

An extremely useful collection of essays, particularly a number of early accounts of film noir translated from French sources.

Richardson, C. (1992) *Autopsy: An Element of Realism in Film Noir* (Scarecrow Press, Metuchen, New Jersey and London).

An important contribution, as Richardson provides a detailed case for the significance of new forms of realistic film-making practices, both to the 'semi-documentaries' and to 'classic' film noir in general.

Schrader, P. (1972), 'Notes on Film Noir', *Film Comment* 8 (1) 8–13.

The most influential single account of film noir, instrumental in reviving interest in the movement, defining its periods and characteristics and in arguing for its relevance to contemporary film-makers and audiences. Reprinted in *Film Noir Reader*, pp.53–64.

Silver, A. and Ursini, J. (eds) (1996) *Film Noir Reader* (Limelight Editions, New York).

An extremely useful anthology of essays, which includes seminal accounts such as Schrader's and a translated section of Borde and Chaumeton, case studies of specific films and directors, and accounts of neo-noir.

Silver, A. and Ursini, J. (eds) (1999a) *Film Noir Reader 2* (Limelight Editions, New York).

A second collection, which includes a number of early accounts of film noir, further essays on neo-noir and Tony Williams's account of British noir.

Silver, A. and Ward, E. (eds) (1980; 1993) *Film Noir: An Encyclopedic Reference to the American Style* (Overlook Press, New York).

The third edition of this important work, first published in Britain in 1980, contains a detailed filmography where each entry is accompanied by an, often highly perceptive, review. The latest edition contains an extensive discussion of neo-noir and an expanded filmography. Appendices give breakdowns of film noir by year, production companies and creative personnel. Indispensable.

Sklar, R. (1992) *City Boys: Cagney, Bogart, Garfield* (Princeton University Press, New Jersey).

Scholarly accounts of stars and performance in Hollywood cinema are all too rare, and Sklar's absorbing and intricate study throws light on the roles and careers of his three chosen actors who each contributed much to film noir.

Stephens, M. (1995) *Film Noir: A Comprehensive Illustrated Reference to Movies, Terms and Persons* (McFarland, Jefferson, North Carolina).

More inclusive than Silver and Ward, but less useful.

BIBLIOGRAPHY

UNPUBLISHED MATERIAL

Arthur, P. (1985) 'Shadows on the Mirror: Film Noir and Cold War America 1945–1957' (PhD thesis, New York University).

Biesen, S. (1998) 'Film Noir and World War II: Wartime Production, Censorship and the "Red Meat" Crime Cycle' (PhD thesis, University of Texas, Austin).

Dimendberg, E. (1992) 'Film Noir and Urban Space' (PhD thesis, University of California, Santa Cruz).

Nelson, J.S. (2001) 'Noir and Forever: Politics as if Hollywood Were Everywhere' (paper given at the Annual Meeting of the American Political Science Association San Francisco: http://papers.tcnj.edu/abstracts/088/088001NelsonJohn.htm).

Plouffe, P.F. (1979) 'The Tainted Adam: The American Hero in Film Noir' (PhD thesis, University of California, Berkeley).
Porfirio, R. (1979) 'The Dark Age of American Film: A Study of American Film Noir 1940–1960' (PhD thesis, Yale University).

BOOKS

Alloway, L. (1971) *Violent America: The Movies 1946–1964* (Museum of Modern Art, New York).
Alpi, D. (1998) *Robert Siodmak* (McFarland, North Carolina and London).
Alton, J. (1995 [1949]) *Painting with Light* (University of California Press, Los Angeles and London).
Andrew, D. (1995) *Mists of Regret: Culture and Sensibility in Classic French Film* (Princeton University Press, New Jersey).
Andrew, G. (1998) *Stranger Than Paradise: Maverick Film-makers in Recent American Cinema* (Prion Books, London).
Arnold, E.T. and Miller, E.L. (1986) *The Films and Career of Robert Aldrich* (University of Tennessee Press, Knoxville).
Atkinson, M. (1997) *Blue Velvet* (British Film Institute, London).
Austin, G. (1999) *Claude Chabrol* (Manchester University Press, Manchester).

Bade, P. (1979) *Femmes Fatales: Images of Evil and Fascinating Women* (Ash & Grant, London).

Balio, T. (1976) *United Artists: The Company Built by the Stars* (University of Wisconsin Press, Wisconsin).

Barefoot, G. (2001) *Gaslight Melodrama: From Victorian London to 1940s Hollywood* (Continuum, New York and London).

Basinger, J. (1979) *Anthony Mann* (Twayne, Boston).

Basinger, J. (1993) *A Woman's View: How Hollywood Spoke to Women 1930–1960* (Knopf, New York.)

Bassoff, L. (1997) *Crime Scenes: Movie Posters of the Film Noir – The Classic Period: 1941–1959* (Lawrence Bassoff Collection Inc., Beverley Hills).

Belton, J. (1992) *Widescreen Cinema* (Harvard University Press, Massachusetts and London).

Belton, J. (1994) *American Cinema/American Culture* (McGraw-Hill, New York).

Bergan, R. (2000) *The Coen Brothers* (Orion, London).

Bernstein, M. (2000), *Walter Wanger: Hollywood Independent* (University of Minnesota Press, Minneapolis and London).

Biskind, P. (1998) *Easy Riders, Raging Bulls: How the Sex 'N' Drugs 'N' Rock 'N' Roll Generation Saved Hollywood* (Bloomsbury, London).

Bogdanovich, P. (1967) *Fritz Lang in America* (Praeger, New York).

Bogle, D. (1994) *Toms, Coons, Mulattoes, Mammies and Bucks: An Interpretive History of Blacks in American Films* (Roundhouse, Oxford).

Borde, R. and Chaumeton, E. (1955) *Panorama du film noir américain (1941–1953)* (Editions de Minuit, Paris).

Bordwell, D. (1985) *Narration in the Fiction Film* (Methuen, London).

Bordwell, D., Staiger, J. and Thompson, K. (1985) *The Classical Hollywood Cinema: Film Style and Mode of Production to 1960* (Routledge & Kegan Paul, London).

Branigan, E. (1984) *Point of View in the Cinema: A Theory of Narration and Subjectivity in Classical Cinema* (Mouton, New York).

Bruzzi, S. (1997) *Undressing Cinema: Clothing and Identity in the Movies* (Routledge, London).

Buhle, P. and Wagner, D. (2001) *A Very Dangerous Citizen: Abraham Lincoln Polonsky and the Hollywood Left* (University of California Press, Los Angeles and London).

Bukatman, S. (1997) *Blade Runner* (British Film Institute, London).

Buss, R. (1994) *French Film Noir* (Marion Boyars, London).

Carey, G. (1981) *All the Stars In Heaven: Louis B. Mayer's MGM* (E.P. Dutton, New York).

Carringer, R.L. (1985) *The Making of 'Citizen Kane'* (University of California Press, Los Angeles).

Cavell, S. (1979) *The World Viewed: Reflections on the Ontology of Film* (Harvard University Press, Cambridge, Mass. and London).

Cawelti, J. (1976) *Adventure, Mystery and Romance: Formula Stories as Art and Popular Culture* (University of Chicago Press, Chicago).

Ceplair, L. and Englund, S. (1983) *The Inquisition in Hollywood: Politics in the Film Community, 1930–1960* (University of California Press, Los Angeles).

Charyn, J. (1996) *Movieland: Hollywood and the Great American Dream* (New York University Press, New York and London).

Christopher, N. (1997), *Somewhere in the Night: Film Noir and the American City* (The Free Press, New York).

Ciment, M. (1985) *Conversations with Losey* (Methuen, London).

Ciment, M. (1986) *John Boorman*, trans. Gilbert Adair (Faber and Faber, London).

Cochran, D. (2000) *America Noir: Underground Writers and Filmmakers of the Postwar Era* (Smithsonian Institution Press, Washington and London).

Cohan, S. (1997) *Masked Men: Masculinity and the Movies in the Fifties* (Indiana University Press, Bloomington and Indianapolis).

Collins, J. (1989) *Uncommon Cultures: Popular Culture and Post-Modernism* (Routledge, New York and London).

Collins, J. (1995) *Architectures of Excess: Cultural Life in the Information Age* (Routledge, New York and London).

Comito, T. (ed.) (1985) *Touch of Evil* (Rutgers University Press, New Brunswick).

Conant, M. (1960) *Antitrust in the Motion Picture Industry* (University of California Press, Los Angeles).

Cook, D.A. (1990) *A History of Narrative Film* (W.W. Norton, London).

Cook, D.A. (1999) *Lost Illusions: American Cinema in the Shadow of Watergate and Vietnam 1970–1979* (Scribners, New York).

Cormack, M. (1994) *Ideology and Cinematography in Hollywood* (Macmillan, London).

Corrigan, T. (1992) *A Cinema Without Walls: Movies and Culture After Vietnam* (Routledge, London).

Creed, B. (1993) *The Monstrous Feminine: Film, Feminism, Psychoanalysis* (Routledge, New York and London).

Crowther, B. (1988) *Film Noir: Reflections in a Dark Mirror* (Columbus, London).

Davis, M. (1990) *City of Quartz: Excavating the Future in Los Angeles* (Verso, London).

Dawson, J. (1995) *Quentin Tarantino: The Cinema of Cool* (Applause Books, New York and London).

Deming, B. (1969) *Running Away from Myself: A Dream Portrait of America Drawn from the Films of the 40s* (Grossman, New York).

Denby, D. (ed.) (1977) *Awake in the Dark: An Anthology of American Film Criticism, 1915 to the Present* (Vintage, New York).

Denning, M. (1987) *Mechanic Accents: Dime Novels and Working Class Culture in America* (Verso, London).

Denning, M. (1997) *The Cultural Front: The Laboring of American Culture in the Twentieth Century* (Verso, London).

Dettmann, B. and Bedford, M. (1976) *The Horror Factory: The Horror Films of Universal 1931–1955* (Gordon Press, New York).

Dick, B. (1989) *Radical Innocence: A Critical Study of the Hollywood Ten* (University Press of Kentucky, Lexington).

Dick, B. (1997) *City of Dreams: The Making and Remaking of Universal Pictures* (University Press of Kentucky, Lexington).

Dick, B. (2001) *Engulfed: The Death of Paramount Pictures and the Birth of Corporate Hollywood* (University Press of Kentucky, Lexington).

Dijkstra, B. (1996) *Evil Sisters: The Threat of Female Sexuality and the Cult of Manhood* (Alfred A. Knopf, New York).

Dmytryk, E. (1978) *It's a Hell of a Life but Not a Bad Living* (Times Books, New York).

Doane, M.A. (1987) *The Desire to Desire: The Woman's Film of the 1940s* (Macmillan, London).

Doane, M.A. (1991) *Femmes Fatales: Feminism, Film Theory, Psychoanalysis* (Routledge, New York and London).

Doherty, T. (1988) *Teenagers and Teenpics: The Juvenilization of American Movies in the 1950s* (Unwin Hyman, London).

Donald, J. (1999) *Imagining the Modern City* (Athlone Press, London).

Dumont, H. (1981) *Robert Siodmak: Le Maître du film noir* (Editions l'Age du Homme, Lausanne)

Dyer, R. (1998) *Stars* (British Film Institute, London).

Dyer, R. (1999) *Seven* (British Film Institute, London).

Eaton, M. (1997) *Chinatown* (British Film Institute, London).

Eisner, L. (1976) *Fritz Lang* (Secker & Warburg, London).

Engelhart, T. (1995) *The End of Victory Culture: Cold War America and the Disillusioning of a Generation* (Basic Books, New York).

Finler, J.W. (1988) *The Hollywood Story* (Octopus, London).

Finler, J.W. (1992) *Hitchcock: The Hollywood Years* (B.T. Batsford, London).

Fishgall, G. (1995) *Against Type: The Biography of Burt Lancaster* (Scribners, New York).

Flinn, C. (1992) *Strains of Utopia: Gender, Nostalgia, and Hollywood Film Music* (Princeton University Press, New Jersey).

Frayling, C. (1992) *Clint Eastwood* (Virgin Publishing, London).

Fujiwara, C. (1998) *The Cinema of Nightfall: Jacques Tourneur* (Johns Hopkins University Press, Baltimore and London).

Gabbard, K. and Gabbard, G.O. (1987) *Psychiatry and the Cinema* (University of Chicago Press, Chicago and London).

Gifford, B. (2001) *Out of the Past: Adventures in Film Noir* (University Press of Mississippi, Jackson).

Gomery, D. (1992) *Shared Pleasures: A History of Movie Presentation in the United States* (British Film Institute, London).

Gorbman, C. (1987) *Unheard Melodies: Narrative Film Music* (British Film Institute, London).

Graebner, W. (1991) *The Age of Doubt: American Thought and Culture in the 1940s* (Twayne, Boston).

Grist, L. (2000) *The Films of Martin Scorsese 1963–77: Authorship and Context* (Macmillan, London).

Handel, L.A. (1950) *Hollywood Looks at its Audience: A Report of Film Audience Research* (University of Illinois Press, Urbana).

Hansberry, K.B. (1998) *Femme Noir: Bad Girls of Film* (McFarland, Jefferson, North Carolina).

Haskell, M. (1987) *From Reverence to Rape: The Treatment of Women in the Movies* (University of Chicago Press, Chicago and London).

Haut, W. (1995) *Pulp Culture: Hardboiled Fiction and the Cold War* (Serpent's Tail, London).

Haut, W. (1999) *Neon Noir: Contemporary American Crime Fiction* (Serpent's Tail, London).

Heisner, B. (1990) *Hollywood Art: Art Direction in the Days of the Great Studios* (St James Press, Chicago and London).

Henriksen, M.A. (1997) *Dr Strangelove's America: Society and Culture in the Atomic Age* (University of California Press, Los Angeles).

Higham, C. and Greenberg, J. (1968), *Hollywood in the Forties* (Tantivy, London).

Hilfer, T. (1990) *The Crime Novel: A Deviant Genre* (University of Texas Press, Austin).

Hillier, J. (1993) *The New Hollywood* (Studio Vista, London).

Hirsch, F. (1983) *The Dark Side of the Screen: Film Noir* (Da Capo: New York).

Howard, J. (1999) *The Stanley Kubrick Companion* (Batsford, London).

Hurst, R.M. (1979) *Republic Studios: Between Poverty Row and the Majors* (Scarecrow Press, Metuchen, New Jersey).

Insdorf, A. (1994) *François Truffaut* (Cambridge University Press, Cambridge).

Izod, J. (1988) *Hollywood at the Box Office, 1895–1986* (Macmillan, London).

Jacobs, D. (1977) *Hollywood Renaissance* (A.S. Barnes, New Jersey).

Jameson, F. (1991) *Postmodernism, or, The Cultural Logic of Late Capitalism* (Verso, London).

Jensen, P. (1969) *The Cinema of Fritz Lang* (Zwemmer, London).

Jewell, R. and Harbin, V. (1982) *The RKO Story* (Arlington House, New Rochelle, New York).

Johnson, D. (1983) *Dashiell Hammett: A Life* (Random House, New York).

Jordan, B. and Morgan-Tamosunas, R. (1998) *Contemporary Spanish Cinema* (Manchester University Press, Manchester).

Kaes, A. (2000) *M* (British Film Institute, London).

Kalinak, K. (1992) *Settling the Score: Music and the Classical Hollywood Film* (University of Wisconsin Press, Madison).

Kapsis, R. (1992) *Hitchcock: The Making of a Reputation* (University of Chicago Press, Chicago and London).

Karimi, A.M. (1970) *Towards a Definition of the American Film Noir* (Arno Press, New York).

Keyssar, H. (1991) *Robert Altman's America* (Oxford University Press, New York).

Kitses, J. (1996) *Gun Crazy* (British Film Institute, London).

Kozloff, S. (1988) *Invisible Storytellers: Voice-Over Narration in the American Fiction Film* (University of California Press, Los Angeles).

Lane, C. (2000) *Feminist Hollywood: From 'Born in Flames' to 'Point Break'* (Wayne State University Press, Detroit).

Lasky, B. (1985) *RKO: The Biggest Little Major of Them All* (Prentice-Hall, New Jersey).

Leab, D.J. (1975) *From Sambo to Superspade: The Black Experience in Motion Pictures* (Secker & Warburg, London).

Leff, L.J. (1987), *Hitchcock and Selznick* (Weidenfeld & Nicolson, London).

Leff, L.J. and Simmons, J.L. (1990) *The Dame in the Kimono: Hollywood, Censorship and the Production Code from the 1920s to the 1960s* (Weidenfeld & Nicolson, London).

Lev, P. (2000) *American Films of the 70s: Conflicting Visions* (University of Texas Press, Austin).

Luhr, W. (1991) *Raymond Chandler and Film* (Florida State University Press, Tallahassee).

Lyons, A. (2000), *Death on the Cheap: The Lost B Movies of Film Noir* (Da Capo, New York).

Lyotard, J.-F. (1984) *The Postmodern Condition: A Report on Knowledge* (Manchester University Press, Manchester).

MacCann, R. Dyer (1962) *Hollywood in Transition* (Greenwood Press, Connecticut).

McArthur, C. (1972) *Underworld USA* (Secker & Warburg, London).

McArthur, C. (1992) *The Big Heat* (British Film Institute, London).

McCann, G. (1996) *Cary Grant: A Class Apart* (Fourth Estate, London).

McGilligan, P. (1986) *Backstory: Interviews with Screenwriters of Hollywood's Golden Age* (University of California Press, Los Angeles).

McGilligan, P. (1997) *Fritz Lang: The Nature of the Beast* (Faber and Faber, London).

Maltby, R. (1983) *Harmless Entertainment: Hollywood and the Ideology of Consensus* (Scarecrow Press, Metuchen, New Jersey).

Maltby, R. (1995) *Hollywood Cinema: An Introduction* (Blackwell, Oxford).

Marling, W. (1995) *The American Roman Noir: Hammett, Cain, and Chandler* (University of Georgia Press, Athens and London).

Maxfield, J. (1996) *The Fatal Woman: Sources of Male Anxiety in American Film Noir, 1941–1991* (Associated University Presses, London).

Millikins, S.F. (1976) *Chester Himes: A Critical Appraisal* (Columbia University Press, New York).

Mitry, J. (1998) *The Aesthetics and Psychology of the Cinema*, trans. Chris King (Athlone Press, London).

Modleski, T. (1982) *Loving with a Vengeance: Mass-Produced Fantasies for Women* (Methuen, London).

Monaco, J. (1980) *The New Wave: Truffaut, Godard, Chabrol, Rohmer, Rivette* (Oxford University Press, New York).

Mordden, E. (1988) *The Hollywood Studios: House Style in the Golden Age of the Movies* (Alfred A. Knopf, New York).

Morrison, J. (1999) *Passport to Hollywood: Hollywood Films, European Directors* (State University of New York Press, New York).

Mottram, J. (2000) *The Coen Brothers: The Life of the Mind* (B.T. Batsford, London).

Muller, E. (1998) *Dark City: The Lost World of Film Noir* (Titan Books, London).

Muller, E. (2001) *Dark City Dames: The Wicked Women of Film Noir* (Regan Books, New York).

Munby, J. (1999a) *Public Enemies, Public Heroes: Screening the Gangster from 'Little Caesar' to 'Touch of Evil'* (University of Chicago Press, Chicago and London).

Naremore, J. (1989) *The Magic World of Orson Welles* (Southern Methodist University Press, Dallas).

Nevins, F.M. Jr (1988), *Cornell Woolrich: First You Dream, Then You Die* (Mysterious Press, New York).

O'Brien, G. (1997) *Hardboiled America: Lurid Paperbacks and the Masters of Noir* (Da Capo, New York).

Orr, J. (1993) *Cinema and Modernity* (Polity Press, Cambridge).

Orr, J. (1998) *Contemporary Cinema* (Edinburgh University Press, Edinburgh).

Orr, J. (2000) *The Art and Politics of Film* (Edinburgh University Press, Edinburgh).

Ott, F.W. (1979) *The Films of Fritz Lang* (The Citadel Press, New Jersey).

Ottoson, R. (1981) *A Reference Guide to the American Film Noir, 1940–1958* (Scarecrow Press, Metuchen, New Jersey).

Pell, R.H. (1985) *The Liberal Mind in a Conservative Age: American Intellectuals in the 1940s and 1950s* (Harper & Row, New York).

Phillips, G.D. (2000), *Creatures of Darkness: Raymond Chandler, Detective Fiction and Film Noir* (University Press of Kentucky, Lexington).

Polan, D. (1986) *Power and Paranoia: History, Narrative and the American Cinema, 1940–1950* (Columbia University Press, New York).

Polan, D. (1993) *In a Lonely Place* (British Film Institute, London).

Polan, D. (2000) *Pulp Fiction* (British Film Institute, London).

Polito, R. (1996) *The Savage Art: A Biography of Jim Thompson* (Alfred A. Knopf, New York).

Porter, D. (1981) *The Pursuit of Crime: Art and Ideology in Detective Fiction* (Yale University Press, New Haven and London).

Praz, M. (1970 [1933]) *The Romantic Agony* (Oxford University Press, Oxford).

Prince, S. (1999) *A New Pot of Gold: American Cinema 1980–1989* (Scribners, New York).

Punter, D. (1996) *The Literature of Terror vol. 1: The Gothic Tradition* (Longman, London).

Pye, M. and Myles, L. (1979) *The Movie Brats: How the Film Generation Took Over in Hollywood* (Holt, Rinehart & Winston, New York).

Ray, R. (1985) *A Certain Tendency of the Hollywood Cinema, 1930–1980* (Princeton University Press, New Jersey).

Read, J. (2000) *The New Avengers: Feminism, Femininity and the Rape–Revenge Cycle* (Manchester University Press, Manchester).

Rubin. M. (1999) *Thrillers* (Cambridge University Press, Cambridge).

Ruth, D.E. (1996) *Inventing the Public Enemy: The Gangster in American Culture, 1918–1934* (University of Chicago Press, Chicago).

Ryan, M. and Kellner, D. (1988) *Camera Politica: The Politics and Ideology of Contemporary Hollywood Film* (Indiana University Press, Bloomington and Indianapolis).

Salt, B. (1992) *Film Style and Technology: History and Analysis* (Starword, London).

Sammon, P.M. (1996) *Future Noir: The Making of 'Blade Runner'* (HarperPrism, London).

Schatz, T. (1981) *Hollywood Genres: Formulas, Filmmaking, and the Studio System* (McGraw-Hill, New York).

Schatz, T. (1983) *Old Hollywood/New Hollywood: Ritual, Art, and Industry* (UMI Research Press, Ann Arbor, Michigan).

Schatz, T. (1989) *The Genius of the System: Hollywood Filmmaking in the Studio Era* (Simon & Schuster, London).

Schatz, T. (1997) *Boom and Bust: American Culture in the 1940s* (University of California Press, Los Angeles).

Schickel, R. (1992) *Double Indemnity* (British Film Institute, London).

Schumach, M. (1975) *The Face on the Cutting Room Floor: The Story of Movie and Television Censorship* (Da Capo, New York).

Schwartz, R. (2001) *Noir Now and Then: Film Noir Originals and Remakes (1944–1999)* (Greenwood Press, Connecticut and London).

Selby, S. (1997) *Dark City: The Film Noir* (McFarland, Jefferson, North Carolina).

Server, L. (1994) *Over My Dead Body: The Sensational Age of the American Paperback: 1945–1955* (Chronicle Books, San Francisco).

Server, L., Gorman, E. and Greenberg, M.H. (1998) (eds) *The Big Book of Film Noir* (Carroll and Graf, New York).

Shadoian, J. (1977) *Dreams and Dead Ends: The American Gangster/Crime Film* (MIT Press, Massachusetts).

Siegel, J.E. (1972) *Val Lewton: the Reality of Terror* (Secker & Warburg, London).

Silver, A. and Ursini, J. (1999b) *The Noir Style* (Aurum Press, London).

Silverman, K. (1992), *Male Subjectivity at the Margins* (Routledge, New York).

Simpson, P.L. (2000) *Psychopaths: Tracking the Serial Killer Through Contemporary American Film and Fiction* (Southern Illinois University Press, Carbondale).

Sklar, R. (1978), *Movie-Made America: A Cultural History of American Movies* (Chappell, London).

Solomon, A. (1988) *Twentieth Century-Fox: A Corporate and Financial History* (Scarecrow Press, Metuchen, New Jersey).

Tallack, D. (1991) *Twentieth-Century America: The Intellectual and Cultural Context* (Longman, London).

Tasker, Y. (1993) *Spectacular Bodies: Gender, Genre and the Action Cinema* (Comedia/ Routledge, London).

Taubin, A. (2000) *Taxi Driver* (British Film Institute, London).

Taylor, J. Russell (1983) *Strangers in Paradise: The Hollywood Emigres 1933–1950* (Faber and Faber, London).

Telotte, J.P. (1985) *Dreams of Darkness: Fantasy and the Films of Val Lewton* (University of Illinois Press, Urbana and Chicago).

Telotte, J.P. (1989) *Voices in the Dark: The Narrative Patterns of Film Noir* (University of Chicago Press, Urbana).

Thomson, D. (1997) *The Big Sleep* (British Film Institute, London).

Thompson, D. and Christie, I. (eds) (1989) *Scorsese on Scorsese* (Faber and Faber, London).

Thompson, P. and Usukawa, S. (1992) *The Little Black and White Book of Film Noir* (Arsenal Pulp Press, Vancouver).

Thompson, P. and Usukawa, S. (1995) *Hard-Boiled: Great Lines from Classic Noir Films* (Chronicle Books, San Francisco).

Truffaut, F. (1986) *Hitchcock* (Paladin, London).

Turim, M. (1989) *Flashbacks in Film* (Routledge, New York and London).

Tuska, J. (1984) *Dark Cinema: American 'Film Noir' in a Cultural Perspective* (Greenwood Press, Westport, Connecticut and London).

Vincendeau, G. (2000) *Stars and Stardom in French Cinema* (Continuum, London and New York).

Wager, J.B. (1999) *Dangerous Dames: Women and Representation in the Weimar Street Film and Film Noir* (Ohio University Press, Athens).

Walsh, A.S. (1985) *Women's Film and Female Experience 1940–1950* (Praeger, New York).

Wexman, V.W. (1985) *Roman Polanski* (Twayne, Boston).

Whitfield, S.J. (1991) *The Culture of the Cold War* (Johns Hopkins University Press, Baltimore and London).

Wilinsky, B. (2001) *Sure Seaters: The Emergence of Art House Cinema* (University of Minnesota Press, Minneapolis and London).

Willett, R. (1996) *The Naked City: Urban Crime Fiction in the USA* (Manchester University Press, Manchester).

Williams, J. (1991) *Into the Badlands: A Journey Through the American Dream* (Grafton Books, London).

Willis, S. (1997) *High Contrast: Race and Gender in Contemporary Hollywood Film* (Duke University Press, Durham, North Carolina).

Wilson, E. (1962) *Classics and Commercials: A Literary Chronicle of the Forties* (Vintage Books, New York).

Wolfenstein, M. and Leites, N. (1950) *Movies: A Psychological Study* (The Free Press, Glencoe).

Woods, P.A. (ed.) (2000a) *Joel and Ethan Coen: Blood Siblings* (Plexus Books, London).

Woods, P.A. (ed.) (2000b) *Quentin Tarantino: The Film Geek Files* (Plexus Books, London).

Worpole, K. (1983) *Dockers and Detectives* (Verso, London).

Wyatt, J. (1994) *High Concept: Movies and Marketing in Hollywood* (University of Texas Press, Austin).

JOURNAL ARTICLES AND CHAPTERS FROM BOOKS

Allyn, J. (1978) '*Double Indemnity*: A Policy that Paid Off', *Literature/Film Quarterly* (6) 118–20.

Andersen, T. (1986) 'Red Hollywood' in Ferguson, S. and Groseclose, B. (eds) *Literature and the Visual Arts in Contemporary Society* (Ohio University Press, Columbus) 141–96.

Appel, A. (1974) 'Fritz Lang's American Nightmare', *Film Comment* 10 (6) 12–17.

Arthur, P. (1996a) 'Los Angeles as Scene of the Crime', *Film Comment* 32 (4) 20–6.

Arthur, P. (1996b) 'Out of the Depths: *Citizen Kane*, Modernism and the Avant-Garde Impulse' in Gottesman, R. (ed.) *Perspectives on 'Citizen Kane'* (G.K. Hall, New York) 367–82.

Arthur, P. (1996c) 'The Gun in the Briefcase; or, The Inscription of Class in Film Noir' in James, D.E. and Berg, R. (eds) *The Hidden Foundation: Cinema and the Question of Class* (University of Minnesota Press, Minneapolis) 90–113.

Arthur, P. (2001) 'Murder's Tongue: Identity, Death and the City in Film Noir' in Slocum, J.D. (ed.) *Violence and American Cinema* (Routledge, New York and London) 153–75.

Balio, T. (1985) 'Retrenchment, Reappraisal, and Reorganization' in Balio, T. (ed.) *The American Film Industry* (University of Wisconsin Press, Madison) 401–47.

Balio, T. (1990) 'Introduction to Part II' in Balio, T. (ed.) *Hollywood in the Age of Television* (Unwin Hyman, London) 259–96.

Balio, T. (1998) '"A major presence in all of the world's important markets": the globalization of Hollywood in the 1990s' in Neale, S. and Smith, M. (eds) *Contemporary Hollywood Cinema* (Routledge, London and New York) 58–73.

Baudrillard, J. (1983) 'The Ecstasy of Communication' in Foster, H. (ed.) *Postmodern Culture* (Pluto Press, 1985) 126–34.

Belton, J. (1980–1) 'The Bionic Eye: Zoom Esthetics', *Cineaste* 9 (1) 20–7.

Bernstein, M. (1999) 'A Tale of Three Cities: The Banning of *Scarlet Street*' in Bernstein, M. (ed.) *Controlling Hollywood: Censorship and Regulation in the Studio Era* (Rutgers University Press, New Jersey) 157–85.

Brackett, L. (1974) 'From *The Big Sleep* to *The Long Goodbye* and More or Less How We Got There', *Take One* 1 (1) 26–8.

Brinton, J.P. III (1947) 'Subjective Camera or Subjective Audience?', *Hollywood Quarterly* (2) 359–66.

Buchsbaum, J. (1992) 'Tame Wolves and Phoney Claims: Paranoia and Film Noir' in Cameron (ed.) 88–97 (first pub. in *Persistence of Vision* 3 (4) 1986).

Buckley, R. (1986) 'Richard Widmark', *Films in Review* xxxvii (5) and xxxvii (6/7) 222–9; 259–70.

Butler, J. (1996 [1985]) '*Miami Vice*: the Legacy of *Film Noir*' in *Film Noir Reader* 289–305 (first pub. *Journal of Popular Film and Television* (13) 3 1985).

Cawelti, J. (1995 [1979]) '*Chinatown* and Generic Transformation in Recent American Films' in Grant, B.K. (ed.) *Film Genre Reader II* (University of Texas Press, Austin) 183–201.

Chandler, R. (1964 [1950]) 'The Simple Art of Murder', in *Pearls Are a Nuisance* (Penguin, Harmondsworth) 181–99.

Chute, D. (1981) 'Tropic of Kasdan', *Film Comment* 17 (5) 49–52.

Cohan, S. (1998) 'Censorship and Narrative Indeterminacy in *Basic Instinct*' in Neale, S. and Smith, M. (eds) *Contemporary Hollywood Cinema* (Routledge, London and New York) 263–79.

Cohen, A.J.-J. (2001) 'Virtual Hollywood and the Genealogy of its Hyper-Spectator' in Stokes, M. and Maltby, R. (eds) *Hollywood Spectatorship: Changing Perceptions of Cinema Audiences* (British Film Institute, London) 152–63.

Cohen, M. (1974) 'The Actor: Villains and Victims', *Film Comment* 10 (6) 27–9.

Cohen, M. (1992–3) 'The Homme Fatal', *Cultural Critique* (23) 111–36.

Collins, J. (1993) 'Genericity in the Nineties: Eclectic Irony and the New Sincerity' in Collins, J. *et al.* (eds) *Film Theory Goes to the Movies* (Routledge, New York and London) 242–63.

Conley, T. (2000) 'Noir in the Red and Nineties in the Black' in Dixon, W.W. (ed.) *Film Genre 2000: New Critical Essays* (State University of New York Press, New York) 193–210.

Cook, P. (1998) 'Duplicity in *Mildred Pierce*' in Kaplan, E. Ann (ed.) *Women in Film Noir* (British Film Institute, London) 69–80.

Cowie, E. (1993) 'Film Noir and Women' in Copjec, J. (ed.) *Shades of Noir* (Verso, London) 121–66.

Couvares, F.G. (1996) 'Hollywood Main Street: Trying to Censor Movies before the Production Code' in Couvares, F.G. (ed.) *Movie Censorship and American Culture* (Smithsonian Institution Press, Washington and London).

Damico, J. (1996) '*Film Noir*: A Modest Proposal' in *Film Noir Reader* 95–105 (first pub. *Film Reader* 3 1978).

Darke, C. (1996) 'Inside the Light – Interview with Darius Khondji', *Sight and Sound* 6 (4) 18–20.

Darke, C. (2000) 'Mr Memory', *Sight and Sound* 10 (11) 42–3.

Davis, M. (2001) 'Bunker Hill: Hollywood's Dark Shadow' in Shiel, M. and Fitzmaurice, T. (eds) *Cinema and the City: Film and Urban Societies in a Global Context* (Blackwell, Oxford) 33–45.

Diawara, M. (1993) 'Noir by Noirs: Toward a New Realism in Black Cinema' in Copjec, J. (ed.) *Shades of Noir* (Verso, London) 261–78.

Dimendberg, E. (1996) 'Kiss the City Goodbye', *Lusitania* (7) 56–66.

Dimendberg, E. (1997) 'From Berlin to Bunker Hill: Urban Space, Late Modernity, and Film Noir in Fritz Lang's and Joseph Losey's *M*', *Wide Angle* 19 (4) 62–93.

Dittmar, L. (1988) 'From Fascism to the Cold War: *Gilda*'s "Fantastic" Politics', *Wide Angle* 10 (3) 5–18.

Dixon, W.W. (2000) 'Introduction: The New Genre Cinema' in Dixon, W.W. (ed.) *Film Genre 2000: New Critical Essays* (State University of New York Press, New York) 1–12.

Douglass, W. (1981) 'The Criminal Psychopath as Hollywood Hero', *Journal of Popular Film and Television* 8 (4) 30–9.

Durgnat, R. (1970) 'Paint it Black: The Family Tree of the *Film Noir*', *Cinema* (6/7) 48–56.

Dyer, R. (1993 [1977]) 'Homosexuality and Film Noir' in *The Matter of Images* (Routledge, London) 52–72.

Dyer, R. (1998) 'Resistance Through Charisma: Rita Hayworth and *Gilda*' in Kaplan, E. Ann (ed.) *Women in Film Noir* (British Film Institute, London) 115–22.

Elsaesser, T. (1998) 'Spectacularity and Engulfment: Francis Ford Coppola and *Bram Stoker's Dracula*' in Neale, S. and Smith, M. (eds) *Contemporary Hollywood Cinema* (Routledge, London and New York) 191–208.

Erickson, T. (1996 [1990]) 'Kill Me Again: Movement Becomes Genre' in *Film Noir Reader* 307–30.

Fischer, L. (1993) 'Mama's Boy: Filial Hysteria in *White Heat*' in Cohan, S. and Hark, I. Rae (eds) *Screening the Male: Exploring Masculinities in Hollywood Cinema* (Routledge, London) 70–86.

Flynn, C. and McCarthy, T. (1975) 'The Economic Imperative: Why Was the B Movie Necessary?' in McCarthy, T. and Flynn, C. (eds) *Kings of the Bs: Working Within the Hollywood System: An Anthology of Film History and Criticism* (E.P. Dutton, New York) 13–43.

Forbes, J. (1992) 'The "Série Noire" in Rigby, B. and Hewitt, N. (eds) *France and the Mass Media* (Macmillan, London) 85–97.

Frank, N. (1999) 'Un Nouveau Genre "Policier": l'Aventure Criminelle' in *Film Noir Reader 2* 15–19 (first pub. *L'Ecran Français* August 1946).

Fuller, G. (1994) 'Kasdan on Kasdan' in Boorman, J. and Donohue, W. (eds) *Projections 3: Film-makers on Film-making* (Faber and Faber, London) 111–50.

Gach, G. (1996) 'John Alton: Master of the Film Noir Mood', *American Cinematographer* 77 (9) 87–92.

Glancy, H.M. (1995) 'Warner Bros. Film Grosses, 1921–51: the William Schafer Ledger', *Historical Journal of Film, Radio and Television* 15 (1) 55–71.

Gledhill, C. (1998) '*Klute* 1: A Contemporary Film Noir and Feminist Criticism' in Kaplan, E. Ann (ed.) *Women in Film Noir* (British Film Institute, London) 20–34.

Gomery, D. (1998) 'Hollywood's corporate business practice and periodizing contemporary history' in Neale, S. and Smith, M. (eds) *Contemporary Hollywood Cinema* (Routledge, London and New York) 47–57.

Graham, M. (1981) 'The Inaccessibility of *The Lady from Shanghai*', *Film Criticism* 5 (2) 21–37.

Grant, B.K. (1998) 'Rich and Strange: The Yuppie Horror Film' in Neale, S. and
Smith, M. (eds) *Contemporary Hollywood Cinema* (Routledge, London and
New York) 280–93.

Gross, L. (1976) 'Film Après Noir', *Film Comment* 12 (2) 44–9.

Haralovich, M.B. (1997) 'Selling *Mildred Pierce*: A Case Study in Movie Promotion' in
Schatz, T., *Boom and Bust: American Cinema in the 1940s* (University of California
Press, Los Angeles and London) 196–202.

Harvey, S. (1998) 'Woman's Place: The Absent Family of Film Noir' in Kaplan, E.
Ann (ed.) *Women in Film Noir* (British Film Institute, London) 35–46.

Hinson, H. (1986) 'Bloodlines', *Film Comment* 21 (2) 14–16.

Hollinger, K. (1996 [1990]) 'Film Noir, Voice-Over and the Femme Fatale', *Film Noir
Reader* 243–59.

Holmlund, C. (1993) 'A Decade of Deadly Dolls: Hollywood and the Woman Killer'
in Birch, H. (ed.) *Moving Targets: Women, Murder and Representation* (Virago,
London) 127–51.

Hugo, C. (1992) '*The Big Combo*: Production Conditions and the Film Text' in
Cameron, I. (ed.) *The Movie Book of Film Noir* (Studio Vista, London) 247–53.

Jacobs, L. (1992) 'The B Film and the Problem of Cultural Distinction', *Screen* 33 (1)
1–13.

Jameson, F. (1993) 'The Synoptic Chandler' in Copjec, J. (ed.) *Shades of Noir*
(Verso, London) 33–56.

Jameson, R. (1999) 'Film Noir Today: Son of Noir' in *Film Noir Reader 2* 197–205
[first pub. *Film Comment* 1974].

Jewell, R.B. (1996) 'Orson Welles and the Studio System: The RKO Context' in
Gottesman, R. (ed.) *Perspectives on 'Citizen Kane'* (G.K. Hall, New York) 122–31.

Jones, A. (1991) '"She Was Bad News": Male Paranoia and the Contemporary New
Woman', *Camera Obscura* (26–7) 297–320.

Kemp, P. (1986) 'From the Nightmare Factory: HUAC and the Politics of Noir',
Sight and Sound 55 (4) 266–70.

Kerr, P. (1996 [1979–80]) 'Out of What Past? Notes on the B Film Noir', in *Film Noir
Reader* 107–27.

Klinger, B. (2001) 'The Contemporary Cinephile: Film Collecting in the Post-Video
Era', in Stokes, M. and Maltby, R. (eds) *Hollywood Spectatorship: Changing
Perceptions of Cinema Audiences* (British Film Institute, London) 132–51.

Kobal, J. (1972) 'The Time, the Place, and the Girl: Rita Hayworth', *Focus on Film*
(10) 15–29.

Krutnik, F. (1997) 'Something More Than Night: Tales of the Noir City' in Clarke,
D.B. (ed.) *The Cinematic City* (Routledge, London) 83–109.

Lafferty, W. (1983) 'A Reappraisal of the Semi-Documentary in Hollywood,
1945–1948', *Velvet Light Trap* 22–6.

Lang, F. (1948) 'Happily Ever After', *Penguin Film Review* (5) 22–9.

Lang, R. (1988) 'Looking for the "Great Whatzit": *Kiss Me Deadly* and Film Noir',
Cinema Journal 27 (3) 32–44.

Lee, A.R. (1990) 'The View from the Rear Window: The Fiction of Cornell Woolrich'
in Bloom, C. (ed.) *Twentieth-Century Suspense: The Thriller Comes of Age*
(Macmillan, London) 174–88.

Lightman, H. and Patterson, R. (1982) 'Blade Runner: Production Design and Photography', American Cinematographer 684-7, 715-25.

Lott, E. (1997) 'The Whiteness of Film Noir' in Hill, M. (ed.) Whiteness: A Critical Reader (New York University Press, New York and London).

McConnell, F. (1973) 'Pickup on South Street and the Metamorphosis of the Thriller', Film Heritage 8 (3) 9-18.

Maltby, R. (1992 [1984]) 'Film Noir: The Politics of the Maladjusted Text' in Cameron, I. (ed.) The Movie Book of Film Noir (Studio Vista, London) 39-48 (first pub. Journal of American Studies 18 1984).

Maltby, R. (1993) 'The Production Code and the Hays Office' in Balio, T. (ed.) Grand Design: Hollywood as a Modern Business Enterprise 1930-1939 (Scribners, New York) 37-72.

Maltby, R. (1998) ' "The search for hidden propaganda": Hollywood, Politics and Ideology' in Chapman, J. (ed.) Popular American Film 1945-1995 (Open University, Milton Keynes).

Maltby, R. (1999) 'Sticks, Hicks and Flaps: Classical Hollywood's Generic Conception of its Audiences' in Stokes, M. and Maltby, R. (eds) Identifying Hollywood's Audiences: Cultural Identity and the Movies (British Film Institute, London) 23-41.

Margolis, H. (1993) 'Blue Steel: Progressive Feminism in the 90s?', Postscript 13 (1) 67-76.

Marks, M. (2000) 'Music, Drama, Warner Brothers: The Case of Casablanca and The Maltese Falcon' in Buhler, J., Flinn, C. and Neumeyer, D. (eds) Music and Cinema (Wesleyan University Press, Hanover, New England) 161-86.

Martin, A. (1998) 'Gilda Didn't Do Any of Those Things You've Been Losing Sleep Over!: The Central Women of 40s Films Noirs' in Kaplan, E. Ann (ed.) Women in Film Noir (British Film Institute, London) 202-28.

May, L. (1989) 'Movie Star Politics: The Screen Actors Guild, Cultural Conversion and the Red Scare' in May, L. (ed.) Recasting America: Culture and Politics in the Age of the Cold War (Johns Hopkins University Press, Baltimore and London) 125-53.

Meisel, M. (1975) 'Edgar Ulmer: The Primacy of the Visual' in McCarthy, T. and Flynn, C. (eds) Kings of the Bs: Working Within the Hollywood System: An Anthology of Film History and Criticism (E.P. Dutton, New York).

Miller, D. (1978) 'Eagle-Lion: The Violent Years', Focus on Film (31) 27-39.

Monk, G. (1973) 'Laird Cregar', Film Fan Monthly (150) 6-11.

Moreno, J. (1953) 'Subjective Camera: And the Problem of Film in the First Person', Quarterly of Film, Radio and Television (7) 341-58.

Morgan, J. (1996) 'Scarlet Street: Noir Realism from Berlin to Paris to Hollywood', Iris (21) 31-53.

Munby, J. (1999b) 'Heimat Hollywood: Billy Wilder, Otto Preminger, Edgar Ulmer, and the Criminal Cinema of the Austro-Jewish Diaspora' in Good, D.F. and Wodak, R. (eds) From World War to Waldheim: Culture and Politics in Austria and the United States (Berghahn Books, New York and Oxford) 138-62.

Nachbar, J. (1988) 'Film Noir' in Gehring, W. (ed.) Handbook of American Genres (Greenwood Press, New York) 66-85.

Naremore, J. (1973) 'John Huston and The Maltese Falcon', Literature/Film Quarterly 1 (3) 239-49.

Naremore, J. (1995-6) 'American Film Noir: The History of an Idea', Film Quarterly 49 (2) 12-28.

Naremore, J. (1999) 'Hitchcock at the Margins of Noir' in Allen, R. and Gonzalès, S.I. (eds) *Alfred Hitchcock: Centenary Essays* (British Film Institute, London) 263–78.

O'Brien, C. (1996) 'Film Noir in France: Before the Liberation', *Iris* (21) 7–20.

O'Brien, G. (2000) 'Dana Andrews, or the Male Mask' in Sante, L. and Pierson, M.H. (eds) *O.K. You Mugs: Writers on Movie Actors* (Granta Books, London) 35–46.

Ogle, B. (1972) 'Technological and Aesthetic Influences Upon the Development of Deep Focus Cinematography in the United States', *Screen* 13 (1) 45–72.

Ohmer, S. (1999) 'The Science of Pleasure: George Gallup and Audience Research in Hollywood' in Stokes, M. and Maltby, R. (eds) *Identifying Hollywood's Audiences: Cultural Identity and the Movies* (British Film Institute, London) 61–80.

Onosko, T. (1972) 'Monogram: Its Rise and Fall in the 1940s', *Velvet Light Trap* (5) 5–9.

Orr, C. (1997) 'Genre Theory in the Context of the Noir and Post-Noir Film', *Film Criticism* 22 (1) 21–37.

Pidduck, J. (1995) 'The 1990s Hollywood Femme Fatale: (Dis)Figuring Feminism, Family, Irony, Violence', *CineAction!* September 65–72.

Place, J. (1998) 'Women in Film Noir' in Kaplan, E. Ann (ed.) *Women in Film Noir* (British Film Institute, London) 47–68.

Place, J.A. and Peterson, L.S. (1996) 'Some Visual Motifs in Film Noir' in *Film Noir Reader* 65–76 (first pub. *Film Comment* January–February 1974).

Porfirio, R. (1996) 'No Way Out: Existential Motifs in the Film Noir' in *Film Noir Reader* 77–93 (first pub. *Sight and Sound* 45 (4) 1976).

Porfirio, R. (1999 [1979]) 'Dark Jazz: Music in the Film Noir', *Film Noir Reader 2* 177–88.

Randall, R.S. (1985) 'Censorship: From *The Miracle* to *Deep Throat*' in Balio, T. (ed.) *The American Film Industry* (University of Wisconsin Press, Wisconsin) 432–57.

Reid, D. and Walker, J.L. (1993) 'Strange Pursuit: Cornell Woolrich and the Abandoned City of the Forties' in Copjec, J. (ed.) *Shades of Noir* (Verso, London) 57–96.

Russ, J. (1973) 'Somebody's Trying to Kill Me and I Think It's My Husband: The Modern Gothic', *Journal of Popular Culture* 6 (4) 666–91.

Schatz, T. (1993) 'The New Hollywood' in Collins, J. *et al.* (eds) *Film Theory Goes to the Movies* (Routledge, London and New York) 8–36.

Sharrett, C. (1993) 'The American Apocalypse: Scorsese's *Taxi Driver*' in Sharrett, C. (ed.) *Crisis Cinema: The Apocalyptic Idea in Postmodern Narrative Film* (Maisonneuve Press, Washington) 220–35.

Shearer, L. (1999) 'Crime Certainly Pays on the Screen', *Film Noir Reader 2* 9–13 (first pub. *New York Times Magazine* 5 August 1945).

Silver, A. (1996) 'Son of *Noir*: Neo-*Film Noir* and the Neo-B Picture', *Film Noir Reader* 331–8 (first pub. *DGA Magazine* 17 (3) June–July 1992).

Siodmak, R. (1959) 'Hoodlums: The Myth', *Films and Filming* 5 (9) 10, 35.

Sklar, R. (1999) ' "The Lost Audience": 1950s Spectatorship and Historical Reception Studies' in Stokes, M. and Maltby, R. (eds) *Identifying Hollywood's Audiences: Cultural Identity and the Movies* (British Film Institute, London) 81–92.

Smith, A.L. (1996) 'Postmodernism/Gothicism' in Sage, V. and Smith, A.L. (eds) *Modern Gothic: A Reader* (Manchester University Press, Manchester) 6–19.

Smith, E. (1997) 'Subtropical Film Noir' in Glassman, S. and O'Sullivan, M. (eds) *Crime Fiction and Film in the Sunshine State: Florida Noir* (Popular Press, New York) 151–64.

Smith, R.E. (1996) 'Mann in the Dark: The Films Noir of Anthony Mann', *Film Noir Reader* 189–202 (first pub. *Bright Lights* 5 (2:1) 1977).

Sobchak, V. (1998) 'Lounge Time: Postwar Crises and the Chronotope of Film Noir' in Brown, N. (ed.) *Refiguring American Film Genres* (University of California Press, Los Angeles) 129–70.

Stables, K. (1998) 'The Postmodern Always Rings Twice: Constructing the Femme Fatale in 90s Cinema' in Kaplan, E. Ann (ed.) *Women in Film Noir* (British Film Institute, London) 164–82.

Stanley, F. 'Hollywood Crime and Romance', *New York Times* 19 November 1944.

Straw, W. (1997) 'Urban Confidential: The Lurid City of the 1950s' in Clarke, P.B. (ed.) *The Cinematic City* (Routledge, London) 110–28.

Susman, W. with Griffin, E. (1989) 'Did Success Spoil the United States? Dual Representations in Postwar America' in May, L. (ed.) *Recasting America: Culture and Politics in the Age of the Cold War* (University of Chicago Press, Chicago and London) 19–37.

Tarantino, Q. (1994) 'Quentin Tarantino on *Pulp Fiction*', *Sight and Sound* 4 (5) 10–11.

Taves, B. (1993) 'The B Film: Hollywood's Other Half' in Balio, T. (ed.) *Grand Design: Hollywood as a Modern Business Enterprise 1930–1939* (Scribners, New York) 313–50.

Telotte, J.P. (1992) 'Film Noir at Columbia: Fashion and Innovation' in Dick, B. (ed.) *Columbia Pictures: Portrait of a Studio* (University Press of Kentucky, Lexington) 106–17.

Thomas, D. (1992) 'Psychoanalysis and Film Noir' in Cameron, I. (ed.) *The Movie Book of Film Noir* (Studio Vista, London) 71–87.

Turner, G. (1988) ' "I Want to Report a Murder" ', *American Cinematographer* August 35–40.

Ursini, J. (1996) 'Angst at Sixty Fields Per Second' in *Film Noir Reader* 275–87.

Vernet, M. (1993) 'Film Noir on the Edge of Doom' in Copjec, J. (ed.) *Shades of Noir* (Verso, London) 1–32.

Vincendeau, G. (1992a) 'France 1945–65 and Hollywood: The Policier as International Text', *Screen* 33 (1) 50–80.

Vincendeau, G. (1992b) 'Noir is also a French Word: The French Antecedents of Film Noir' in Cameron, I. (ed.) *The Movie Book of Film Noir* (Studio Vista, London) 49–58.

Waldman, D. (1983) 'At Last I Can Tell It to Someone! Feminine Point-of-view and Subjectivity in the Gothic Romance Film of the 1940s', *Cinema Journal* 23 (2) 29–40.

Walker, M. (1992a) 'Film Noir: Introduction' in Cameron, I. (ed.) *The Movie Book of Film Noir* (Studio Vista, London) 8–38.

Walker, M. (1992b) 'Robert Siodmak' in Cameron, I. (ed.) *The Movie Book of Film Noir* (Studio Vista, London) 110–51.

Ward, E. (1996) 'The Post-Noir P.I.: *The Long Goodbye* and *Hickey and Boggs*' in *Film Noir Reader* 237–41 (first pub. ASUCLA Program Notes, Spring 1974).

Warner, M. (1997) 'Voodoo Road', *Sight and Sound* 7 (8) 6–10.

Warshow, R. (1962 [1948]) 'The Gangster as Tragic Hero', *Partisan Review* reprinted in *The Immediate Experience* (Doubleday, New York) 127–33.

Wicking, C. and Pattison, B. (1969) 'Interview with Anthony Mann', *Screen* 10 (4) 32–54.

Williams, L. (1993) 'Erotic Thrillers and Rude Women', *Sight and Sound* 3 (7) 12–15.

Williams, T. (1996) '*Phantom Lady*, Cornell Woolrich and the Masochistic Aesthetic' in *Film Noir Reader* 129–44 (first pub. *CineAction!* 13–14 Summer 1988).

BRITISH FILM NOIR

Addison, P. (1995) *Now the War Is Over: A Social History of Britain 1945–51* (Pimlico, London).

Allsop, K. (1958) *The Angry Decade* (Peter Owen, London).

Barr, C. (1986) 'Introduction: Amnesia and Schizophrenia' in Barr, C. (ed.) *All Our Yesterdays: 90 Years of British Cinema* (British Film Institute, London) 1–30.

Bennett, R. (1995) 'Lean, Mean and Cruel', *Sight and Sound* 5 (1) 34–6.

Chapman, J. (1998) 'Celluloid Shockers' in Richards J. (ed.) *The Unknown 1930s: An Alternative History of the British Cinema, 1929–1939* (I.B. Tauris, London) 75–98.

Chibnall, S. (1995) 'Pulp Versus Penguins: Paperbacks Go to War' in Kirkham, P. and Thoms, D. (eds) *War Culture: Social Change and Changing Experience in World War Two Britain* (Lawrence & Wishart, London) 131–49.

Chibnall, S. (1999) 'Ordinary People: "New Wave" Realism and the British Crime Film' in Chibnall, S. and Murphy, R. (eds) *British Crime Cinema* (Routledge, London) 94–109.

Chibnall, S. (2000) *J. Lee Thompson* (Manchester University Press, Manchester).

Chibnall, S. (2001) 'Travels in Ladland: The British Gangster Film Cycle, 1998–2001' 281–91 in Murphy (ed.) *The British Cinema Book* (British Film Institute, London).

Clay, A. (1998) 'When the Gangs Came to Britain: The Postwar Crime Film', *Journal of Popular British Cinema* (1) 76–86.

Clay, A. (1999) 'Men, Women and Money: Masculinity in Crisis in the British Professional Crime Film 1946–1965' in Chibnall, S. and Murphy, R. (eds) *British Crime Cinema* (Routledge, London) 51–65.

Darke, C. (2001) 'Mike Hodges: "The only thing I like are the credits"', *Independent*, 20 May.

Drazin, C. (2000) *In Search of the Third Man* (Methuen, London).

Everson, W. (1987) 'British Film Noir', *Films in Review* 38 (5) 285–89; and 38 (6) 341–7.

Eyles, A. (1971) 'Ken Hughes: A Passion for Cinema', *Focus on Film* 42–51.

Falk, Q. (1990) *Travels in Greeneland: The Cinema of Graham Greene* (Quartet Books, London).

Gans, H. (1959) *American Films and Television Programs on British Screens: A Study of the Functions of American Popular Culture Abroad* (University of Pennsylvania Institute for Urban Studies, Pennsylvania).

Gilbey, R. (2001) 'Who Killed *Croupier?*', *Financial Times* 25 May.

Gomez, J.A. (1971) 'The Theme of the Double in *The Third Man*', *Film Heritage* (vi) 7–12.

Gough-Yates, K. (1989) 'The British Feature Film as a European Concern: Britain and the Emigré Film-Maker, 1933–1945' in Berghaus, G. (ed.) *Theatre and Film in Exile: German Artists in Britain, 1933–1945* (Oswald Wolff Books, Oxford) 135–66.

Higson, A. (1997) *'Pool of London'* in Burton, A., O'Sullivan, T. and Wells, P. (eds) *Liberal Directions: Basil Dearden and Postwar British Film Culture* (Flicks Books, Trowbridge) 162–71.

Hill, J. (1999a) *British Cinema in the 1980s* (Clarendon Press, Oxford).

Hill, J. (1999b) 'Allegorising the Nation: British Gangster Films of the 1980s' in Chibnall, S. and Murphy, R. (eds) *British Crime Cinema* (Routledge, London) 160–71.

Holland, S. (1993) *The Mushroom Jungle: A History of Postwar Paperback Publishing* (Zeon Books, Westbury, Wiltshire).

James, L. (1976) *Print and the People 1819–1851* (Allen Lane, London).

Knight, S. (1995) 'Murder in Wartime' in Kirkham, P. and Thoms, D. (eds) *War Culture: Social Change and Changing Experience in World War Two Britain* (Lawrence & Wishart, London) 161–77.

MacCabe, C. (1998) *Performance* (British Film Institute, London).

McFarlane, B. (1996) 'Pulp Fictions: The British B Film and the Field of Cultural Production', *Film Criticism* 21 (1) 48–70.

McFarlane, B. (1997) *An Autobiography of British Cinema* (Methuen/BFI, London).

McFarlane, B. (1998) 'Losing the Peace: Some British Films of Postwar Adjustment' in Barta, T. (ed.) *Screening the Past* (Praeger Press, Westport, Connecticut) 93–107.

Marwick, A. (1998) *The Sixties: Cultural Revolution in Britain, France, Italy, and the United States, c.1958–c.1974* (Oxford University Press, Oxford).

Mighall, R. (1999) *A Geography of Victorian Gothic Fiction: Mapping History's Nightmares* (Oxford University Press, Oxford).

Miller, L. (1994) 'Evidence for a British Film Noir Cycle' in Dixon, W.W. (ed.) *Re-Viewing British Cinema, 1900–1992* (State University of New York Press, New York) 155–64.

Monk, C. (1999) 'From Underworld to Underclass: Crime and the British Cinema in the 1990s' in Chibnall, S. and Murphy, R. (eds) *British Crime Cinema* (Routledge, London) 172–88.

Murphy, R. (1986) 'Riff-Raff: British Cinema and the Underworld' in Barr, C. (ed.) *All Our Yesterdays: 90 Years of British Cinema* (British Film Institute, London) 286–305.

Murphy, R. (1989) *Realism and Tinsel: Cinema and Society in Britain 1939–49* (Routledge, London).

Murphy, R. (1992) *Sixties British Cinema* (British Film Institute, London).

Murphy, R. (1993) *Smash & Grab: Gangsters in the London Underworld 1920–60* (Faber and Faber, London).

Park, J. (1990) *British Cinema: The Lights That Failed* (Batsford, London).

Petley, J. (1986) 'The Lost Continent' in Barr, C. (ed.) *All Our Yesterdays: 90 Years of British Cinema* (British Film Institute, London) 98–119.

Pirie, D. (1973) *A Heritage of Horror: The English Gothic Cinema 1946–1972* (Gordon Fraser, London).

Richards, J. (1986) *Thorold Dickinson: The Man and his Films* (Croom Helm, London).

Richards, J. (1997) *Films and British National Identity: From Dickens to 'Dad's Army'* (Manchester University Press, Manchester).

Ripley, M. and Jakubowski, S. (1998) 'Fresh Blood: British Neo-Noir' in Server, L., Gorman, E. and Greenberg, M.H. (eds) *The Big Book of Film Noir* (Carroll and Graf, New York) 317–22.

Sinyard, N. (1991) *The Films of Nicolas Roeg* (Charles Letts, London).

Spicer, A. (1999) 'The Emergence of the British Tough Guy: Stanley Baker, Masculinity and the Crime Thriller' in Chibnall, S. and Murphy, R. (eds) *British Crime Cinema* (Routledge, London) 81–93.

Spicer, A. (2000) 'The BBFC Reports at the British Film Institute: The Case of the Macabre Film', *Journal of Popular British Cinema* (3) 121–4.

Spicer, A. (2001) *Typical Men: The Representation of Masculinity in Popular British Cinema* (I.B. Tauris, London).

Spicer, A. (forthcoming) 'Fisher and Genre II: The Crime Films' in Chapman, J. (ed.) *Fantastic Vision: Terence Fisher and British Film Culture* (Flicks Books, Trowbridge).

Vesselo, A. (1947) 'Films of the Quarter', *Sight and Sound* 120.

Walker, A. (1986) *Hollywood, England: The British Film Industry in the Sixties* (Harrap, London).

Williams, T. (1999) 'British Film Noir' in *Film Noir Reader 2* 242–69.

Worpole, K. (1983) Dockers and Detectives (Verso, London).

Zweiniger-Bargielowska, I. (2000) *Austerity in Britain: Rationing, Controls and Consumption, 1939–1955* (Oxford University Press, Oxford).

MAGAZINES AND JOURNALS

There is no journal specifically devoted to film noir, but articles on film noir appear in most film journals, including *Film Comment, Journal of Popular Film and Television* and others cited in the bibliography.

AUDIO-VISUAL

Century of Cinema: A Personal Journey with Martin Scorsese through American Movies (1995) (three-part documentary, broadcast on Channel 4, 21 May to 4 June).

The Film Noir Story (1995) (broadcast on BBC 2, 4 August).

Dark and Deadly (1995) (broadcast on Channel 4, 19 October).

Big Shots (2001) (broadcast on Channel 4, 27 October).
Second Sight Films Ltd. have brought out a number of 'classic' noirs on video, with accompanying explanatory material, including *D.O.A.*, *Scarlet Street*, *He Walked By Night* and *Force of Evil*.

WEBSITES

Any search engine will provide a large number of film noir pages and references. The three that stand out are:

Martin's Film Noir Page: http://www.martinsfilmnoir.com, which has links to articles, images and other noir sites.

Media Resources Center, University of California, Berkeley: http://www.lib.berkeley.edu/mrc/noirtext.html, which contains the text of academic articles.

'The Dark Room': http://www.cinepad.com/filmnoir/noir_intro.htm, Jim Emerson's enjoyable and imaginative site which introduces noir iconography and archetypes.

OTHER RESOURCES

The British Film Institute Library, 21 Stephen Street, London, W1P 2LN has the most important collection of books and other materials for the study of film in the United Kingdom. It holds runs of all the important journals and has collections of (British) reviews of classic and contemporary films noirs on microfiche. The BFI has published a brief bibliographic guide to 'Modern Noir' (1999). The library catalogue can be accessed online: http://www.bfi.org.uk/nationallibrary/olib/index.html

Film noir is the frequent subject of retrospectives at 'art house' cinemas in this country and abroad. The National Film Theatre's 'Crime Scene', is an annual festival held in July devoted to the crime and mystery genre that includes screenings and discussions of film noir. There is an annual event devoted specifically to Film Noir – 'Noir in Festival' – held in December in Courmayeur, in northern Italy (for details see: www.noirfest.com).

FILMOGRAPHY

(Films arranged chronologically by category; country of origin America unless stated)

ANTECEDENTS

1912 *The Musketeers of Pig Alley* d. D.W. Griffith.

1915 *Alias Jimmy Valentine* d. Maurice Tourneur.

1919 (Germany) *Das Cabinet des Dr Caligari* (*The Cabinet of Dr Caligari*) d. Robert Wiene.

1922 (Germany) *Dr Mabuse der Spieler* (*Dr Mabuse the Gambler*) Parts 1 & 2 d. Fritz Lang.

1923 (Germany) *Die Freudlose Gasse* (*The Joyless Street*) d. G.W. Pabst.

1923 (Germany) *Die Strasse* (*The Street*) d. Karl Grune.

1926 (Germany) *Metropolis* d. Fritz Lang.

1926 (Germany) *Der Student von Prag* (*The Student of Prague*) d. Henrik Galeen.

1927 *Sunrise* d. F.W. Murnau.

1927 *Underworld* d. Joseph Von Sternberg.

1928 *The Docks of New York* d. Joseph Von Sternberg.

1928 (Germany) *Asphalt* d. Joe May.

1929 *The Great Gabbo* d. Eric Von Stroheim.

1929 *Thunderbolt* d. Joseph Von Sternberg.

1930 (Germany) *Der Blaue Engel* (*The Blue Angel*) d. Joseph Von Sternberg.

1930 *Little Caesar* d. Mervyn LeRoy.

1931 (France) *La Chienne* (*The Bitch*) d. Jean Renoir.

1931 *Dracula* d. Tod Browning.

1931 *Frankenstein* d. James Whale.

1931 (Germany) *M* d. Fritz Lang.

1931 *The Maltese Falcon* d. Roy del Ruth.

1931 (Germany) *Der Mann, Der Seinen Mörder Sucht* (*The Man Who Searched for His Own Murderer*) d. Robert Siodmak.

1931 *The Public Enemy* d. William Wellman.

1931 (Germany) *Stürme der Liedenschaft* (*Storms of Passion*) d. Robert Siodmak.

1932 *Beast of the City* d. Charles Brabin.

1932 *The Mummy* d. Karl Freund.

1932 *Murders in the Rue Morgue* d. Robert Florey.

1932 *The Old Dark House* d. James Whale.

1932 *Scarface* d. Howard Hawks.

1932 (Germany) *Das Testament von Dr Mabuse* (*The Last Will of Dr Mabuse*) d. Fritz Lang.

1934 *The Black Cat* d. Edgar Ulmer.
1935 *The Bride of Frankenstein* d. James Whale.
1936 *Fury* d. Fritz Lang.
1936 *Satan Met a Lady* d. William Dieterle.
1937 (France) *Pépé le Moko* d. Julien Duvivier.
1937 *You Only Live Once* d. Fritz Lang.
1938 *Dead End* d. William Wyler.
1939 (France) *Le dernier tournant* (*The Final Twist*) d. Pierre Chenal.
1938 (France) *Quai des brumes* (*Port of Shadows*) d. Marcel Carné.
1939 *Blind Alley* d. Charles Vidor.
1939 (France) *Le Jour se lève* (*Daybreak*) d. Marcel Carné.
1939 *Let Us Live* d. John Brahm.
1939 (France) *Pièges* (*Traps*) d. Robert Siodmak.
1939 *Rio* d. John Brahm.
1939 *The Roaring Twenties* d. Raoul Walsh.
1939 *Son of Frankenstein* d. Rowland V. Lee.
1940 *They Drive by Night* d. Raoul Walsh.
1941 *The Shanghai Gesture* d. Joseph Von Sternberg.
1942 *Cat People* d. Jacques Tourneur.
1943 *The Leopard Man* d. Jacques Tourneur.
1943 *The Seventh Victim* d. Mark Robson.
1943 *Son of Dracula* d. Robert Siodmak.
1945 (Italy) *Rome, Open City* d. Roberto Rossellini.

'CLASSICAL NOIR': 1940–59

1940 *Citizen Kane* d. Orson Welles.
1940 *Rebecca* d. Alfred Hitchcock.
1940 *Stranger on the Third Floor* d. Boris Ingster.
1941 *Among the Living* d. Stuart Heisler.
1941 *High Sierra* d. John Huston.
1941 *I Wake Up Screaming* d. H. Bruce Humberstone.
1941 *The Maltese Falcon* d. John Huston.
1941 *Man Hunt* d. Fritz Lang.
1941 *Suspicion* d. Alfred Hitchcock.
1942 *Crossroads* d. Jack Conway.
1942 *Dr Broadway* d. Anthony Mann.
1942 *Escape from Crime* d. D. Ross Lederman.
1942 *The Falcon Takes Over* d. Irving Reiss.
1942 *The Glass Key* d. Stuart Heisler.
1942 *Street of Chance* d. Jack Hively.
1942 *This Gun for Hire* d. Frank Tuttle.
1943 *Casablanca* d. Michael Curtiz.
1943 *The Fallen Sparrow* d. Richard Wallace.
1943 *Hangmen also Die* d. Fritz Lang.
1943 *Journey into Fear* d. Orson Welles.
1943 *Secret Enemies* d. Benjamin Stoloff.
1943 *Shadow of a Doubt* d. Alfred Hitchcock.

1944 *Christmas Holiday* d. Robert Siodmak.
1944 *Double Indemnity* d. Billy Wilder.
1944 *Experiment Perilous* d. Jacques Tourneur.
1944 *Gaslight* d. George Cukor.
1944 *Laura* d. Otto Preminger.
1944 *The Mask of Dimitrios* d. Jean Negulesco.
1944 *Ministry of Fear* d. Fritz Lang.
1944 *Murder, My Sweet* d. Edward Dmytryk.
1944 *Phantom Lady* d. Robert Siodmak.
1944 *The Suspect* d. Robert Siodmak.
1944 *The Woman in the Window* d. Fritz Lang.
1945 *Conflict* d. Curtis Bernhardt.
1945 *Cornered* d. Edward Dmytryk.
1945 *Detour* d. Edgar Ulmer.
1945 *The Great Flamarion* d. Anthony Mann.
1945 *Hangover Square* d. John Brahm.
1945 *The House on 92nd Street* d. Henry Hathaway.
1945 *Lady on a Train* d. Charles David.
1945 *Mildred Pierce* d. Michael Curtiz.
1945 *My Name Is Julia Ross* d. Joseph H. Lewis.
1945 *Scarlet Street* d. Fritz Lang.
1945 *Spellbound* d. Alfred Hitchcock.
1945 *The Strange Affair of Uncle Harry* d. Robert Siodmak.
1945 *Strange Illusion* d. Edgar Ulmer.
1945 *To Have and Have Not* d. Howard Hawks.
1946 *13 Rue Madeleine* d. Henry Hathaway.
1946 *The Big Sleep* d. Howard Hawks.
1946 *Black Angel* d. Roy William Neill.
1946 *The Blue Dahlia* d. George Marshall.
1946 *The Chase* d. Arthur Ripley.
1946 *Cloak and Dagger* d. Fritz Lang.
1946 *Crack-Up* d. Irving Reis.
1946 *The Dark Corner* d. Henry Hathaway.
1946 *The Dark Mirror* d. Robert Siodmak.
1946 *Deadline at Dawn* d. Harold Clurman.
1946 *Gilda* d. Charles Vidor.
1946 *The Killers* d. Robert Siodmak.
1946 *Leave Her to Heaven* d. John M. Stahl.
1946 *Nobody Lives Forever* d. Jean Negulesco.
1946 *Notorious* d. Alfred Hitchcock.
1946 *The Postman Always Rings Twice* d. Tay Garnett.
1946 *Somewhere in the Night* d. Joseph L. Mankiewicz.
1946 *The Spiral Staircase* d. Robert Siodmak.
1946 *A Stolen Life*, d. Curtis Bernhardt.
1946 *The Stranger* d. Orson Welles.
1946 *Strange Impersonation* d. Anthony Mann.
1946 *The Strange Love of Martha Ivers* d. Lewis Milestone.
1946 *Undercurrent* d. Vincente Minnelli.
1947 *The Arnelo Affair* d. Arch Oboler.
1947 *Body and Soul* d. Robert Rossen.

1947 *Born to Kill* d. Robert Wise.

1947 *Brute Force* d. Jules Dassin.

1947 *Crossfire* d. Edward Dmytryk.

1947 *Dark Passage* d. Delmer Daves.

1947 *Dead Reckoning* d. John Cromwell.

1947 *Desperate* d. Anthony Mann.

1947 *Fall Guy* d. Reginald LeBorg.

1947 *Fear in the Night* d. Maxwell Shane.

1947 *The Gangster* d. Gordon Wiles.

1947 *The Guilty* d. John Reinhardt.

1947 *High Wall* d. Curtis Bernhardt.

1947 *Kiss of Death* d. Henry Hathaway.

1947 *Lady in the Lake* d. Robert Montgomery.

1947 *The Locket* d. John Brahm.

1947 *The Long Night* d. Anatole Litvak.

1947 *Nora Prentiss* d. Vincent Sherman.

1947 *Out of the Past* d. Jacques Tourneur.

1947 *The Paradine Case* d. Alfred Hitchcock.

1947 *Possessed* d. Curtis Bernhardt.

1947 *Railroaded* d. Anthony Mann.

1947 *Ride the Pink Horse* d. Robert Montgomery.

1947 *The Two Mrs Carrolls* d. Peter Godfrey.

1947 *The Unsuspected* d. Michael Curtiz.

1947 *The Woman on the Beach* d. Jean Renoir.

1948 *The Big Clock* d. John Farrow.

1948 *The Black Book* d. Anthony Mann.

1948 *Call Northside 777* d. Henry Hathaway.

1948 *Cry of the City* d. Robert Siodmak.

1948 *The Dark Past* d. Rudolph Maté.

1948 *Easter Parade* d. Charles Walters.

1948 *Force of Evil* d. Abraham Polonsky.

1948 *He Walked by Night* d. Alfred Werker.

1948 *Hollow Triumph* d. Steve Sekely.

1948 *I Walk Alone* d. Byron Haskin.

1948 *Key Largo* d. John Huston.

1948 *Kiss the Blood off My Hands* d. Norman Foster.

1948 *The Lady from Shanghai* d. Orson Welles.

1948 *The Naked City* d. Jules Dassin.

1948 *The Pitfall* d. André de Toth.

1948 *Raw Deal* d. Anthony Mann.

1948 *Secret Beyond the Door* d. Fritz Lang.

1948 *Sorry, Wrong Number* d. Anatole Litvak.

1948 *The Street with No Name* d. William Keighley.

1948 *T-Men* d. Anthony Mann.

1948 *White Heat* d. Raoul Walsh.

1949 *Act of Violence* d. Fred Zinnemann.

1949 *Border Incident* d. Anthony Mann.

1949 *The Bribe* d. Robert Z. Leonard.

1949 *Caught* d. Max Ophuls.

1949 *City Across the River* d. Maxwell Shane.

1949 *The Clay Pigeon* d. Richard Fleischer.

1949 *Criss Cross* d. Robert Siodmak.

1949 *The Crooked Way* d. Robert Florey.

1949 *The File on Thelma Jordon* d. Robert Siodmak.

1949 *The Set-Up* d. Robert Wise.

1949 *Thieves Highway* d. Jules Dassin.

1949 *Too Late for Tears* d. Byron Haskin.

1949 *The Undercover Man* d. Joseph H. Lewis.

1950 *The Asphalt Jungle* d. John Huston.

1950 *The Breaking Point* d. Michael Curtiz.

1950 *D.O.A.* d. Rudolph Maté.

1950 *The Damned Don't Cry* d. Vincent Sherman.

1950 *Dark City* d. William Dieterle.

1950 *Gun Crazy* d. Joseph H. Lewis.

1950 *House by the River* d. Fritz Lang.

1950 *In a Lonely Place* d. Nicholas Ray.

1950 *Manhandled* d. Lewis R. Foster.

1950 *No Way Out* d. Joseph L. Mankiewicz.

1950 *Panic in the Streets* d. Elia Kazan.

1950 *711 Ocean Drive* d. Joseph M. Newman.

1950 *Side Street* d. Anthony Mann.

1950 *Sunset Boulevard* d. Billy Wilder.

1950 *They Live by Night* d. Nicholas Ray.

1950 *The Underworld Story* d. Cy Endfield.

1950 *Union Station* d. Rudolph Maté.

1950 *Where Danger Lives* d. John Farrow.

1950 *Where the Sidewalk Ends* d. Otto Preminger.

1950 *Woman on the Run* d. Norman Foster.

1951 *Clash by Night* d. Fritz Lang.

1951 *Detective Story* d. William Wyler.

1951 *The Enforcer* d. Bretaigne Windt.

1951 *He Ran All the Way* d. John Berry.

1951 *I Was a Communist for the F.B.I.* d. Gordon Douglas.

1951 *M* d. Joseph Losey.

1951 *The Man Who Cheated Himself* d. Felix Feist.

1951 *The Prowler* d. Joseph Losey.

1951 *The Racket* d. John Cromwell.

1952 *Angel Face* d. Otto Preminger.

1952 *Beware, My Lovely* d. Harry Horner.

1952 *The Blue Gardenia* d. Fritz Lang.

1952 *Captive City* d. Robert Wise.

1952 *High Noon* d. Fred Zinnemann.

1952 *Kansas City Confidential* d. Phil Karlson.

1952 *Macao* d. Joseph Von Sternberg.

1952 *On Dangerous Ground* d. Nicholas Ray.

1952 *The Steel Trap* d. Andrew L. Stone.

1952 *Sudden Fear* d. David Miller.

1952 *The Thief* d. Russell Roe.

1952 *Walk East on Beacon* d. Alfred Werker.

1953 *The Big Heat* d. Fritz Lang.

1953 *City That Never Sleeps* d. John H. Auer.

1953 *The Hitch-Hiker* d. Ida Lupino.

1953 *99 River Street* d. Phil Karlson.

1953 *Pickup on South Street* d. Samuel Fuller.

1954 *Human Desire* d. Fritz Lang.

1954 *Private Hell 36* d. Don Siegel.

1954 *Pushover* d. Richard Quine.

1954 *Rogue Cop* d. Roy Rowland.

1954 *Suddenly* d. Lewis Allen.

1954 *Witness to Murder* d. Roy Rowland.

1954 *World for Ransom* d. Robert Aldrich.

1955 *The Big Combo* d. Joseph H. Lewis.

1955 *The Desperate Hours* d. William Wyler.

1955 *House of Bamboo* d. Samuel Fuller.

1955 *Killer's Kiss* d. Stanley Kubrick.

1955 *Kiss Me Deadly* d. Robert Aldrich.

1955 *Mr Arkadin* d. Orson Welles.

1955 *The Night Holds Terror* d. Andrew L. Stone.

1955 *Night of the Hunter* d. Charles Laughton.

1955 *The Phenix City Story* d. Phil Karlson.

1955 *The Trouble with Harry* d. Alfred Hitchcock.

1955 *While the City Sleeps* d. Fritz Lang.

1956 *Beyond a Reasonable Doubt* d. Fritz Lang.

1956 *The Harder They Fall* d. Mark Robson.

1956 *The Killer Is Loose* d. Bud Boetticher.

1957 *The Brothers Rico* d. Phil Karlson.

1957 *The Burglar* d. Paul Wendkos.

1957 *Crime of Passion* d. Gerd Oswald.

1957 *Nightfall* d. Jacques Tourneur.

1958 *Murder by Contract* d. Irving Lerner.

1958 *Touch of Evil* d. Orson Welles.

1958 *Vertigo* d. Alfred Hitchcock.

1959 *Odds Against Tomorrow* d. Robert Wise.

MODERNIST NEO-NOIR AND ITS ANTECEDENTS

1947 (France) *Quai des Orfèvres* d. Henri-Georges Clouzot.

1949 (France) *Mission à Tangier* d. André Hunebelle.

1954 (France) *Les Diaboliques* (*The Fiends*) d. Henri-Georges Clouzot.

1954 (France) *Touchez pas au grisbi* d. Jacques Becker.

1955 (France) *Du Rififi chez les hommes* (*Rififi*) d. Jules Dassin.

1959 (France) *À bout de souffle* (*Breathless*) d. Jean-Luc Godard.

1959 (France) *Pickpocket* d. Robert Bresson.

1960 (France) *Tirez sur le pianiste* (*Shoot the Piano Player*) d. François Truffaut.

1961 (France) *L'Année dernière à Marienbad* (*The Last Year at Marienbad*) d. Alain Resnais.

1961 *Underworld U.S.A.* d. Samuel Fuller.

1962 (France) *Le Doulos* (*The Finger Man*) d. Jean-Pierre Melville.

1963 *Shock Corridor* d. Samuel Fuller.

1964 *The Naked Kiss* d. Samuel Fuller.

1966 (Italy) *The Battle of Algiers* d. Gillo Pontecorvo.

1967 *Bonnie and Clyde* d. Arthur Penn.

1967 *Point Blank* d. John Boorman.

1967 *Le Samourai* d. Jean-Pierre Melville

1968 *If He Hollers Let Him Go* d. Charles Martin.

1969 *Easy Rider* d. Dennis Hopper.

1969 (France) *Z* d. Costa-Gavras.

1970 *Cotton Comes to Harlem* d. Ossie Davis.

1971 *Death Wish* d. Michael Winner.

1971 *Dirty Harry* d. Don Siegel.

1971 *The French Connection* d. William Friedkin.

1971 *Klute* d. Alan J. Pakula.

1971 *Shaft* d. Gordon Parks.

1972 *Chandler* d. Paul Magwood.

1972 *Hickey and Boggs* d. Robert Culp.

1973 *Coffy* d. Jack Hill.

1973 *Executive Action* d. David Miller.

1973 *The Long Goodbye* d. Robert Altman.

1973 *Mean Streets* d. Martin Scorsese.

1973 *The Outfit* d. John Flynn.

1973 *Shamus* d. Buzz Kulik.

1973 *Walking Tall* d. Phil Karlson.

1974 *Chinatown* d. Roman Polanski.

1974 *The Conversation* d. Francis Ford Coppola.

1974 *Foxy Brown* d. Jack Hill.

1974 *The Parallax View* d. Alan J. Pakula.

1975 *French Connection II* d. John Frankenheimer.

1975 *Hustle* d. Robert Aldrich.

1975 *Night Moves* d. Arthur Penn.

1975 *Sheba Baby* d. William Gerdler.

1975 *Three Days of the Condor* d. Sidney Pollack.

1975 *The Yakuza* d. Sidney Pollack.

1976 *All the President's Men* d. Alan J. Pakula.

1976 *The Domino Principle* d. Stanley Kramer.

1976 *The Drowning Pool* d. Stuart Rosenberg.

1976 *The Killer Inside Me* d. Burt Kennedy.

1976 *Taxi Driver* d. Martin Scorsese.

1977 *The Late Show* d. Robert Benton.

1977 *Twilight's Last Gleaming* d. Robert Aldrich.

1978 *The Big Fix* d. Jeremy Paul Kagan.

1978 *The Driver* d. Walter Hill.

POSTMODERN FILM NOIR

1981 *Body Heat* d. Lawrence Kasdan.

1981 *The Postman Always Rings Twice* d. Bob Rafelson

1982 *Blade Runner* d. Ridley Scott.

1984 *Blood Simple* d. Joel Coen.

1984 *Tightrope* d. Richard Tuggle.

1985 *Jagged Edge* d. Richard Marquand.

1986 *Blue Velvet* d. David Lynch.

1986 *Manhunter* d. Michael Mann.

1987 *Black Widow* d. Bob Rafelson.

1987 *Siesta* d. Mary Lamb.

1988 *Betrayed* d. Costa-Gavras.

1988 *Masquerade* d. Bob Swain.

1989 *Fatal Attraction* d. Adrian Lyne.

1989 *Kill Me Again* d. John Dahl.

1989 *The Kill-Off* d. Maggie Greenwald.

1990 *After Dark My Sweet* d. James Foley.

1990 *Bad Influence* d. Curtis Hanson.

1990 *Blue Steel* d. Kathryn Bigelow.

1990 *Body Chemistry* d. Kristine Peterson.

1990 *The Grifters* d. Stephen Frears.

1990 *The Hot Spot* d. Dennis Hopper.

1990 *Impulse* d. Sondra Locke.

1990 *Internal Affairs* d. Mike Figgis.

1990 *Presumed Innocent* d. Alan J. Pakula.

1991 *Basic Instinct* d. Paul Verhoeven.

1991 *Deceived* d. Damian Harris.

1991 *The Hand That Rocks the Cradle* d. Curtis Hanson.

1991 *A Kiss Before Dying* d. James Dearden.

1991 *Love Crimes* d. Lizzie Borden.

1991 *Mortal Thoughts* d. Alan Rudolph.

1991 *New Jack City* d. Mario Van Peebles.

1991 *A Rage in Harlem* d. Bill Duke.

1991 *Reservoir Dogs* d. Quentin Tarantino.

1991 *Shattered* d. Wolfgang Petersen.

1991 *Silence of the Lambs* d. Jonathan Demme.

1991 *Sleeping with the Enemy* d. Joseph Ruben.

1991 *V.I. Warshawski* d. Jeff Kanew.

1992 *Body of Evidence* d. Uli Edel.

1992 *Boyz 'N the Hood* d. John Singleton.

1992 *Deep Cover* d. Bill Duke.

1992 *Night and the City* d. Irwin Winkler.

1992 *One False Move* d. Carl Franklin.

1992 *Poison Ivy* d. Katt Shea.

1992 *Red Rock West* d. John Dahl.

1992 *Single White Female* d. Barbet Schroeder.

1992 *Unlawful Entry* d. Jonathan Kaplan.

1993 *Guilty as Sin* d. Sidney Lumet.

1993 *Guncrazy* d. Tamra Davis.

1993 *Kalifornia* d. Dominic Sena.

1993 *Killing Zoe* d. Roger Avery.

1993 *The Temp* d. Tom Holland.

1994 *Disclosure* d. Barry Levinson.

1994 *The Getaway* d. Roger Donaldson.
1994 *The Last Seduction* d. John Dahl.
1994 *Natural Born Killers* d. Oliver Stone.
1994 *Pulp Fiction* d. Quentin Tarantino.
1994 *Romeo Is Bleeding* d. Peter Medak.
1994 *Sexual Malice* d. Jag Mundra.
1995 *Bodily Harm* d. James Lemmo.
1995 *Copycat* d. John Amiel.
1995 *Dead Presidents* d. Allen and Albert Hughes.
1995 *Devil in a Blue Dress* d. Carl Franklin.
1995 *Eye for an Eye* d. John Schlesinger.
1995 *The Glass Shield* d. Charles Burnett.
1995 *Seven* d. David Fincher.
1995 *Strange Days* d. Kathryn Bigelow.
1995 *The Underneath* d. Steven Soderbergh.
1995 *Unforgettable* d. John Dahl.
1995 *The Usual Suspects* d. Bryan Singer.
1996 *Fargo* d. Joel Coen.
1997 *Breakdown* d. Jonathan Mostow.
1997 *Copland* d. James Mangold
1997 *Face/Off* d. John Woo.
1997 *The Gingerbread Man* d. Robert Altman.
1997 *Jackie Brown* d. Quentin Tarantino.
1997 *Kiss the Girls* d. Gary Fleder.
1997 *L.A. Confidential* d. Curtis Hanson.
1997 *Lost Highway* d. David Lynch.
1997 *This World Then the Fireworks* d. Michael Oblowitz.
1997 *U Turn* d. Oliver Stone.
1999 *The Bone Collector* d. Phillip Noyce.
1999 *Double Jeopardy* d. Bruce Beresford.
2000 *Memento* d. Christopher Nolan.
2001 *Along Came a Spider* d. Lee Tamahori.
2001 *Hannibal* d. Ridley Scott.
2001 *The Man Who Wasn't There* d. Joel Coen.

BRITISH FILM NOIR

Antecedents/Experimental Period

1926 *The Lodger* d. Alfred Hitchcock.
1929 *Blackmail* d. Alfred Hitchcock.
1932 *The Frightened Lady* d. T. Hayes Hunter.
1935 *The 39 Steps* d. Alfred Hitchcock.
1937 *The Green Cockatoo* d. William Cameron Menzies.
1937 *Young and Innocent* d. Alfred Hitchcock.
1938 *They Drive by Night* d. Arthur Woods.
1939 *On the Night of the Fire* d. Brian Desmond Hurst.
1940 *The Case of the Frightened Lady* d. George King.

1940 *Gaslight* d. Thorold Dickinson.
1941 *Hatter's Castle* d. Lance Comfort.
1942 *The Night Has Eyes* d. Leslie Arliss.
1944 *Fanny by Gaslight* d. Anthony Asquith.
1945 *Dead of Night* d. Robert Hamer/Alberto Cavalcanti.
1945 *Great Day* d. Lance Comfort.
1945 *Murder in Reverse* d. Montgomery Tully.
1945 *Pink String and Sealing Wax* d. Robert Hamer.
1945 *Waterloo Road* d. Leslie Gilliat.

'Classical British Noir'

1946 *Carnival* d. Stanley Haynes.
1946 *Daybreak* d. Compton Bennett.
1946 *Great Expectations* d. David Lean.
1946 *Wanted for Murder* d. Lawrence Huntington.
1947 *Blanche Fury* d. Marc Allégret.
1947 *Dancing with Crime* d. John Paddy Carstairs.
1947 *Dear Murderer* d. Arthur Crabtree.
1947 *The Fallen Idol* d. Carol Reed.
1947 *Frieda* d. Basil Dearden.
1947 *The Mark of Cain* d. Brian Desmond Hurst.
1947 *Mine Own Executioner* d. Anthony Kimmins.
1947 *It Always Rains on Sunday* d. Robert Hamer.
1947 *Jassy* d. Bernard Knowles.
1947 *Nicholas Nickleby* d. Alberto Cavalcanti.
1947 *The October Man* d. Roy Ward Baker.
1947 *Odd Man Out* d. Carol Reed.
1947 *Temptation Harbour* d. Lance Comfort.
1947 *They Made Me a Fugitive* d. Alberto Cavalcanti.
1947 *The Upturned Glass* d. Lawrence Huntington.
1948 *Brighton Rock* d. John Boulting.
1948 *Corridor of Mirrors* d. Terence Young.
1948 *The Flamingo Affair* d. Horace Shepherd.
1948 *Good Time Girl* d. David Macdonald.
1948 *Night Beat* d. Harold Huth.
1948 *No Orchids for Miss Blandish* d. St John L. Clewes.
1948 *Noose* d. Edmond T. Greville.
1948 *Oliver Twist* d. David Lean.
1948 *The Small Back Room* d. Michael Powell.
1948 *The Small Voice* d. Fergus McDonnell.
1948 *So Evil My Love* d. Lewis Allen.
1948 *Uneasy Terms* d. Vernon Sewell.
1949 *Boys in Brown* d. Montgomery Tully.
1949 *Forbidden* d. George King.
1949 *Kind Hearts and Coronets* d. Robert Hamer.
1949 *Madeleine* d. David Lean.
1949 *Obsession* d. Edward Dmytryk.
1949 *The Queen of Spades* d. Thorold Dickinson.

1949 *Silent Dust* d. Lance Comfort.

1949 *The Third Man* d. Carol Reed.

1950 *The Blue Lamp* d. Basil Dearden.

1950 *Night and the City* d. Jules Dassin.

1950 *There Is Another Sun* d. Lewis Gilbert.

1951 *The Pool of London* d. Basil Dearden.

1952 *Wide Boy* d. Ken Hughes.

1953 *The Flanagan Boy* d. Reginald LeBorg.

1953 *The Intruder* d. Guy Hamilton.

1953 *The Long Memory* d. Robert Hamer.

1953 *The Man Between* d. Carol Reed.

1953 *Marilyn* d. Wolf Rilla.

1953 *Street of Shadows* d. Richard Vernon.

1954 *Black 13* d. Ken Hughes.

1954 *The Good Die Young* d. Lewis Gilbert.

1954 *The House Across the Lake* d. Ken Hughes.

1954 *The Stranger Came Home* d. Terence Fisher.

1954 *Thirty-Six Hours* d. Montgomery Tully.

1954 *The Weak and the Wicked* d. J. Lee Thompson.

1955 *The Brain Machine* d. Ken Hughes.

1955 *Confession* d. Ken Hughes.

1955 *Impulse* d. Cy Endfield.

1955 *Joe Macbeth* d. Ken Hughes.

1955 *The Ship That Died of Shame* d. Basil Dearden.

1956 *Tiger in the Smoke* d. Roy Ward Baker.

1956 *Yield to the Night* d. J. Lee Thompson.

1957 *Hell Drivers* d. Cy Endfield.

1957 *The Long Haul* d. Ken Hughes.

1958 *Tread Softly Stranger* d. Gordon Parry.

1958 *Violent Playground* d. Basil Dearden.

1959 *Beyond this Place* d. Jack Cardiff.

1959 *In the Wake of a Stranger* d. David Eady.

1959 *Passport to Shame* d. Alan Rakoff.

1959 *Room at the Top* d. Jack Clayton.

1959 *The Rough and the Smooth* d. Robert Siodmak.

1960 *The Criminal* d. Joseph Losey.

1960 *Hell Is a City* d. Val Guest.

1961 *The Man in the Back Street* d. Vernon Sewell.

1961 *Payroll* d. Sidney Hayers.

1961 *Taste of Fear* d. Seth Holt.

1963 *Cairo* d. Wolf Rilla.

1963 *A Place to Go* d. Basil Dearden.

1964 *Face of a Stranger* d. John Moxey.

British Neo-Noir

1965 *The Spy Who Came in from the Cold* d. Martin Ritt.

1966 *The Deadly Affair* d. Sidney Lumet.

1967 *Blow-up* d. Michelangelo Antonioni.

1968 *The Strange Affair* d. David Greene.
1969 *The Looking Glass War* d. Frank R. Pierson.
1970 *Performance* d. Donald Cammell/Nicolas Roeg.
1971 *Get Carter* d. Mike Hodges.
1971 *Villain* d. Mike Tuchner.
1972 *Frenzy* d. Alfred Hitchcock.
1972 *The Offence* d. Sidney Lumet.
1972 *Sitting Target* d. Douglas Hickox.
1975 *Farewell My Lovely* d. Michael Winner.
1978 *The Big Sleep* d. Michael Winner.
1980 *The Long Good Friday* d. John Mackenzie.
1985 *Dance with a Stranger* d. Mike Newell.
1986 *Mona Lisa* d. Neil Jordan.
1987 *Empire State* d. Ron Peck.
1988 *Scandal* d. Michael Caton-Jones.
1989 *Stormy Monday* d. Mike Figgis.
1990 *The Krays* d. Peter Medak.
1990 *Tank Malling* d. James Marc.
1991 *'Let Him Have It'* d. Peter Medak.
1992 *The Crying Game* d. Neil Jordan.
1993 *The Young Americans* d. Danny Cannon.
1994 *Beyond Bedlam* d. Vadim Jean.
1994 *Shopping* d. Paul Anderson.
1995 *The Near Room* d. David Hayman.
1995 *The Innocent Sleep* d. Scott Michell.
1995 *Shallow Grave* d. Danny Boyle.
1996 *Darklands* d. Julian Richards.
1997 *Face* d. Antonia Bird.
1997 *Hard Men* d. J.K. Amalou.
1997 *Mojo* d. Jez Butterworth.
1997 *Resurrection Man* d. Marc Evans.
1998 *Killing Time* d. Bernt Amade Capra.
1998 *Lock, Stock and Two Smoking Barrels* d. Guy Ritchie.
1999 *Croupier* d. Mike Hodges.
2000 *Circus* d. Rob Walker.
2000 *The Criminal* d. Julian Simpson.
2000 *Essex Boys* d. Terry Winsor.
2000 *Gangster No. 1* d. Paul McGuigan.
2000 *Sexy Beast* d. Jonathan Glazer.

MISCELLANEOUS

1943 (GB) *The Man in Grey* d. Leslie Arliss.
1944 *Wilson* d. Henry King.
1945 *The Bells of St Mary's* d. Leo McCarey.
1946 *The Best Years of Our Lives* d. William Wyler.
1946 *Blue Skies* d. Stuart Heisler.

1949 *Samson and Delilah* d. Cecil B. de Mille.
1950 *Devil's Doorway* d. Anthony Mann.
1951 *A Streetcar Named Desire* d. Elia Kazan.
1953 *The Band Wagon* d. Vincente Minnelli.
1957 (GB) *The Curse of Frankenstein* d. Terence Fisher.
1958 *Man of the West* d. Anthony Mann.
1967 *Dr Dolittle* d. Richard Fleischer.
1967 *The Graduate* d. Mike Nichols.
1968 *Star!* d. Robert Wise.
1969 *Easy Rider* d. Dennis Hopper.
1969 *Hello Dolly* d. Gene Kelly.
1974 *The Texas Chainsaw Massacre* d. Tobe Hooper

INDEX OF NAMES

INDEX OF FILMS